THE ROMANCE OF TEA
Tea and Tea-Drinking Through Sixteen Hundred Years

BENJAMIN PRESS

Tea and Coffee Trade Journal Founder
WILLIAM H. UKERS

THE ROMANCE OF TEA
Tea and Tea-Drinking Through Sixteen Hundred Years

New Introduction, Notes & Timeline of Tea History by
JAMES NORWOOD PRATT

Copyright © 2017 by Benjamin Press

All rights reserved. No part of this book, in whole or in part, may be reproduced by any means without prior written permission of the copyright holder.

Senior Editor: Bruce Richardson
Research Editor: Lou Berkley
Associate Editor: Sara Loy
Copy Editor: Ben Sheene

James Norwood Pratt gratefully acknowledges the collaboration and indefatiguable assistance of his friend and fellow tea scholar Lou Berkley.

Contains material adapted and abridged from *The Romance of Tea* by William H. Ukers, M.A., originally published by Alfred A. Knopf in 1936.

ISBN 978-0-9836106-9-4

Printed in Canada

BENJAMIN PRESS
135 North Second Street
Danville, Kentucky 40422 USA
www.BenjaminPress.com
800.765.2139

William H. Ukers dedicated his 1936 edition —

To my wife Helen De Graff Ukers

This new and expanded edition is dedicated to the
memory of two leading pioneers of America's Tea Renaissance —

JOHN HARNEY, founder of Harney & Sons Fine Teas
and
DEVAN SHAH, founder of International Tea Importers.

A Qing Dynasty watercolor showing tea harvesting in China. Courtesy British Library.

CONTENTS

INTRODUCTION — James Norwood Pratt

I The Genesis of Tea - 15
Its legendary origin and etymology. Early history of tea propagation. The first book on tea; Lu Yu and his Tea Classic. *Its botany. Mother Nature's tea garden. The legend of Daruma, Buddhism's patron saint of tea. Its culture spread by Buddhist priests.*

II Tea's Conquest of the Orient - 33
The thrilling adventures of J. I. L. L. Jacobson, founder of the tea industry in Netherlands India. The far-flung kingdom of India tea. Tea's dramatic triumph over coffee in Ceylon.

III Tea Comes to Europe and America - 51
Its introduction into Holland, France and England. The story of the colonial tea parties and the tea tax that divided an empire.

IV Ships in Azure - 79
The world's greatest tea monopoly. The golden age of the tea clippers. The great tea race of 1866.

V How Tea Grows and How It is Manufactured - 109
Tea Gardens of China, Japan, Formosa, Java, Sumatra, Ceylon, India and Africa.

VI Tea Manners and Customs - 117
The social history of tea. The art and practice of Chanoyu. London tea gardens of the eighteenth century. Tea drinking round the world.

VII Tea and the Fine Arts - 143
How tea has been celebrated in painting, ceramics, silver, music, poetry and literature.

VIII The Shining Hour of the Day - 173
Teatime reflections. Chemistry and pharmacology of tea.

TIMELINE OF TEA HISTORY — James Norwood Pratt - 183

Index - 206

A Qing Dynasty watercolor showing tea packing at Canton. Courtesy of the British Library.

TEA AS ROMANCE
James Norwood Pratt

The novelist is the historian of the present and the historian is the novelist of the past. History must have as much entertainment value as intellectual content if it's to be read for long. Consider, for example, Edward Gibbon's *Decline & Fall of the Roman Empire*. Over two centuries after its completion, Gibbon's is still the most widely enjoyed and liberally quoted work on the subject. Unsurprisingly, it was the work of decades.

> "It was in Rome, on the fifteenth of October 1764, as I sat musing among the ruins of the Capitol while the barefoot friars were singing Vespers in the temple of Jupiter, that the idea of writing the decline and fall of the City first started into my mind."

According to Gibbon's memoirs:

> "It was on the day, or rather the night, of 27 June 1787 between the hours of eleven and twelve, that I wrote the last lines of the last page in a summer house in my garden."

Gibbon can be compared, for the pleasure of his writing, his clarity and grasp of a vast subject, to the great historian of tea, William Harrison Ukers. In the preface of his monumental *All About Tea*, Ukers declares:

> "Twenty-five years ago, the author made his first visit to the tea countries of the Orient and began to collect materials for a work on tea. After the initial surveys, researching started in the principal European and American libraries and museums; this work continued up to the return of the final proofs to the printer in 1935. The sorting and classification of the material was begun twelve years ago. Subsequently, the author spent a year in travel among the tea countries, to revise and bring up to date the data already in hand. The actual writing of the manuscript extended over ten years. …it was found impossible to do justice to the subject in one volume."

For sheer scope, Ukers ranks with Gibbon, however, unlike Gibbon, Ukers went on to abridge the work of his lifetime for our entertainment. His tale of how humanity acquired its favorite habit first attracts us, then absorbs us and casts a spell over us and teaches us. Ukers regales us, in his quaint way and measured tones, with a little known epic romance—how the whole world learned to love drinking tea. Who was this great but forgotten chronicler of the greatest story never told before him?

The future historian of tea was born in 1878 in William Penn's Quaker metropolis Philadelphia. America's elderly and aristocratic first capital, Philadelphia had been a center of colonial culture since before Ben Franklin's day. The city's famous schools upheld the highest standards of behavior and learning. The Quaker community avoided alcohol and supported a thriving tea trade. On Dock Street, John Wagner set up shop in 1847 as an importer of wine, cigars, spices and, especially, tea. At the request of a customer recorded as "Mr. Borie," Wagner imported America's first Lapsang Souchong on one of the first clipper ships arriving from China. Over the following century Wagners sold tons of tea to generations of Biddles, Duponts and other prominent Philadelphia families. Writers and artists like Thomas Eakins at the Pennsylvania Academy of Art also bought tea from Wagners.

A product of this cultured milieu, William Ukers all his life took great pride in the classical education he received from Philadelphia's famous Central High School. The school was equally proud of William and, in 1922, bestowed upon him its honorary degree, the M. A., for "exceptional scholarly attainment." From that day forward, he would proudly sign himself "W. H. Ukers, M. A." Every inch a gentleman and scholar, he was a young Victorian with ambitions to match his intelligence and nerve enough to seek his fortune in the scribbler's trade.

The written word ruled the world William Ukers entered when he finished high school in 1893. Editors like Horace Greeley, Joseph Pulitzer and William Randolph Hearst seemed more powerful than presidents. Above them all, William admired England's poet-editor W. E. Henley. To enter the ranks of men like these, William, at 16, moved to Manhattan and began honing his craft as a reporter until he landed his first job as an editor editing "The Spice Mill," the house organ of Jabez Burns' company Burns Coffee Roasting Machines.

Working for Burns, William got to know the principal sources, types, companies and customers involved in the world embracing coffee and tea trades. He also learned the printing and publishing business and—just as vital—realized "practical" writing could be profitable. The young visionary rapidly outgrew his position. Jabez Burns simply wanted an in-house publication for his company, a company which William saw as simply a single member of a larger commercial community. Having envisioned a publication to serve that community's needs, he became the father of business journalism in 1901 when, with "youthful enthusiasm," as he was to say later of another adventurer, he founded the monthly *Tea and Coffee Trade Journal* with offices at 70 Wall Street. It was the earliest trade journal and the editor was 23 years old.

Queen Victoria died the year *Tea and Coffee Trade Journal* was founded. That was two years after she had knighted Thomas Lipton and one year after the last Russian caravan left Beijing carrying tea to Moscow. Ukers quickly became friends with the coffee and tea professionals in his vicinity and developed a nodding acquaintance with passers-by like J.P. Morgan, who bought choice teas from Ukers' friend Lester Vail. Tea importer William Sullivan, around whom the myth of "inventing" the teabag sprang up, did business a few blocks from the magazine offices. Ukers routinely met visiting professionals like Richard Blechynden, soon to popularize iced tea at the 1904 St. Louis World's Fair. Encountering such senior colleagues, William was invariably correct and, though younger, always stood on his dignity. "Everybody always called him 'Mr. Ukers,' including Sir Thomas Lipton," recalled an employee. "Even his wife called him 'Mr. Ukers.'"

As scribe of the far-flung tribe composed of the world's tea and coffee men (women were few), William filled a need and his trade journal prospered from the first. And right from the beginning Mr. Ukers insisted his small staff hoard every scrap of information he could acquire about his beloved tea and coffee community.

In those days, the U.S. coffee and tea trades were centered on Front Street in downtown Manhattan near the New York Stock Exchange, with leading banks located only blocks away. Ukers' office was between the two, on the corner of Wall and Pearl Streets. It was not unusual to see a tea or coffee trader walk down this block with a tray of samples and get three or four bids on a full ship's cargo, based on the samples alone. Entire shiploads of coffee and tea changed hands several times during the week before and after the vessel arrived in the Port of New York. Serious money was constantly exchanged on those few blocks and it was exciting to be an insider chronicling the non-stop activity. Gathering and publishing market intelligence from abroad was no small task. Eventually, the harder task of keeping this material organized fell to William's fellow hoarder-of-lore and long-time secretary Helen.

"I knew he had married his secretary Helen De Graff," said James P. Quinn long after the fact. Quinn, who had eventually succeeded Ukers as editor, was interviewed in 2001 on the magazine's centenary. "He told me he and Mrs. Ukers were determined to make the magazine a success so they never had any children and devoted themselves to their continuing work with the magazine and his other projects."

Besides *Tea and Coffee Trade Journal,* William's "projects" included starting a separate business, the Audit Board of Circulation, which made them modestly wealthy, but mostly his projects were books. In 1922, ten years after they were married, William dedicated "his" first book to Helen, his unacknowledged co-author. The encyclopedic *All About Coffee* was followed by other books but telling the full story of tea, "far-fetched and dear bought," remained beyond them. Its origins and history in China were inaccessible and its very cultivation and trade were shrouded in Asian languages. One imagines William and Helen poring over *The Book of Tea* by Okakura Kakuzo again and again.

Japan and India by the 1920's were supplying most of America's tea and in 1924 Ukers' colleagues willingly sponsored his second fact-finding mission to Asia. Leaving Helen in charge of the magazine, he left on a leisurely visit to the tea producing countries, making friends and crossing borders of color and race to a degree usually impossible in his day. Besides Japan's unique tea culture, his hosts there supplied him with a panoramic view of China's ancient tea history and lore. He visited Taiwan, then a Japanese possession, and his photo with the leading family of Taiwan tea was still on display when I visited eighty years after him. Then Java, Sri Lanka and India: he returned to New York with something like reverence for the leaf. William and Helen had taken on a subject as vast as the Grand Canyon. Ten years later, in 1935, they were finally able to publish *All About Tea* with its heartfelt opening sentence, "Tea is a treasure of the world." After the magazine, the tea "project" was their other love child.

The Romance of Tea is the essence of *All About Tea*. Ukers wrote it for recreation, like play after work is done. It is written to interest Helen and dedicated to her. William is telling Helen a story, re-telling a story they both know well but telling it anyway for fun, how a simple, healthful beverage could inspire high deeds, create empires and art, lead to war and peace. We readers are listening in on a saga spun out to entertain an intelligent companion, full of quaint and curious lore and high endeavor. His voice is even but fresh, the story-telling steady and clear. *The Romance of Tea* is not just the original version of one of the greatest stories ever told. It is also a work of love and the telling must be understood as an act of love. Old-fashioned only superficially, it is really a ripping yarn, told with the beauty that is of many days "steady and clear" like William and Helen's married life and work together.

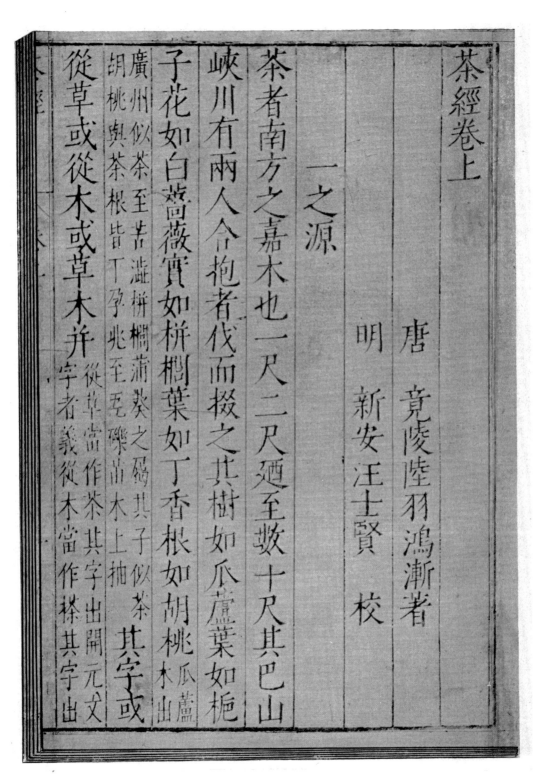

The Cha Ching by Lu Yu was the first written book on tea. Image courtesy of the University of London.

THE GENESIS OF TEA

Tea had its genesis in China untold centuries ago; its early history is lost in the obscurity of China's venerable antiquity and for the most part is traditional. Everything known of its beginning is so inextricably intertwined with things patently mythical and fabulous that we can only vaguely surmise what is fact and what is fancy.

Probably it will never be known when tea was first used as a beverage nor how it was discovered that tea leaves could be treated and used to make a palatable drink.[1] It is equally doubtful whether we shall ever know, with anything like reasonable accuracy, when and how the cultivation of the plant began. Just as coffee has been known and used as food and drink in Ethiopia since time out of mind, so too, the Chinese have known the tea plant and have used its leaves for food and their extract for a beverage from time immemorial.

The Chinese have dramatized the vague and obscure advent of tea by ascribing it to the reign of a legendary emperor, Shen Nung, called the "Divine Healer," who lived about 2737 B.C. "This," says Samuel Ball,[2] with a sympathetic understanding of the Eastern habits of thought, "is not so much from the vanity of assigning it to a high antiquity, as to a kind of courtesy sanctioned by ancient usage and oral tradition, which ascribes the discovery of numerous medicinal plants, and of tea among the rest, to Shen Nung."[3]

According to Dr. Emil Bretschneider,[4] the use of the ideograph *cha* for tea was not general before the publication of the *Cha Ching,* or *Tea Classic* (A.D. 780). The strokes of the character *cha* are inscribed in the order set forth in the illustration on page 16; beginning at the top and writing downward, after the Chinese fashion.

The translation of the Chinese word for "tea" into other languages began with the earliest sale of the commodity to a foreign people. So, the Arabs called it *shai* and the Turks *chay*. The Japanese adopted the Chinese ideograph. The Persians and the Portuguese also called it *cha*; the Russians *chai;* the Dutch followed the Amoy dialect[5] and Romanized it as *thee,* the English "tea," originally pronounced "tay," being derived through the Dutch.[6]

The word is not to be found in the Bible, the works of Shakespeare, or any other publication in English previous to the latter half of the seventeenth century. In the known references to

The Genesis of Tea

How the Chinese character "cha" is inscribed.

tea in English during the years 1650-9 the word appears in its earlier form of "tee" but pronounced "tay." It was first spelled "tea" in 1660,[7] but still pronounced "tay" until the middle of the eighteenth century.

The languages of the civilized world derive their respective words for "tea" direct from China, the home of its earliest cultivation and preparation. The native name for tea in China is 茶, Romanized as *cha,* pronounced "chah," in Cantonese; and changing to *te,* pronounced "tay," in the dialect of Amoy. From one or the other of these two sources the term has found its way with little or no alteration into practically every modern language.

The Chinese were forced to borrow the names of other shrubs for their earliest references to tea, as it did not receive its present appellation (*cha*) until about A.D. 725; consequently, there is some uncertainty whether tea or something else was meant in certain references to plants by authors who wrote before that time.

In Shen Nung's *Pen tsao,* or *Medical Book,* a reference reads: "Bitter *tu* is called *cha, hsuan,* and *yu.* It grows in winter in the valleys by the streams, and on the hills of Ichow [in the province of Szechwan], and does not perish in severe winter. It is gathered on the third day of the third month [in April] and then dried." Another reference mentions the tea leaf as "good for tumours or abscesses that come about the head, or for ailments of the bladder. It dissipates heat caused by the phlegms, or inflammation of the chest. It quenches thirst. It lessens the desire for sleep. It gladdens and cheers the heart."

The *Pen tsao* of Shen Nung has been cited time and time again as a proof of the great antiquity of tea. To the popular mind this seems a *prima facie* case, for here, it may be argued, is a quotation from an author who flourished as far back as 2700 B.C. What a pity to destroy such an enchanting myth, even though historical accuracy compels us to do so! Shen Nung's book was not actually written in its earliest form until the Neo-Han dynasty (A.D. 23-220), and the reference to tea was not added until after the seventh century, when the word *cha* came into use. This was thirty-four hundred years after the time of the fabled Emperor to whom the authorship of the book is ascribed.[8]

This is but one of many errors which have crept into the history of tea. There is a supposed reference to tea in the *Shih Ching,* or *Book of Odes,* edited by Confucius, about 550 B.C., but this has been discredited, as have several others. Often quoted, too, is the legend of Gan Lu, who is said to have brought back from his Buddhist studies in India seven tea bushes which he planted on Meng Mountain, in Szechwan, during the Later Han dynasty (A.D. 23-220). There are several third century notices in which the words *ku tu* or *chuan* are possibly used to refer to tea, but it is in the *Erh Ya,* the Chinese dictionary annotated by Kuo Po, a celebrated Chinese scholar of about A.D. 350, that we find the first recognizable definition of tea under the name of *kia,* or *ku tu,* with the additional information that "a beverage is made from the leaves by boiling." The same work states the earliest gathering of the leaves was called *tu,* and the latest, *ming.*[9]

The Genesis of Tea

The reference in the *Erh Ya* is accepted by many authorities on the history of tea as the earliest credible record of tea cultivation. As revised by Kuo Po it forms the basis for the often-published statement that the tea plant was first cultivated about A.D. 350. The tea drink of Kuo Po's time was a medicinal decoction—and probably a bitter one—of unprepared green tea leaves, but its aroma attracted favorable attention, for Pau Ling-hui, a Chinese authoress, wrote of it under the title *Fragrant Ming*. Mention of the tea drink is also found in the *Chin Shu,* a history of the Chin dynasty, where the statement is made that the Governor of Yangchow, Huan Wen (A.D. 312-373), "was frugal; he employed only seven receptacles for tea and fruit when he dined."

Some light on the manufacturing process of the period, and on the drink made from tea, is to be found in an extract from the *Kuang Ya,* a dictionary by Chang I, of the Later Wei dynasty (A.D. 386-535), which states that the leaves were plucked and made into cakes in the district between the provinces of Hupeh and Szechwan; the cakes were roasted until reddish in color, pounded into tiny pieces, and placed in a chinaware pot. Boiling water was then poured over them, after which onion, ginger and orange were added.[10]

By the fifth century tea had become an article of trade. The custom of reserving special teas for Imperial use began about this time, for we find the *Wu Hsing chi,* by Shan Chien-chih, of the Northern Sung dynasty (A.D. 420-479), stating: "Twenty lis [a li is 705 yards] west from the city of Wucheng, in the province Chekiang,[11] there is the Wen mountain, on which grows the tea reserved to the Emperor as tribute tea."

Late in the sixth century the Chinese generally began to regard tea as something more than a medicinal drink.[12] Its use as a refreshing beverage was epitomized by the poet Chang Meng-yan, of the Chin dynasty (A.D. 557-589), in his poem *On the Chengtu Terrace* (in Szechwan). "Fragrant *tu,*" he wrote, "superimposes the six passions: the taste for it spreads over the nine districts." The six passions are: content and anger, sorrow and joy, like and dislike. The nine districts included the entire kingdom.

The transition of the tea drink at this time from medicinal uses to use as a beverage is confirmed by the author of the *Kuen Fang Pu*. Tea, according to this account, was first used as a beverage in the reign of Wen Ti, of the Sui dynasty (A.D. 589-620), and was acknowledged to be good, though not much esteemed. Tea continued in high repute as a remedy, however, for the "noxious gases of the body, and as a cure for lethargy."

While tea propagation became more general in the sixth century, it was not until A.D. 780 that the horticultural and other aspects of tea-growing were first published in a work exclusively devoted to tea. In this year appeared the *Cha Ching,* or *Tea Book,* written by Lu Yu, a noted Chinese author and tea expert, at the request of the tea merchants. It treats, among other things, of the qualities and effects of the beverage. In an allegory, the book quotes one of the emperors of the Han dynasty as saying: "The use of tea grows upon me surprisingly; I know not how it is, but my fancy is awakened and my spirits exhilarated as if with wine." This makes it evident that tea as a drink had progressed in Lu Yu's time from the earlier rank decoction of unprepared green tea leaves to a more inviting infusion. With methods of improving the leaf came better quality in the drink as a beverage, making the use of certain ingredients, such as spices, no longer necessary for improving its flavor. During the greater part of the time that the cultivation of tea was spreading through China, such meager knowledge as existed regarding its culture and manufacture was disseminated almost entirely by word of mouth. While some slight mention of tea had been made in contemporary writings, most of these references to tea were fragmentary and could furnish little or no practical guidance to the agriculturist.

To Lu Yu the early Chinese agriculturists were heavily indebted. And if their debt was heavy, how much more so is the debt which all the world owes! But for the knowledge imparted by the *Cha Ching* concerning the cultivation and manufacture of tea, the world might have remained in ignorance of the joys of tea-drinking until long after the time of Jacobson, Gordon, Ball, Fortune, and other explorers,[13] who learned much from this work at a time when tight-lipped Chinamen found it convenient to be mute. For it must be remembered that tea,

The *Cha Ching*, *or* Tea Book, *was written by* Lu Yu, *a noted Chinese author and tea expert, at the request of the tea merchants in A.D. 780.*

The Genesis of Tea

then as precious as rubies, was not a subject to be lightly discussed with foreigners, nor were the secrets of its growth and preparation to be disclosed. Yet disclosed they were, for the *Cha Ching* opened the closely guarded mystery to the prying Westerners.

These people from other lands would undoubtedly have learned all the essential facts in time, but the *Cha Ching* simplified their quest and hastened the day of universal knowledge. Logically, the situation was incongruous. This is apparent when we consider that the very merchants who were most jealous in guarding the secrets of tea from foreigners were themselves responsible for the written record which disseminated the vital facts among them.

The tea merchants, in casting about for someone to gather together the fragmentary knowledge of their industry, happily hit upon Lu Yu, a colorful personality of high ability and wide versatility. From fugitive references, here and there in Chinese literature, it is easy to piece together the story of Lu Yu's adventurous life.

According to the fanciful story of his origin—a story savoring of the Biblical account of Moses in the bulrushes—he was a foundling. A native of Foochow, in Hupeh,[14] he is thought to have been found by a Buddhist priest and to have been adopted by him. Later, when Lu Yu refused to join the priesthood, he was set at menial tasks in the hope that the discipline would tame his proud spirit, teach him true humility, and fit him for the practicalities of a staid and proper eighth century conventionalism.

Irked by such servile duties, Lu Yu, always an extreme individualist, heard the call of the open road and fled. He became a clown, a long-cherished ambition. Wherever he went, delighted crowds acclaimed him for his antics, but he was far from being happy. His is the old, old story of the saddened heart beneath the motley jacket. Lu Yu's discontent, however, came from a frustrated ambition for learning. He was a pantaloon, if you will, but with a deep yearning for knowledge. One of his many admirers, an official, became his patron and supplied him with books with which to educate himself. China's world of books, that vast storehouse of ancient wisdom, was opened to him. He absorbed it greedily.

Lu Yu then became fired with further ambition; he wanted to add to the national store of knowledge he yearned to create. The tea merchants offered the very opportunity he sought. They needed someone who could put together the disconnected knowledge of their growing industry; they needed his genius to emancipate tea from crude commercialism and lead to its final idealization.

Lu Yu saw in the tea service the same harmony and order that rule in all things. He became the first apostle of tea. In the *Cha Ching* he gave his patrons the *Tea Memoir,* or, as it is sometimes called, the *Tea Scripture* or *Tea Classic.* He was the first to formulate a Code of Tea, out of which, later on, the Japanese developed the Tea Ceremony.

If, as Ruskin[15] said, "to see a thing and tell it in plain words is the greatest thing a soul can do," then no one will deny Lu Yu his place among the immortals.

The Genesis of Tea

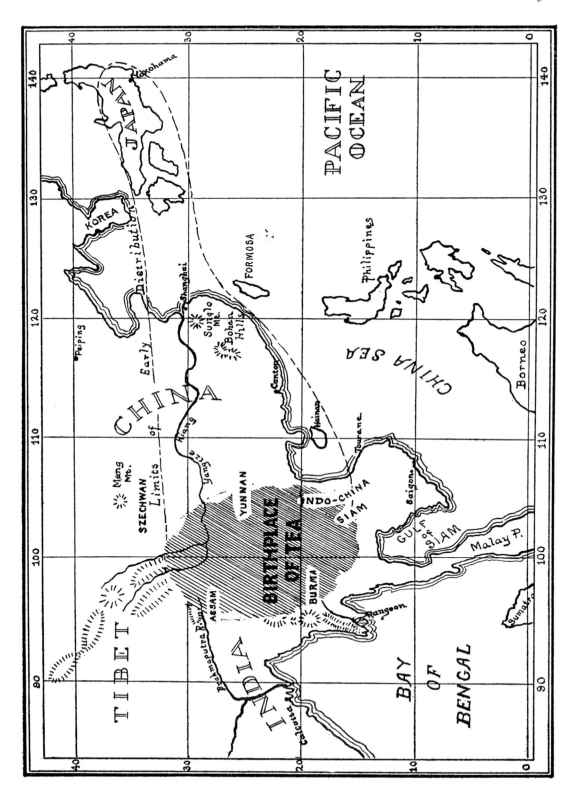

The Genesis of Tea

Lu Yu found himself famous in his own country. It was futile for him to insist that his feet were of clay; his admirers knew better. They literally canonized him, and he has been worshipped ever since as the patron saint of the Chinese tea merchants.

The last years of his life were sweet, or should have been. Lu Yu was befriended by the Emperor, and none were too rich or too poor to pay him reverence. But disillusionment stalked his footsteps. Life was a comedy, yes, but too much of a comedy not to be taken seriously. Was that, after all, its hidden meaning? He must think it out. Were the sages right? Only in meditation could he find the way. He would seek the truth in the belief that it would make him whole. He would withdraw into the solitudes and try to solve the mystery of life. And so, he arrived back at his starting-point; his life had come full circle. Had not the great Confucius taught that "they who know the truth are not equal to those who love it, and they who love it are not equal to those who find pleasure in it?"

In 775, Lu Yu became a hermit. Five years later the *Cha Ching* was published and, in 804, he died.

The *Cha Ching* consists of three volumes with ten parts. In the first part, Lu Yu speaks of the nature of the tea plant, in the second of the utensils for gathering the leaves, and in the third of the manipulation of the leaves. The fourth is devoted to enumerating and describing the twenty-four implements of tea equipage. In this part, Lu Yu's predilection for Taoist symbolism and the influence of tea upon Chinese ceramics may be noticed. In the fifth part, Lu Yu describes the method of infusion. The remaining chapters include descriptions of the ordinary methods of tea-drinking, a historical summary, enumeration of famous tea plantations, and illustrations of tea utensils.

The introduction of tea into general use may be said to have taken place in the two centuries between the reign of the Emperor Wen Ti, of the Sui dynasty (A.D. 589-620), to whose reign the author of the *Cha Pu,* another book on tea, ascribes the first use of the beverage, and the reign of Tih Tsung in the Tang dynasty, A.D. 780, when the first tea duty was levied.[16]

One account of the manner of preparing it in this period is supplied by two Arabian travelers who visited China about A.D. 850. The travelers speak of tea as the common beverage of China and tell how the Chinese boil water and pour it scalding hot upon the leaf, adding: "The infusion preserves them from all distempers."[17] It is evident that the Chinese of the ninth century infused the leaf much the same as today, and that they continued to regard it as possessing medicinal properties.

By the time of the Sung dynasty (A.D. 960-1280), tea, according to the *Kuen Fang Pu,* was used throughout all the provinces, and whipped tea had made its appearance as the fashionable mode among tea exquisites. The dried leaf was ground to a fine powder and whipped in hot water with a light bamboo whisk. Salt disappeared as a flavoring agent and, for the first time, the beverage was enjoyed for its own delicate flavor and aroma.

The enthusiasm of tea epicures now became lyrical and was reflected in the social and intellectual intercourse of the period. New varieties were eagerly sought, and tournaments were held to decide their merits. The Emperor Hwei Tsung (A.D. 1101-26), who was extremely artistic in temperament, counted no cost too great for the attainment of new and rare varieties. A dissertation on the twenty kinds of tea by this royal connoisseur specifies the "white tea" as of the rarest and most delicate flavor.

Elaborate tea houses appeared in all of the cities, and in the temples Buddhist priests of the southern Zen sect, founded in India by Bodhidharma[18] and brought by him to China, A.D. 519, gathered before the image of Bodhidharma and drank tea in solemn ceremonial from a single bowl. One or two centuries later, in the Ming dynasty (A.D. 1368-1644), the second book on tea appeared, the *Cha Pu*, by Ku Yuan-ching, a Chinese scholar. This work has been judged of slight historical value.

Thea is the botanical name for the tea plant, first used by Dr. Engelbert Kaempfer (1651-1716), a German naturalist. It is the Latinized version of Θεά, the Greek word meaning "a goddess," hence, perhaps, "the divine herb." The tea plant was first classified by the Swedish botanist Carl von Linne (1707-78), best known as Linnaeus, as *Thea sinensis,* in 1753. Since then the genus *Thea* has come to include the Linnæan genus *Camellia,* which is chiefly known for the familiar white or red flowers of the *Thea japonica*.

Botanists now consider Assam and China tea as equivalent tea-yielding plants, and so, with a bow to J. Sims, who first joined several species under a common name, the complete name of the tea plant is *Thea sinensis*.

Its botanical classification is as follows: Division—*Angiospermae;* Class—*Dicotyledones;* Order—*Parietales;* Family—*Theaceae;* Genus—*Thea;* Species—*sinensis*.

The tea plant is an evergreen shrub, which in its natural state grows to a height from fifteen to thirty feet, but the tea-planter keeps it pruned down to a height from three to five feet. In its general appearance and the form of its leaf it resembles the myrtle; its blossoms are white with yellow anthers and suggest the wild rose. These are succeeded by the tea fruit, containing three seeds.

The plant grows in the tropics from sea-level up to six thousand feet; in more temperate zones, where there is danger of frost, it must be kept to low elevations. As with coffee, however, it does best in the higher altitudes of the tropics.

Tea is cultivated over a range of seventy-five degrees of latitude—from 42° N., in Russian Transcaucasia, to 33° S., in northern Argentina. But all the most important tea-producing areas lie within a restricted range of about forty-three degrees of latitude—from 8° S. in Java, to 35° N. in Japan—and sixty degrees of longitude—from 80° E. to 140° E. This area includes China, Japan, Formosa, Java, Sumatra, Ceylon and India.

The Genesis of Tea

Besides the leaves of the tea shrub, the flowers are sometimes dried and a beverage made from them in the same way as from the leaves. Tea from the flowers may be said to represent a surrogate for tea. Perhaps the most important surrogate is maté, also known as yerba maté, Paraguay tea, or Brazilian tea. It is prepared from the leaf of *ilex paraguayensis* by roasting and crushing; hot water is poured upon it, and the infusion is imbibed through a tube with a strainer from a bottle-shaped gourd. Sugar and milk or the juice of oranges, limes, or lemons is sometimes added.

The list of tea substitutes is well-nigh endless.[19] Most countries have their peculiar "teas," and the exigencies of the World War caused numerous ancient formulas to be raked up and new ones added.

For many years, controversies raged among scientific men as to whether the tea plant originated in China or in India. Plants of the China variety had been painstakingly carried to India for a long time after the native *assamica* was found

In fact, tea is nowhere plucked by monkeys and it never has been, but the Englishman Aeneas Anderson accepted the myth on a 1793 embassy to China and carried the story home with him to England. It has been handed down ever since in the West.

there in 1823, and there are ancient stories of how tea came to China from India. Now we know the plant was indigenous to both countries. Specimens of the jungle or wild tea plant are still to be found growing in the forests of the Shan States of northern Siam, eastern Burma, Yunnan, Upper Indo-China, and British India–Nature's original tea garden. Consequently, the tea plant may be said to be indigenous to that portion of southeast Asia which includes China and India. The political boundaries of the various countries where wild tea has been found are purely imaginary lines which men have traced to mark the confines of India, Burma, Siam, Yunnan, and Indo-China. Before any thought was given to dividing this land into separate states, it consisted of one primeval tea garden where the conditions of soil, climate, and rainfall were happily combined to promote the natural propagation of tea.

Contemporary Chinese records establish that tea cultivation began in the interior province of Szechwan about A.D. 350, gradually extending down the Yangtze valley to the seaboard provinces. The author of the *Cha Pu,* however, writing at a much later date, assigns the first discovery of tea to the Bohea hills, partly in deference to prevailing popular opinion and partly, perhaps, to give greater éclat to his story by connecting it with one of the most celebrated and widely known tea districts in China. During the Tang dynasty (A.D. 620-907) tea cultivation spread through the present provinces of Szechwan, Hupeh, Hunan, Honan, Chekiang, Kiangsu, Kiangsi, Fukien, Kwangtung, Anhwei, Shensi, and Kweichow. Hupeh and Hunan tea plants became famous for quality, and tea from these plants was reserved for the Emperor.

Early legends, thought to be inspired by Buddhist priests, relate that monkeys were used to gather the tea leaves from inaccessible places. Sometimes they were trained for the work or, when seen among the rocks where the tea bushes grew, the Chinese would throw stones at them. The monkeys, becoming angry, would break off branches of the tea bushes and throw them down at their tormentors.[20]

After the cultivation of tea had spread through the provinces, it came to the attention of travelers from other shores, and China became the fountainhead whence tea culture spread to other countries. The first of these was Japan, where it was destined to assume an even more important social position than in China.

Knowledge of tea was probably introduced into the Island Empire along with Chinese civilization, the fine arts, and Buddhism, about A.D. 593, in the reign of Prince Shotoku. Actual tea cultivation was introduced later by Japanese priests of the Buddhist religion. These priests, many of them famous in Japanese tea history, became acquainted with the cultivation of the tea plant while pursuing religious studies in China. Upon their return to Japan they carried with them some of the seeds, and from these Chinese seeds are descended the cultivated teas of Japan.

Japanese mythology credits the origin of tea in China to Daruma—or Bodhidharma, as he was known in India. He was the founder of the Dhyan, or Zen, sect of Buddhism, and was the twenty-eighth Buddhist patriarch. Leaving India, he reached Canton early in the reign of the Emperor Wu Ti, about A.D. 520, bringing with him the sacred bowl of the patriarchs. The Emperor invited the sage to his capital at Nanking and gave him as sanctuary a cave-temple in the mountains. Here Daruma, or the "White Buddha," as he was called by the Chinese, is said to have remained seated before a wall in meditation for nine years; wherefore he has been called the "wall-gazing saint."

The Daruma legend runs that during one of his meditations the saint fell asleep. Upon awakening, he was so chagrined that he cut off his eyelids to assure himself of no recurrence of the sin. Where the severed eyelids dropped to earth, a strange plant came up. From its leaves, it was found a drink could be prepared that would banish sleep. And so, the divine herb was born and the tea beverage came into being.

Later, Daruma offended his Emperor patron by asserting that real merit could be found, not in works, but solely in purity and wisdom. Whereupon he is said to have retired to Lo-yang, crossing the turbulent Yangtze on a reed.

The Genesis of Tea

According to the *Koji Kongen* and *Ogisho,* authoritative historical records, the Japanese Emperor Shomu bestowed some *hiki-cha,* or powdered tea, upon one hundred priests whom he summoned for a four day reading of the Buddhist scriptures at the Imperial palace, in the first year of the Tempei era (A.D. 729).

The introduction of this rare and costly beverage to these ritualists apparently aroused in them a desire to grow their own plants, as the records show the monk Gyoki (A.D. 658-749) crowned his life work by building forty-nine temples and planting tea shrubs in the temple gardens. This is the first recorded cultivation of tea in Japan.

In the thirteenth year of the Yenryaku era (A.D. 794) the Emperor Kammu erected an Imperial palace at Heian-kyō [Kyoto], the Capital of Peace, adopting Chinese architecture and enclosing a tea garden. For the administration of the tea garden a governmental post was created under the medical bureau, indicating that the tea plant was then regarded as a medicinal shrub.

Subsequently, in the twenty-fourth year of the Yenryaku era (A.D. 805) the Buddhist saint Saicho, better known by his posthumous name, Dengyo Daishi, returned from studies in China, bringing tea seeds which he planted at the foot of Mount Hiyei in the village of Sakamoto, province of Omi. The present-day tea garden of Ikegami is said to be located on the site of Dengyo Daishi's original planting.

The following year, the first of the Daido era (A.D. 806), Kobo Daishi, another Buddhist monk, returned from studies in China. Like his illustrious predecessor, Dengyo Daishi, he was so impressed with this friendly plant and with the advance of civilization marking its progress in palaces and temples in the neighboring Chinese Empire that he aspired to see it take an equal or greater place in his own country. He, too, brought a quantity of tea seeds and planted them at various places. He is said to have brought home and imparted as well a knowledge of the process of manufacturing.

Yeisai (Eisai) was Japan's first tea planter, this Japanese brushwork upon a panel records Yeisai's reverance for tea: "Cha. The soil where the tea plant grows is sacred and when a man takes tea he enjoys a long life."

The Genesis of Tea

Evidently the attempt of the priests to grow tea in the temple gardens was a success. The ancient Japanese histories *Nihon-Koki* and *Ruishu Kokushi* record that in the sixth year of Konin (A.D. 815) the Emperor Saga paid a visit of state to the Bonshaku Temple at Karasaki, Shiga, in the province of Omi, where the abbot Yeichu regaled him with tea.

It is further recorded that the temple beverage so pleased the Emperor that he decreed the cultivation of the plant in the five home provinces near the capital, stipulating an annual tribute of the leaf for the use of the Imperial household.

Tea cultivation was successful also at the Genko Temple of Yamato for, according to the same histories, the retired Emperor Uda, while visiting there in the first year of Shotai (A.D. 898), was served with scented tea by the abbot Seiju Hos-shi.

At this time, when the tea drink was well on the way to becoming a popular social beverage of the capital at Heian-kyō, although still used extensively for medicinal purposes by those in high circles, it had a dramatic set-back. Civil wars broke out in Japan and tea was practically forgotten for nearly two hundred years. The tea-drinking custom was neglected, and no attention was paid to tea cultivation during this period.

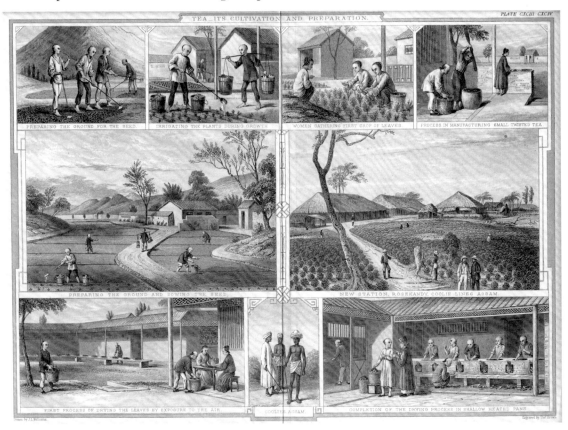

Illustrations from Samuel Ball's Cultivation and Manufacture of Tea in China, *published in London (1848).*

The Genesis of Tea

With the return of peace, tea-drinking was again revived in the second year of the Kempo era (A.D. 1191) by one of the brightest figures in Japanese tea history, the Buddhist abbot Yeisai, chief of the Zen sect, whose posthumous name is Senko-soshi. He reintroduced the tea plant to Japan, bringing new seeds from China and planting them on the slope of the Seburi Mountain, southwest of the Castle of Fukuoka, in the province of Chikuzen. Others he planted in the temple grounds of Shofukuji at Hakata.

Yeisai not only planted and raised tea, but envisioned the plant as the source of a sacred remedy, writing a book–the first Japanese work on tea–called *Kitcha Yojoki,* literally, the *Book of Tea Sanitation.* In his book, Yeisai acclaimed tea a "divine remedy and a supreme gift of heaven" for preserving human life. After this the use of tea, previously restricted to a few priests and members of the nobility, began to extend to the people at large.

The popularity of tea was no doubt considerably helped by a spectacular incident which focused attention upon it as a miraculous elixir. The mighty Minamoto Shogun Sanetomo (A.D. 1203-19) became desperately ill from over-feasting and summoned Yeisai to offer prayers for his recovery. Never doubting the efficacy of his petitions, the good abbot supplemented his prayers with his favorite beverage, sending in all haste to his temple for some of the tea grown there. He administered to the sufferer a drink prepared by his own hands, and lo! the great general's life was spared. Naturally enough, Sanetomo wanted to know more about tea; so Yeisai presented him with a copy of his book and subsequently the shogun became a devotee to tea. The fame of the new remedy spread far and wide, nobles and commoners alike seeking its healing virtues.[21]

Its appeal as a social agent was enhanced by the appearance of a tea service provided by a skilled potter, Tashiro, who imported a special glaze from China, then under the Sung dynasty (A.D. 960-1280). Applying this to tea sets helped to bring tea as a drink into fashionable vogue.

It was about this time, too, that to the abbot Myōe, chief of the Mantra sect, at Togano-o, near Kyoto, Yeisai presented some tea seeds with instructions for their cultivation and manufacture. Myōe carefully observed the directions, and the tea produced from this garden was used in his temple and elsewhere.

As the use of the tea beverage became more general, tea cultivation gradually spread to other districts. The invention of the green tea manufacturing process by Soichiro Naga-tani, better known as San-no-jo, in the third year of Genbun (A.D. 1738) gave the final impetus to its propagation in all parts of the Japanese Empire.

NOTES

1. In January 2016, organic analysis of the contents of a wooden box unearthed from the tomb of the Han dynasty Emperor Jing, revealed that tea had been among the royal possessions important in the afterlife. Jing Di died in 141 BCE.

The appearance of this tea is of a very high quality pluck, almost entirely of unopened buds, as well displaying a refined processing that resulted in a well-formed and consistent leaf. The agricultural skills required to manufacture such a product, as well as the development of the cultural importance needed to establish tea as a 'tribute-worthy' luxury reserved for royalty, would almost certainly have required several generations to mature, so it is plausible that tea cultivation had become an important practice well in advance of Jing Di's death. Tribute Tea was reportedly given to the first Zhou dynasty emperor in 1046.

2. Samuel Ball was assuredly the Western world's leading tea expert in his day. He was an executive of the "Honorable United East India Company" in China, where he resided from 1804 until 1826 at the company's compound in Canton (Guangzhou) as "inspector of teas" or chief buyer. He had retired, very comfortably we may be sure, to England before the Company lost its monopoly on trade with China in 1834. Then in 1848, eight years after the Assam Company was launched, he published *Cultivation and Manufacture of Tea in China,* which was, at the time, the most comprehensive book written about tea and the Chinese tea industry by a non-Chinese author.

3. Samuel Ball: *Cultivation and Manufacture of Tea in China* (London, 1848), p. 1.

4. Dr. Emil Breschneider: "Botanicum Sinicum," Part II, Journal of the China Branch of the Royal Asiatic Society, Vol. XXXV, pp. 130-1 (Shanghai, 1893).

5. The dialect spoken in the port of Amoy (Xiamen) and throughout much of the province of Fujian is called Hokkien. It is as far removed from Cantonese or Mandarin as Sicilian dialect is from standard Italian. Hokkien preserves the ancient word Confucius used, "tu," pronounced "tay," which the Dutch in Java learned and took back to Europe in 1610 along with the first tea ever sold in the West. The Portuguese, based at Macao in the Cantonese-speaking province of Guangdong, learned the word "cha" by which they still know tea today. Probably some of Portugal's elite had experienced tea before 1610, by which date Asians had already known tea for perhaps four thousand years. In Hokkien, one is said to "eat"—not "drink"—tea, further proof of tea's antiquity in the region.

6. In 1610 the Dutch not only brought the first tea to Europe but also brought the name by which it has been known ever since. Tea is *cha* to the Chinese—but not all to all of them. Denied access to Canton or Macao, the Dutch conducted their early China trade from Java, now in Indonesia. Java was then a regular port of call for

The Genesis of Tea

Chinese merchant junks out of Fujian, the Chinese province opposite Taiwan. The Dutch obviously obtained their first tea from these speakers of Hokkien. This Fujian dialect retains the word *t'e* in direct descent from the word found in an ancient ode which Confucius (Kongfuzi 551-479 BCE) anthologized in his *Book of Songs*.

7. In his diary written in the 1660's, Samuel Pepys *(Peeps)* presents various culturally-attributed spellings: *Tcha, Tay, Tee,* and finally, *Tea*.

8. According to Chinese legend, civilization was founded by the nation's first four emperors, the second of whom taught men farming and the use of plants for medicine. This demi-god was called Shen Nung, the "divine" farmer or healer. The legend of Shen Nung (or Yan Di) harks back into China's Neolithic pre-history, 1000 years or more before the earliest surviving Chinese writing is found on the Oracle Bones of the Shang dynasty (1600–1046 BCE). Besides legends, we also have noteworthy ancient evidence of tea.

An account is given of the overthrow of the Shang dynasty in *Records of the State Huayang* (now Sichuan). Written circa 350 CE, this document describes King Wu's victory which established the Zhou dynasty in 1046 BCE; the list of tribute gifts offered him include notation of a *possible* character for tea. Tea was probably a royal, possibly sacred, offering to the highest powers under the Zhou, as it very certainly was under the succeeding Han dynasty.

In *The Manual of the Zhou Dynasty Rituals*, written during the Han dynasty (206 BCE–220 CE), is a record of the previous Zhou period (794-221 BCE), which describes religious tea rituals held at the Zhou court.

Additionally, in his 59 BCE *Tong Yue* (*Instructions to the Slave*), writer and poet Wang Bao (84–53 BCE) gives explicit details regarding proper tea service, even stipulating tea purchased in Wuyang, near Chengdu in Sichuan. The author's careful directions resolve any possible ambiguity regarding his wishes. Although he employs the older, more general Chinese character "tu," it seems hard to doubt that to him it means "tea."

9. Historians have diligently sought for the first distinct reference to tea meaning Camellia sinensis, as opposed to other popular herbs. No such clarification existed in Chinese literature before tea's development and widespread popularity attained "critical mass". This is simply another example of the lexicographer's dilemma; culture getting ahead of its linguistic codification. Buddhism, and with it tea, had been spreading for over five hundred years before tea drinking become commonplace under the Tang dynasty (616-907 CE). Writing the first book about tea, Lu Yu (733-804 CE) obviously gave China's literate, urban class the word for the thing—tea, as opposed to anything else infused in water. *Cha*, the name he gave it, had long been in use among Buddhist monks and farmers and in 725 CE finally appeared in a Chinese dictionary. Human speech and human thought are always coincident.

Before Lu Yu wrote during the Tang dynasty (616-907 CE), there existed five different sobriquets for our desired beverage, and likely more than one of them were used describing the same drink:

The *Erh Ya (Approaching Refinement)* is an ancient compendium of Chinese lore, natural history, and culture, dated by modern researchers to as early as the fourth century BCE and including matter from as far back as the sixth century BCE. This ancient work contains ambiguous references to a bitter vegetable "jia," as well as "tu."

The *Guangya* by Chang Yi (Zhang Yi) was an edition or version of the Erh Ya written circa 230 CE by the doctor of the Han Emperor Ming. In the fourth century CE, Kuo Po (Guo Pu, 276–322 CE); historian, poet and, most importantly, the seer who formulated Feng Shui, wrote commentaries and translations on early Chinese texts. He spent eighteen years writing annotations to the *Guangya*. The terms this learned authority used for "teas" of various types are *jia, tu, ming, chuan,* and *kutu*.

10. Chang Yi (Zhang Yi) also served Emperor Ming as Doctor to the Imperial Academy.

11. Chekiang (*Zhejiang*).

12. It is recorded that during the reign of Han Emperor Xuan (91-49 BCE) Buddhist monk Wu Lizhen first planted seven tea bushes on Mount Mengdeng (*Mengdengshan*) in Sichuan around the year 50 BCE. Only 360 leaves were harvested yearly, and exclusively dedicated for tribute to the Emperor. These plants and Mengdengshan tea became so prized that, more than 1,200 years later, Wu Lizhen was to be awarded the title Master Ganlu ("Master of the Sweet Dew") by Emperor Xiaozong of the Song dynasty. The earliest known tea poem dates from circa 300 CE and exalts tea as "Marvelous plants from magnificent mountains." It was during this same period Buddhists established monasteries on Lushan and planted tea there that was to inspire visiting poets century after century.

13. Jacobson, J.I.L.L.; author, early Dutch tea plantation farmer in Jakarta, Indonesia, "Handhoeli v. cl. Kultuur en fabrikatie von Thee," d. J. J. L. L. Jacobson. Batavia (Jakarta), 1843.

Gordon, George James; Secretary to the Tea Committee of the East India Company, acquired China tea plants, seeds and experienced Chinese tea hands for tea planting in Assam in 1834.

Ball, Samuel; author of *An Account of the Cultivation and Manufacture of Tea in China,* 1848, and former Tea Inspector to the British East India Tea Company.

Fortune, Robert; Scottish botanist and adventurer, author of several tea books, including *Two Visits to the Tea Countries of China,* 1853.

14. Lu Yu is said to have been born in 733 CE in Tianmen county of Hubei province.

15. John Ruskin, 1819-1900, prolific English author, artist, critic, social thinker and philanthropist of the Victorian era, also a progenitor of environmentalism. He was a major intellectual influence on W. H. Ukers.

16. Gong Cha (Tribute Tea) was first received around 1066 BCE, according to *Records of the lands south of Mt. Hua (Hua Yang Guo Zhihe),* as transcribed centuries after the event. It came from Bashu-speaking people of present-day Sichuan, the earliest tea growing region. Lu Yu claimed tea was first taxed by decree of the Emperor Taihe (477-499 CE).

17. Sulayman al-Tajir (Eusebius Renaudot, translator): *Accounts of India and China by Two Mohammedan Travellers Who Went to Those Parts in the Ninth Century* (London, 1733).

18. Bodhidharma is called *Daruma* by the Japanese.

19. One of today's most popular herbal is rooibos from South Africa. Others include three representatives of the Holly species: yerba maté (South America), guayusa (Ecuador) and yaupon (North America).

The Genesis of Tea

20. In fact, tea is nowhere plucked by monkeys and it never has been, but the Englishman Aeneas Anderson accepted the myth of simian assisted tea while on a 1793 embassy to China and carried the story home with him to England. It has been handed down ever since in the West.

21. Japan and China had developed trade and cultural ties from Han dynasty days when Nero ruled Rome. Not surprisingly, two monks returning from Buddhist studies in China (Dengyo Daishi in 805 and Kobo Daishi in 806) brought with them the seeds of Japan's very first tea gardens. The arc of time in Japan's eventual adoption of tea is bookended by a pair of emperor/priest relationships, each with a focus on a different Chinese dynasty and different tea style. The *Nihon Kōki* (later *Chronicles of Japan*) documents Emperor Saga's introduction to tea in 815 by Dengyo Daishi, just returned from thirty years in China. Their manner of tea drinking was borrowed from Tang China which they regarded as the height of civilized culture. They prepared their beverage Tang-style, boiling leaf crumbled from tea cakes. For a time, tea culture developed in Japan.

Following centuries of disruption by ongoing civil wars, tea was once again taught to Japan's royalty by a priest under the influence of Chinese culture and practices—this time not Tang, but Song dynasty China. In a reprise of tea's earlier introduction to Japan, Yeisai (1141-1215) brought back from a trip to China tea seed which he distributed to other Buddhists. He also grew adept at cultivating tea. He composed *Kissa yojo ki*, Japan's first book on tea and its health benefits, both physical and spiritual. It was heavily indebted to China's Song dynasty culture. By administering his tea cure, the new style matcha (steamed leaf ground into a powder and whipped into a frothy broth), Yeisai cured an Emperor's hangover from wine drinking, sparing him the wrath of grapes. Yeisai's Zen-style tea drinking attracted the attention of Japan's samurai class. Japan's tea culture was revived.

Tea roasting depicted in an early nineteenth century Chinese watercolor.

TEA'S CONQUEST OF THE ORIENT

For many years, it was thought that tea could not be grown and manufactured successfully except in China and Japan, so it was a long time after the Portuguese navigators had shown the way to the Indies and the Far East that the Dutch and the English were inspired to try to grow it in their Indian possessions.

The Dutch were more enterprising in developing a tea cultivation of their own than were the English. However, tea had been known in the Netherlands and traded in by Dutch merchants for seventy-four years before the Dutch drove the English out of Java, and Andreas Cleyer, the German naturalist, smuggler, and doctor of medicine, first thought of growing Japan tea in Java. This was in 1684. Although nothing ever came of his experiment (he used the plants to ornament his palatial home in Batavia), this gesture entitles him to the honor of being the first to grow tea in Java.

So tea's conquest of Java and Sumatra started with tea from Japan, followed by plants from China; but it was not until Assam tea seed was brought from British India in 1878 that the victory was complete. Indeed, it took over two hundred years for tea to accomplish the subjugation of Java; some forty years elapsed after Cleyer's importation of Japanese tea seed before the Dutch East India Company decided to grow its own tea with tea seed brought from China. The company was undoubtedly actuated by jealousy of the competition from Austrian Netherlands merchants in the China-Japan trade, and was looking for a means to thwart it.

The "Seventeen Lords," the Board of Directors of the Dutch East India Company, in certain representations made to the Government of Netherlands Indies in 1728, argued that China tea seed should be sown not only in Java, but also at the Cape of Good Hope, in Ceylon, and at Jaffanapatnam.

The Dutch East Indian Government viewed the project coldly, promising little encouragement. It doubted if tea could be grown in Java; however, it would make the experiment by offering a bonus to the first producer of a pound of the finished native product, as suggested by the "Honourable and Noble Lords." Apparently, the Dutch East India Company did not pursue the matter, for a few years later it had regained its monopoly of the tea trade of Europe and had ceased worrying about the growing of tea, satisfied to be sole distributor of the product on the Continent.

The company did not revive the subject of tea growing in Java until 1823, the year the English were discovering the indigenous tea plant in India. The next year, 1824, Dr. Philipp Franz von Siebold, a naturalist attached to the Dutch Embassy in Japan, was instructed to secure seeds of the tea plant and send them to Java. The first shipment was a failure, but from the second, received in 1826, tea plants were successfully grown in that year at the Buitenzorg Botanical Gardens, and in 1827 near Garoet.

J. I. L. L. Jacobson was only 28 years old when he was appointed by the Netherlands Trading Company in 1827 to be the resident tea expert for their lucrative trading station in Canton. He was being paid a handsome salary of four thousand dollars annually.

Also, in 1827, Commissioner General L. P. J. Viscount du Bus de Gisignies, late Governor of South Brabant, was sent out to Java to promote private enterprise. He opened experimental gardens and set the stage for the entrance of the real founder and father of tea culture in Java, Jacobus Isidorus Lodewijk Levien Jacobson, or, as he is more familiarly known, J. I. L. L. Jacobson.

Jacobson was an expert tea taster *en route* from Holland to Canton to sample tea from the Netherlands Trading Company. When he arrived in Java the tea plants were doing well in the moist climate around Buitenzorg and Garoet, but search among the Chinese population of Java had failed to discover anyone who knew how the leaf should be prepared for market.

Commissioner General du Bus de Gisignies gave Jacobson his great opportunity by assigning him the task of collecting and forwarding information, implements and workmen from China, with a view to promoting the tea industry of Netherlands Indies. Jacobson travelled back and forth between China and Java for six years, and after that labored at his task in Java for upwards of fifteen years, during which time he achieved more than anyone else in the cultivation of tea in Netherlands Indies.

J. I. L. L. Jacobson was born at Rotterdam, March 13, 1799. He was the son of I. L. Jacobson, a coffee and tea broker whose business was established in Rotterdam, and it was from his father that young Jacobson learned all there was to know of the art of tea tasting at that time. The Netherlands Trading Company appointed him their tea expert for Java and China, and on September 2, 1827 he arrived at Batavia. Invited by Commissioner General du Bus de Gisignies to undertake the mission of collecting information and forwarding tea seed from China for the Government's tea experiments, he proceeded to Canton. There he ingratiated himself with the leading tea merchants. During the following six years, he made annual return journeys to Java, each time bringing with him valuable information and quantities of seeds or tea plants for the enterprise.

From various accounts of Jacobson's activities, we gather that, although he was still in his twenties when he began this work, he was possessed of amazing assurance. He was a positive type who knew how to get things done, although his accomplishments stirred up much jealousy and made many enemies. From the most authoritative biographical sketch of him that has come down to us we learn that he not only gained access to the tea making establishments in Honan, but even penetrated to the interior, where he visited the tea gardens.

Some of Jacobson's critics would have us look upon him as a kind of Baron Munchausen,[1] but the main facts of his career stand out clearly. His contributions to the founding of Java's tea industry were many and salutary, even with necessary allowances made for youthful enthusiasm.[2] He was what is sometimes described in America as a "go-getter." Dr. Ch. Bernard says in his monograph, *The History of Tea Culture in the Dutch East Indies*: "Jacobson must be rightly considered the actual founder of this culture."

Jacobson gained considerable information on his first trip to China, in 1827-8, although he was essentially a tea-taster and trader, not a tea culturist.

At Canton it was Jacobson's duty, in his service to the Netherlands Trading Company, working with a fellow countryman to assist, as tea taster, the supercargo, A. H. Buchler, in buying the return cargoes. For one so young—he was only twenty-eight—he was being paid a handsome salary of four thousand dollars a year. Besides being full of ambition as well as romantic ideas, he knew tea from the buyer's standpoint, and no one else knew much about its cultivation and manufacture. He was young, too, to have thrust upon him the high honour conferred by his Government, although it does not appear that he flinched from the service, fraught though it was with much danger. It was an exceedingly hazardous undertaking to invade an unfriendly country and attempt to carry off men and produce, yet Jacobson did both.

On returning from his second journey, in 1828-9, Jacobson brought back eleven Chinese tea shrubs, from Fukien. His third journey, in 1829-30, yielded no results for tea culture. From his fourth journey, in 1830-1, he brought back 243 tea plants and 150 seeds. From his fifth journey, in 1831-2, he returned with 300,000 seeds and twelve Chinese workmen. This was a success of some significance. When the workmen were subsequently murdered in a row among the coolies, Jacobson went on a sixth journey to China, in 1832-3, and brought back no less than 7,000,000 seeds, fifteen workmen—tea-planters, tea-makers, and box-makers—and a mass of materials and implements which he had collected. It was during this last expedition that he nearly lost his life; for the Chinese government had put a price on his head, and the mandarins attempted to capture his vessel with his tea seed and the Chinese workmen. They succeeded in getting his interpreter, Acheong, who made the voyage in another ship and was mistaken for Jacobson. Acheong was later ransomed by M. J. Senn van Basel, the Dutch consul at Canton, for 502 piastres. Jacobson got away with his precious cargo.

The tasks assigned to Jacobson were from the start recognized by the Government as most difficult, and all who knew Canton with its myriad spies were doubtful of the outcome. From a cabinet letter of Governor General van den Bosch it is apparent that much importance was attached to the 1832-3 charge. Jacobson's return trip was a major triumph. On the arrival of his ship off Anjer,[3] cannon were fired, a swarm of prauws[4] put off to enable him to discharge his cargo, and post-horses were put at his disposal to take him to Batavia. He was the Charles Lindbergh of his day.

Thus in 1833, seven years after the first parcel of Japanese tea seed was safely in the ground, Jacobson began in good earnest his labours for the tea industry in Java. Up to 1833 much of the pioneer work had been carried on by others, but Jacobson brought valuable contributions of seeds, plants, men, materials and technical advice on tea making.

Among others of importance in this period mention should be made of de Serière. As Bus de Gisignies's faithful Boswell, he claimed for himself and for his patron the honor of first promoting tea cultivation in Java. Although never confirmed officially, de Serière's pioneer work for tea was recognized by the award to him of a gold medal at the Paris Exposition of 1867.

For fifteen years following 1833, the indefatigable Jacobson devoted himself to the development of tea cultivation in Java, directing the planting and manufacturing in fourteen provinces. The Dutch Government rewarded his perseverance by appointing him inspector of tea cultivation, with some two hundred hands to help him, and later gave him the Cross of the Dutch Lion. In 1843 he published at Batavia his *Handboek voor de Cultuur en Fabrikatie van Thee (Handbook for the Cultivation and Manufacture of Tea),* and in 1845 his *Over het Sorteeren en Afpakken van de Thee (About the Sorting and Packing of Tea),* the pioneer technical books on tea.

Tea's Conquest of the Orient

The cultivation of tea introduced under his direction throughout the whole of west and middle Java increased rapidly, but he was not destined to see its ultimate triumph. He returned to his native country to work out further plans for the development of the industry, only to meet his death on December 27, 1848. In that same year Robert Fortune sailed for China to bring back tea plants and Chinese workmen to British India, and the first attempt was made to grow tea in the United States. China was still thought of everywhere as the prime source of tea.

The cultivation of tea in Java experienced several varying phases. First it was promoted as a Government monopoly, but that was a failure. Then followed an era of private ownership, which began in 1862 and produced many famous names, among them the Holies and the Kerkhovens, sturdy Dutch pioneers who were the real founders of the tea industry in Java.

John Peet,[5] an Englishman who first introduced Assam tea seed into Java from British India in 1878, started a revolution in the cultivation and preparation of tea. Gradually the old China plants were superseded by the sturdier Assam jats, or types; modern machinery took the place of the old rolling methods, and mechanical dryers drove out the charcoal furnaces. Thus was ushered in the third period of tea's conquest of Java—a period that was marked by great prosperity, when the coffee lands became *koffie moe* (coffee tired). The tea garden areas were extended, quality was improved, and Java tea became as well known in the tea markets of the world as Java coffee had been in the old days.

The third phase, the golden age of sociability and good fellowship, extended from 1875 to 1890. Those were the good old times when an almost royal hospitality was dispensed in the mansions of the tea barons, who lived like feudal lords and were looked up to as Great White Fathers by the thousands of laborers on their estates; when journeys took days to accomplish and were full of adventures; when palanquins, "balloon" carts, and buffalo oxen provided more picturesque if less speedy means of transportation than modern motorcars; the days of thrilling snipe-hunts, of races, soirées, dinner parties and gorgeous Oriental fiestas. Not that the spirit of Dutch hospitality has changed; only we live in a swifter age, wherein railways, airplanes, motorcars, radio, telephones, superb roads, all conspire to rob life of something of the peace and serenity which

Edinburgh botanist Robert Fortune was one of the greatest industrial spies of the 19th century. In 1848, he was commissioned by the English East India Company to go undercover into China for three years in order to learn the secrets to growing and manufacturing tea. His two-volume Two Visits to the Tea Countries of China *details his harrowing adventures.*

In 1859, Fortune returned to China under the auspices of the United States Patent Office to gather and propagate tea seeds for planting research tea gardens in the southern United States. The seedlings were planted in a Washington, D.C. nursery but the onset of the Civil War brought the agricultural project to an abrupt end.

characterized the "old days," and which will always linger in the memories of those of us who knew them without the modern hysteria, our present *perpetuum mobile*.

And a curious thing about it is the ease with which we adapt ourselves to the changing conditions. I must admit I found Dutch hospitality in Java quite as pleasant in 1924, when I covered ten times as much ground and saw and learned much more, as in 1906, when I visited only two or three estates and spent most of my time on the island as a guest of that princely host Mr. L. A. F. H. Baron van Heeckeren tot Waliën, on Sinagar, one of the show places of the "Garden of the East."

During the period between 1880 and 1890 tea completed its conquest of Java by scaling the Pengalengan Plateau, that magnificent table-land which appeared to offer all the advantages of an elevation almost equal to that of Darjeeling, combined with the forcing climate of the equatorial zone. Tea cultivation on this broad elevated tract of rich tropical soil was stimulated largely by the activities of the planter-philanthropist K. A. R. Bosscha (1855-1928),[6] sometimes referred to as the "agricultural king of the Preanger" and as the "tea king of Java." For over thirty years he was associated with Malabar Estate, a name which, like Goal para, is almost synonymous with Java tea. Tea's conquest of Sumatra began in the early nineties and among the pioneers the names of C. A. Lampard and J. H. Marinus stand out prominently. Tea is now in a fair way to repeat in Sumatra on a much more imposing scale what has already been achieved in Java.

The year 1934 marked the hundredth anniversary of the appointment, by Lord William Charles Cavendish Bentinck, of a committee to formulate a plan for the introduction of tea into British India. The event signalized the founding of the far-flung kingdom of India tea, which extends to all the countries of the earth where tea is grown or is used as a beverage: to Ceylon and Java, where Indian jats supplanted the China varieties; to Europe, where India tea took possession of markets held inviolate by China tea for two hundred years; to North America, where first China and then Japan were forced to give way to British-grown tea; to the Latin countries, which for centuries have acknowledged cocoa as queen; to Brazil, where coffee is king; to Paraguay, where maté rules; to Africa, Australia, and New Zealand, where devotees to India tea are legion; and even to China and Japan, which produce their own tea, but where many foreigners, and not a few natives, do India tea homage, morning, noon, and night. Verily, the sun never sets upon India tea's dominions.

The introduction of tea culture into India is in itself quite a stirring tale, for, in the first place, tea was indigenous to India, although only the aborigines knew it. Patriotic Englishmen proposed to import China tea plants and set up an industry of their own in India. Apologetic statesmen of the compromising kind, and all those more or less directly interested in preserving the English East India Company's monopoly of the Eastern trade, promptly objected.

Tea's Conquest of the Orient

For ten years indigenous India tea begged for recognition, only to be met with cynical indifference; and when recognition came, how halting, how half-hearted it was! The glamor of centuries still clung to China tea, and when the bewildered merchants were relieved at last of the incubus of the East India monopoly, they found themselves incapable of thinking of any but China tea. They continued to send thousands of miles to China for tea seeds, plants, and workmen, solemnly and laboriously trying to grow China tea in a country that already possessed a native jat[7] much better suited to its requirements.

This was recognized by only a few soldiers of fortune, statesmen and scientists. These courageous souls eventually won the day for India's indigenous tea, and then private enterprise stepped in where governmental paternalism had failed.

Within the span of three generations British enterprise carved out of the jungles of India an industry which embraces over one million acres, a capital investment of seventy-five million pounds, giving employment to nearly nine hundred thousand workers and exporting 38.4 percent of the world's total exports of tea, thus making India the world's largest tea-exporting country and at the same time creating one of the most lucrative sources of private wealth and Government tax returns in the British Empire. What Brazil is to coffee, India is to tea.

In 1823, eleven years previous to the appointment of the historic tea committee, Major Robert Bruce conducted a trading expedition into Burmese Assam, and reported finding native tea trees growing near Rangpur. This was confirmed the following year by C. A. Bruce, a brother of Major Bruce. Still earlier–about 1780–Governor General Warren Hastings and Colonel Robert Kyd had started an agitation on behalf of indigenous tea. It was not until 1788, however, when the eminent English naturalist Sir Joseph Banks[8] wrote his celebrated memoir on tea, that serious attention began to be paid to the cultivation of tea in India.

There seems to have been a long-maintained reluctance at the Calcutta Botanical Gardens to admit the identity of the Assam tea plant. Following Bruce, others sent specimens, but no recognition was obtained for them. Meanwhile there had been brewing in London a strong sentiment favorable to starting a tea industry in India, despite the unfriendly attitude of the East India Company, which still was enjoying its highly profitable monopoly of the Chinese tea trade.

In 1825 we find the English Society of Arts offering a gold medal for the best British-grown tea. In 1827 Dr. J. F. Royle, scientist and author, urged the introduction of tea culture into the north-west district of the Himalaya range. In 1831 Captain Andrew Charlton reported wild tea trees growing near Beesa, in Assam. In 1832 an experimental tea garden was opened in the Nilgiri hills of southern India by Dr. Christie, a surgeon of the Madras Establishment. The same year C. A. Bruce, the real founder of tea cultivation in Assam, again urged recognition of the native jat through Captain Francis Jenkins, Commissioner of Assam. Finally, after the abolition in 1833 by the British Parliament of the East India Company's monopoly of the China tea trade, came the belated recognition, in 1834, by the Calcutta authorities, of Captain Charlton's specimens as genuine indigenous tea.

Governor General Lord Bentinck's committee was also hard to convince of the nature and virtues of the native product. At first it experimented with tea seeds brought from China by George James Gordon, but after the appointment, in 1835, of C. A. Bruce as superintendent of tea culture in Assam, cultivation of the Assam jat received great impetus. Bruce put Chinese tea makers at work on native leaf and in 1836 sent the first manufactured samples to Calcutta. Three years later the first importation of Assam tea was sold at India House, London, with the East India Company as vendor. The same year the Assam Company, India's pioneer tea-planting company, was formed, with a double board of directors–one in London and one in Calcutta.

Of the scientific commission, which, in 1835-6, explored Assam, guided by C. A. Bruce, the name of botanist Dr. William Griffith stands out because he subsequently wrote and published *Journals of Travels* dealing with his experiences. He, too, for a time, favored the importation of China seed, since characterized by Dr. H. H. Mann as "the curse of the Indian tea industry." Under the commission's auspices the first experimental tea garden—destined to be washed away—was opened near Sadiya, and in 1837 a second garden was opened at Chubwa. Some of the original Chinese plantings are still there, though now abandoned.

Further imports of China tea were demanded by the partisans of the China jat, and several notable shipments of seeds, plants and native workmen were arranged for in 1848-51 by Robert Fortune, agent of the English East India Company, who disguised himself as a Chinaman in order to penetrate the tea districts of North China. These plants were set out in the Himalayas, where they did well, although never achieving a degree of commercial importance comparable with that of the indigenous jat.

It is a curious fact that whenever an attempt has been made to transplant the China jat the result has been disastrous. It was so in Java; it followed in India and in Ceylon. It seems as if that mysterious, hidden force which Couperus[9] talks about in his stories of the East was at work to accomplish the undoing of anyone who sought to carry away the seeds of China's most venerated plant.

It has been charged that before selling it to foreigners the Chinese frequently boiled the tea seed to prevent its germination, and it is known that all kinds of strange tricks were resorted to in order to defeat the propagation of the China tea plant outside of China. Seeds and plants shipped in good condition often arrived improperly packed, moldy, diseased, dead or in a dying condition; and when good seed or healthy plants were successfully imported, the tea manufactured from them was never the same as in China. Indeed, only China's soil and climate seem able to produce year after year, the distinctive China tea which the Celestial accepts as a gift of the gods, designed for him alone. White men for centuries begged it from the Chinese because they liked it, too; but just as soon as the white man tried to produce it outside of its native China, "it bit him like a serpent" or "stung him like an adder."

Tea cultivation spread rapidly after C. A. Bruce demonstrated its commercial possibilities, and we find the Assam jat favored in many localities, notably in Ceylon and Java, where its introduction became responsible for powerful allied tea industries.

In 1842 the English Society of Arts awarded a gold medal to C. A. Bruce for the discovery of tea in Assam, and the Horticultural Society of Bengal presented gold medals to Major Jenkins and Captain Charlton for their part in securing its recognition.[10] Thus was settled a previous controversy over the discoverer of tea in Assam.

Scottish brothers Robert and Charles Bruce were early pioneers in the Assam tea industry. In 1823, Robert (above) visited Rangpur in Upper Assam in search of native tea plants which he confirmed resembled the Chinese cultivar. But he was dead within a year and it fell to Charles to continue his brother's quest for propagating tea plants.

Assam tea was first sold at the London auction in 1839, the same year Charles published his Report on the Manufacture of Tea in Assam.

The early vicissitudes of the Assam Company, the lineal descendant of the East India Company, make interesting reading. In 1840 the Assam Company took over two-thirds of the Government tea gardens in northeastern India. In 1852 its first dividend, of two and one-half percent, was earned. In 1851 the first privately owned tea garden in Assam had been opened by Colonel F. S. Hannay.

The period between 1863 and 1866 was notable for a boom in tea lands and wild speculation in tea shares. It was then that tea acquired much unenviable notoriety from being classed with the South Sea and other bubbles. The Government finally stepped in and appointed a commission to inquire into the state of the industry. This commission confirmed the opinion, held by all thoughtful students and prudent investors, that the industry was basically sound and needed only to forge ahead after ridding itself of unwise inflation and its stock-jobbing companions.

In 1872 William Jackson set up his first mechanical tea roller on the Heeleaka garden of the Scottish Assam Tea Company, at Jorhat. Jackson was the inventor of many rollers, dryers and other epoch-making machines. In 1874 Lieutenant Colonel Edward Money also invented a tea.

In 1877 Samuel C. (later Sir Samuel) Davidson invented his first "Sirocco" tea dryer. This was followed by a number of revolutionizing tea machines.[11]

The 1877 invention of the Sirocco tea dryer by Samuel C. Davidson greatly increased the quantity of tea manufactured across India.

One of the most interesting things in this brief survey of India's tea history is the part which she played in changing England from a coffee-drinking to a tea-drinking nation. The movement was well under way when indigenous tea was discovered in India, but the final fillip was given to the transformation when it became possible, through that discovery, to make it a patriotic duty for Britishers to drink tea. Also, it marked the beginning of the decline of China teas in the English market.

In 1866 the United Kingdom consumed 102,265,000 pounds of tea, of which only 4 percent was Indian; and the annual per-capita consumption of tea in the British Isles was 3.42 pounds. By 1903 this consumption had increased to 6.03 pounds per head, of which only 10 percent was from China, with 59 percent from India and 31 percent from Ceylon. By 1908 tea imports from China had fallen from 104,500,000 pounds to 9,750,000 pounds, and imports of India tea had increased from 6,250,000 pounds to 162,500,000 pounds.

The per-capita consumption of tea in the United Kingdom had risen to 10.56 pounds in 1932. China tea imports were down to approximately 8,200,000 pounds, or less than 2 percent, and the imports of India tea were approximately 253,000,000 pounds, or 57 percent. These shifting figures also show how black teas are displacing greens. Pretty much the same story is repeating itself in America, where a hundred years ago, 99 percent of the tea consumed was China tea (black and green). Today black teas dominate, with over 65 percent, and greens from China and Japan have fallen to about 21 percent.

Tea's triumph over coffee on the plantations of Ceylon is one of the most dramatic stories in the history of the industry. Coffee had been successfully cultivated on the island for nearly fifty years when the dreaded blight, *Hemileia vastatrix,* made its appearance and within a few years destroyed an industry that had represented at its peak a capital value of £16,500,000 ($80,000,000), and exports amounting to 110,000,000 pounds in a single year.

Up to that time tea cultivation had been tried in an experimental way only; when the great blight came, the acreage under tea was practically negligible–between 200 and 300 acres–compared with that of coffee, which covered 275,000 acres. Today there are upwards of 557,000 acres devoted to tea, and the coffee acreage has dwindled to almost nothing. Tea production reached the record of 252,824,000 pounds in 1932. The area now under tea exceeds the vanished area under coffee by some 282,000 acres.

Tea's Conquest of the Orient

When the British finally settled down to develop to the utmost the vast resources of the "brave island, so fruitful and fair," that they had inherited from the Dutch, one of the first things they did was to carve for themselves an astounding coffee enterprise out of the virgin forests of the Kandyan country. Coffee had been known in Ceylon at that time (1796) for nearly a hundred years.

In 1864, when coffee was in its hey-day, Mr. (later Sir) Graeme Hepburn Dalrymple-Horn Elphinstone came out to Ceylon and began his career as a planter in Kotmalie. By 1875 he was the largest coffee estate proprietor in Ceylon. Then came the coffee leaf disease, which, while it destroyed all his great properties, was at the same time responsible for initiating a movement to turn the collapse of coffee into a triumph for tea. Inspired by a former Assam planter named William Cameron (really Campbell), Elphinstone became interested in tea and probably would have figured largely in its further development had not financial difficulties presently overwhelmed him and brought his life to an untimely end in 1900. In 1882 Cameron so improved the local system of pruning and plucking tea as to show a remarkable increase in crop returns.

After the first coffee slump of 1845, due to the hysterical speculative "rush into coffee," many European-owned properties were abandoned, but the village coffee industry still flourished. This suffered with the rest when the coffee blight came in the seventies. The apex of Ceylon's prosperity resulting from the coffee industry was reached in 1877. Ten years later the Government was facing a deficit, and the island seemed derelict, with the coffee smash at its worst. Like rats deserting a sinking ship, large numbers of Jaffna Tamils and frightened burghers joined the crowd of ruined planters who were leaving the island in despair, many going to the Malay States, as the coffee slump was coincident with the opening of that country.

Tea was being tried in an experimental way when the coffee blight struck Ceylon, but the financial outlook for a new industry of this kind was dour indeed. With one highly organized agricultural industry, on which Ceylon was dependent, in ruins, and the coffee trees rotting, there seemed little chance of raising money to promote tea cultivation.

The strange orange-red blots had appeared on the under-side of the coffee leaves only a few years before. One lone scientist, Dr. George Henry Kendrick Thwaites, then director of the Royal Botanic Gardens at Peradeniya, raised his voice in solemn warning, but it was like the voice of one crying in the wilderness. No one heeded him until it was too late. Like a thief in the night the plague had descended upon the all too confident, smiling planters.

There was left only a small band who made a pathetic picture standing together amid the ruins of their fortunes, but stubbornly refusing to accept defeat. To these men, who faced seemingly insurmountable obstacles at the blackest period of Ceylon's history, the world is indebted for the raising of a magnificent industry from the ashes of the coffee estates—an industry conceived in penury and nurtured in economy, yet producing today the finest quality teas that reach the world's markets.

How complete was the ruin of coffee may be gathered from the fact that dead coffee trees were stripped and exported to England to serve as legs for tea tables.

At this time, some of the coffee planters were so poor that they were unable to buy seed; not a few were struggling along on as little as thirty to forty rupees a month. Hence the recovery from the coffee slump was one of the most remarkable and striking achievements in colonial history. Families ruined by coffee returned to Ceylon, took off their coats, and started with a grim determination which has been an example to British colonists ever since.

First, cinchona was tried, with good results until—as always with drugs—the price dropped out of sight. Cinchona seed was secured and planted through the coffee, and this helped to stave off the evil days. Quinine at that time brought about eleven and a half rupees an ounce, but overproduction soon reduced it to three-quarters of a rupee an ounce, and ultimately the bark from which the quinine was extracted was not worth taking off the trees.

Then tea seeds were bought and planted in the rows of coffee trees. The resourcefulness, grit, self-denial and sheer hard work shown by the Ceylon planters in a trying climate during those critical days command unlimited admiration. The experiments with tea were well under way before coffee received its death warrant, although cinchona helped bridge the transition from coffee to tea on not a few estates. In the closing days of 1839 the first tea seeds from the newly discovered Assam indigenous plants, grown by Dr. Nathaniel Wallich in the Botanic Gardens at Calcutta, were received at the Botanic Gardens in Peradeniya. Early in 1840, 205 plants followed. In 1840-2 some of these were planted on the land of Sir Anthony Oliphant, Chief Justice, in the neighborhood of Queens Cottage, Nuwara Eliya and some near Essex Cottage, now the Naseby tea estate.

In the meantime, Mr. Maurice B. Worms, returning from a voyage to China in 1841, brought with him some cuttings of the China tea plant, and these were set out on the Rothschild coffee estate in the Pussellawa district. Later Mr. Worms and his brother, Gabriel B., cousins of the London Rothschilds, planted tea on Sogamma and their other estates, and among them on Condegalla, now a part of the Lahookelle group in the Ramhoda district. Some tea, which is reputed to have cost a guinea a pound to produce, was manufactured by the aid of a Chinaman on the Rothschild estate.

The Worms brothers belonged to a remarkable family. The eldest, Solomon, was the first Baron de Worms, son of Benedict Worms of Frankfurt am Main, and his wife, who was the eldest sister of the Baron de Rothschild. The brothers were born traders and adventurers. Maurice went to England in 1827; Gabriel in 1832; and both became members of the London Stock Exchange. Maurice sailed for the East in 1841, and in 1842 Gabriel joined him in Colombo, where they established a shipping and banking business under the name of G. & M. B. Worms. Gabriel remained in Colombo, and Maurice looked after the planting in the up-country. Their two-thousand-acre Rothschild estate in Pussellawa was famed for its completeness and efficiency, and was held up as a model by William Sabonadiere in his coffee planter's textbook. Their trademark was a standard for quality in Mincing Lane, the center of the tea and coffee trade in London, for over twenty-five years. They reached out until their holdings totaled 7,318 acres. When they sold out, it was for £157,000–a record transfer of European-owned estates. They then retired to England. As one of the brothers expressed it, they "led useful, contented lives." Maurice died in 1865; Gabriel in 1881.

Sir Thomas Lipton took advantage of Ceylon's devastating coffee blight in 1890 when he purchased several plantations and began growing tea to supply his stores across Scotland and England,

About the time that the Worms brothers imported their China cuttings, a Mr. Llewellyn of Calcutta, planted some Assam indigenous shrubs on Penylan estate, Dolosbage. Quite as early in the field, however, and more successful in a quiet way, were the proprietors of Loolecondera estate,

Hewaheta, then Messrs. G. D. B. Harrison and W. M. Leake, now the Anglo-Ceylon & General Estates Co., Ltd., whose produce in the early eighties, under Mr. James Taylor's careful management, acquired a high reputation among Ceylon teas. Loolecondera was also a coffee estate originally. It had been purchased from the crown by Mr. James Joseph Mackenzie in 1841. As far back as 1865, Mr. Taylor, sometimes called the father of tea planting in Ceylon, began collecting tea seed from Peradeniya on Mr. Harrison's order. He planted it in hedgerows, along the roadsides, in 1866.

In that year, Mr. William Martin Leake, being secretary of the Planters' Association, moved that body to get Sir Hercules Robinson's Government to send Mr. Arthur Morice, an experienced Ceylon coffee planter, on a mission to inspect and report on the Assam tea districts. The result

The Pinehurst Tea Farm in South Carolina was one of many attempts by state and federal departments of agriculture to establish tea growing and manufacturing in America. None were successful due to the high cost of labor in comparison to gardens in Indian, Ceylon, China and Japan. This 1898 photo shows Assam hybrid plants being plucked.

was a valuable report which induced Mr. Leake in 1866 to order for his firm, Keir, Dundas & Co., a consignment of Assam hybrid tea seed—the first, probably, of this kind ever imported into Ceylon—and this seed was handed over to the care of Mr. Taylor on Loolecondera.[12]

Mr. Taylor's first clearing, of twenty acres, was made towards the end of 1867. This is generally considered to be the oldest field of tea under continuous cultivation in Ceylon; many of the earlier plantings having been allowed to go out of cultivation, either permanently or temporarily, before Mr. Taylor began planting tea on Loolecondera. The Ceylon Company, now the Eastern Produce and Estates Co., Ltd., imported Assam seed and began planting the hybrid kind in 1869.

Between 1875 and 1930 there was a rush into tea. The tea area increased from 1,080 acres to 467,000 acres. Ceylon teas appeared first on the London market in 1873. In 1891 a parcel of Ceylon tea was sold at the London Tea Auction in Mincing Lane for £25.10s. per pound.[13]

In addition to the major transplantations of the tea bush from China to Japan, Java, India, Ceylon and Sumatra it has been introduced and is cultivated on a commercial scale in For-

Tea's Conquest of the Orient

mosa, French Indo-China, Russian Transcaucasia, Natal, Nyasaland, Kenya and Uganda. On a minor scale, it is cultivated in Siam and Burma, and the plant is grown in British Malaya, Iran, Portuguese East Africa, Rhodesia and the Azores. Experimental cultivation in the Eastern Hemisphere has been attempted in Sweden, England, France, Italy, Bulgaria, and, more recently, in the Cameroons, Ethiopia and Tanganyika Territory.

On the continents of the Western Hemisphere experiments have been conducted in the United States, British Columbia, Mexico, Guatemala, Colombia, Brazil, Peru, Chile, Paraguay and Argentina. The islands where attempts have been made to grow tea include Borneo, the Philippines, Fiji and Mauritius in the Eastern Hemisphere, and Jamaica, Cayenne and Puerto Rico in the Western Hemisphere. Only in Brazil has the cultivation shown any commercial promise.

The introduction of tea culture by Chinese immigrants into Formosa took place in the early part of the nineteenth century. Tea cultivation in Russian Transcaucasia, where alone in Europe it ever reached commercial proportions, dates from 1847. It was introduced into Natal in 1850; Nyasaland in 1878; the United States in 1890; Uganda and Kenya in 1910.

The United States experimented with tea cultivation, under the direction of Dr. Charles U. Shepard, at Summerville, South Carolina, from 1890 to 1915, when it was given up as a bad job. The climate was suitable, but labor was too high and there was no tariff protection after the Spanish-American war tax of ten cents a pound was repealed in 1903.

NOTES

1. Baron Munchhausen, or more properly Hieronymus Karl Friedrich Freiherr von Münchhausen (1720–1797), was a real-life nobleman who told fantastical tales about his military adventures and was fashioned into a fictional character of the same name by Rudolf Erich Raspe (1736-1794) in his 1785 book *Baron Munchausen's Narrative of his Marvellous Travels and Campaigns in Russia*. The book become an international best seller with many sequels.

2. Ukers' droll, Victorian wisdom was acquired over the course of his 35 years of editing and publishing. Ukers was the first since Samuel Ball in 1848 to mention this bold and brilliant Dutch "youth" but he tells us little about him. Jacobson's life awaits a proper biography in English only because he was Dutch and his books and records are in Dutch.

3. Fifty years later, the busy Port of Anjer was destroyed during the catastrophic eruption of the Krakatoa volcano, 75 miles away.

4. A prauw (also *perahu, prau*) is a narrow, outrigger sailing boat indigenous to the waters of Southeast Asia (roughly from Indonesia east to the Mariana Islands). Designs vary according to region but are typically rigged with one proportionally large triangular sail, a pointed head and stern, and a hull which looks as though it has been cut in half lengthwise: a normal curve on one side of the boat, but nearly flat on the opposite side. Accounts contemporary to Jacobson labeled the prauw as "peculiar…, outlandish," and "in direct opposition to the principles of boat-building as adopted in England…," but both the English and Dutch admired its amazing speed as superior to anything they had seen, "worthy of our admiration and meriting a place amongst the mechanical productions of civilized nations where arts and sciences have most eminently flourished." Citations taken from Folkard, *The Sailing boat; a description of English and Foreign boats,* 1870.

5. John Peet was an Englishman who planted the first Assamica tea in Java and achieved great success. It seems unlikely he was kin to Alfred Peet, a Hollander brought up in the Dutch tea trade. Like John, Alfred managed a tea estate on Java but right at the time Indonesia gained its independence and forced the Dutch colonial masters to flee. Alfred had served the customary European apprenticeship in tea and coffee under his father before he emigrated to the Dutch East Indies after World War II. Fleeing Indonesia, he made his way to California and found work as coffee roaster for San Francisco's venerable firm Freed Teller Freed. Peet believed in roasting coffee beans very dark but his employer disagreed and they argued bitterly for years. In frustration, Alfred moved across the Bay to Berkeley and founded Peet's Tea & Coffee in 1966. He inspired his early employees Jerry Baldwin and Howard Schultz to found Starbucks and spread Peet-style dark roast coffee around the world. Peet remained a tea man at heart, or so he told me. He was the first in the United States to sell a Darjeeling by its estate name. This was in the early 1970's and the estate was Selimbong.

6. Ukers occasionally finds an opportunity to pay compliments to especially impressive tea colleagues among the many who had hosted him on his two trips around the world visiting tea and coffee lands. All leading tea professionals down to his own day are to be found in his two-volume *All About Tea*.

7. The tea species of Camellia is subdivided into three principal varietals or strains which are indigenous to different regions of Asia. These varietals are China (C. sinensis sinensis), Assam (C. sinensis assamica) and Indo-China (C. sinensis irrawadiensis). China and Assam are the varietals planted for commercial use. Each varietal over time develops numerous separate "cultivars" or *jat* as they are called in India. China recognizes hundreds.

8. Sir Joseph Banks (1743-1820). The memoir of this eminent British "natural scientist," celebrated in his own day but forgotten in ours, is again attracting readers, proof positive of the growing interest in all aspects of tea. Like Carl Linnaeus and all his fellow botanists, Sir Joseph felt sure green and black tea came from different plants.

Tea's Conquest of the Orient

9. Louis Couperus (1863-1923), was a celebrated Dutch author whose works include *The Hidden Force: A Story of Modern Java*, in which he writes, "The Hidden Force gives back especially the enmity of the mysterious Javanese soul and atmosphere, fighting against the Dutch conqueror." For Couperus, such things as recurrent nightmares arise from the subconscious guilt of the colonial "conqueror."

10. Assam's native tea plant was repeatedly re-discovered after Robert Bruce's initial report in 1823, though it had obviously been known to the people of Assam for centuries. Each early British explorer doubtlessly learned of the tea plant from the interpreter Maniram Barua Dewan, who was a minister to Assam's last Ahom dynasty king. Following the auction of the first nine chests of Assam tea in London in 1839, the Assam Company was hastily incorporated. In best imperial fashion, the British in quick succession deposed Assam's hereditary king, annexed his kingdom and launched their colonial tea industry. Maniram became the first non-European to own a tea plantation, Cinnemara. But, in 1857, he was lynched under cover of law by jealous British rivals in Assam, like George Williamson, who went on to acquire his estates.

11. Samuel Davidson (1846-1921), later "Sir Samuel," left Ireland at age 18 to work at his father's tea estate in the Cachar district of Assam and soon began inventing machinery for tea manufacture, starting with the Sirocco dryer. The Sirocco replaced the traditional Chinese method of drying, or *firing*, tea in baskets over charcoal fires. Together with George Jackson's tea-rolling machines, which could do the work of 80 men, Davidson's dryer enabled British tea growers to vastly increase production. The enterprising entrepreneur imported his own tea into Ireland, sold it at a price designed to undercut the avaricious competition, then closed his stores when he had succeeded in bringing the market price from five shillings per pound down to two shillings a pound.

12. James Taylor (1835-1892) is now revered as the father of Ceylon tea. He arrived in the Crown Colony from Scotland at age 17 at a time when British fortunes were being made from coffee plantations. In less than a generation a blight had wiped out the coffee plants and the fortunes along with them. Planters tried to profit from growing cinchona for quinine, but too many tried and the market collapsed. James Taylor proved tea planting could succeed. As manager of Loolecondera Estate near Kandy, he had, out of curiosity, set out a hedge of assamica plants which thrived in the subtropical climate. This inspired him to plant 21 acres of tea bushes in 1867. By 1872 he had put together a tea factory and, in 1873, began selling Ceylon tea in London. His pioneering example launched the island on its way to becoming the world's fourth largest tea producer today. Although Sri Lanka reclaimed its original name along with independence in 1952, the country's tea industry kept the name *Ceylon* for its most famous product.

13. Records are made to be broken but this one still stands as of 2017. Ceylon Silver Tips and other rarities fetch higher prices but only tiny amounts are produced and these are never sold at auction. A history of top prices paid for tea could be amusing. Record prices were paid in London auctions for the first chests of Assam and later for the first chests of Ceylon. Fresh tea brought in on the year's fastest clipper commanded the highest prices in the mid-1800's. The most valuable of all the tea in China, historically, was Tribute Tea, which was never on the market and therefore priceless except as "gift currency." A Hong Kong tycoon once paid roughly half-million USD for a quarter pound of tea from the original Da Hong Pao shrubs which grow in Nine Dragon's Nest Canyon, located in Fujian's Wuyi Mountains.

Tasting teas in a Yokahama tea brokerage, c.1886.

TEA COMES TO EUROPE AND AMERICA

Tea drinking is one of the great temperance customs that the East shares most generously with the West; yet it was many centuries after tea was commonly used in the Orient that Europeans learned of it. Of the world's three great temperance beverages—cocoa, tea, and coffee—cocoa was the first to be introduced into Europe, in 1528, by the Spanish. It was almost a century later, in 1610, that the Dutch brought tea to Europe. Coffee was introduced into Europe just a few years later, in 1615, by Venetian traders.

The earliest known mention of tea in the literature of Europe appeared about 1559. It occurs as *Chai Catai,* "Tea of China," in *Navigationi e Viaggi,* or *Voyages and Travels,* by Giambattista Ramusio (1485-1557), a noted Venetian author who published a valuable collection of narratives of voyages and discoveries in ancient and modern times.

Ramusio, as secretary to the Venetian Council of Ten, collected some rare commercial information and met many famous travelers, among whom was Hajji Mahommed, or Chaggi Memet, the Persian merchant credited with having brought the first knowledge of tea to Europe. The paragraph containing the tea reference reads:

> "The name of the narrator was Hajji Mahommed.... He told me that all over Cathay they made use of another plant or rather of its leaves. This is called by those people *Chai Catai* and grows in the district of Cathay which is called Cacianfu [Szechwan]. This is commonly used and much esteemed over all those countries. They take of that herb, whether dry or fresh, and boil it well in water. One or two cups of this decoction taken on an empty stomach remove fever, headache, stomach-ache, pain in the side or in the joints, and it should be taken as hot as you can bear it. He said, besides, that it was good for no end of other ailments which he could not remember, but gout was one of them."[1]

An account of Marco Polo's travels, also edited by Ramusio, fails to mention tea, although the drink was in great favor among the Chinese at the time of Marco Polo's visit.

The reason is simple. Polo spent most of his time among the hosts of Kublai Khan, the Tatar invader, and was not much interested in the customs of the subject people.[2]

The Portuguese were the first Europeans to arrive in China by sea, in 1516. A fleet of several ships followed the next year, and an ambassador was sent to Peiping [Beijing]. By 1540 they reached Japan.

The Chinese, looking with suspicion upon the Portuguese, held out no welcome, but the Portuguese ambassador finally convinced the Chinese Emperor that the newcomers had come to barter and exchange and not to invade. The Chinese then permitted them to settle at Macao, a narrow peninsula projecting from the island of Hiang Shang, on the western side of the estuary of the Canton River.

During the early years of European commerce with China and Japan there is no record of tea having been transported, but the Jesuit missionaries, who early penetrated both countries, became acquainted with the tea drink and sent accounts of it to Europe.[3]

Of these missionaries, Father Gasper da Cruz published the first notice of tea in Portuguese. It reads: "Whatsoever person or persons come to any man's house of quality, he hath a custom to offer him ... a kind of drink called *ch'a,* which is somewhat bitter, red, and medicinal, which they are wont to make with a certain concoction of herbs."

Further news of tea reached Italy in 1565 in a letter from Father Louis Almeida, a missionary to Japan. Father Almeida wrote: "The Japanese are very fond of an herb agreeable to the taste, which they call *chia.*"

Two years later, in 1567, the first account of tea reached Russia. The news was carried there by Ivan Petroff and Boornash Yalysheff upon their return from travels in China. They casually described the tea plant as a wonder of China, but they brought back neither specimens of the bush nor samples of tea.

Although an account of tea had been published at Venice in 1559, it was not until 1588 that it was again noted in an Italian work. This was when Giovanni Maffei, an eminent Italian author, printed at Florence Father Almeida's 1565 letter in an extensive collection of papers, entitled *Four Books of Selected Letters from India.*

In Maffei's frequently quoted *Historica Indica,* published at Rome the same year, are two other references to tea.

Next in point of time was Giovanni Botero, a Venetian ecclesiast and author, who in 1589, in his work *On the Causes of Greatness in Cities,* stated: "The Chinese have an herb from which they press a delicate juice which serves them instead of wine. It also preserves the health and frees them from all those evils that the immoderate use of wine doth breed in us." At this time tea had been a medicinal and social beverage in China for approximately eight hundred years, so it is fairly certain that Botero is referring to tea.

Writing thirteen years after Botero, in 1602, on the etiquette of China, Father Diego de Pantoia, another Portuguese missionary, makes this reference to tea: "When they have ended their salutations, they straightway cause a drink to be brought, which they call *ch'a,* which is water boiled with a certain herb which they much esteem . . . and they must drink of it twice or thrice."

Padre Matteo Ricci travelled to China and published one of the first Western recollections of tea in 1610.

The next reference to tea to appear is perhaps the most important of all early accounts, for it gives not only the details as to the price of tea, but briefly contrasts the Chinese and Japanese methods of making the drink. It was found among the letters of an Italian missionary, Padre Matteo Ricci (1552-1610), a scientific adviser to the Chinese court at Peiping from 1601 until his death. The letters were published in 1610 by Padre Nicolas Trigault (d. 1628), a French Jesuit. The account reads:

> "I cannot pass by some rarities, as their shrub whence they make their *Cia* [tea—obsolete Italian]. ... The most excellent is sold at ten and more, often at twelve gold escus a pound in Japan, where its use is also somewhat different from that of China; for the Japanese mix the leaves, reduced to a powder, in a cup of boiling water, to the amount of two or three tablespoonfuls, and swallow this potion mixed in this manner; but the Chinese throw a few leaves into a pot of boiling water; then when it is tinctured with the strength and virtue of the same, they drink it quite hot and leave the leaves."[4]

The same year, 1610, in which Padre Ricci's account appeared in Italy, a Portuguese traveler and scholar published *An Account of the Kings of Persia and Ormuz* which contained a notice of tea, reading: "*Cha* is a small leaf of a herb, from a certain plant brought from Tartary, which was shown me while I was at Malacca." Following this there were several less important references by Portuguese and French missionaries.

Tea Comes to Europe & America

The Portuguese had the sea trade of the Orient to themselves up to 1596, carrying silks and other rich produce on their return voyages to Lisbon, where Dutch ships became the principal carriers to the ports of France, the Netherlands, and the Baltic.

In 1595-6 Jan Huyghen van Linschoten (1563-1611), a Dutch navigator who had sailed to India with the Portuguese, published an account of his travels, a work which fired the Dutch merchants and ship captains with a desire for a share of the rich Oriental trade. His account is notable because it contains the first notice of tea (as *chaa*) in the Dutch language and throws an informing light on early Japanese manners and customs. In his English translation, printed in London in 1598, Linschoten says, in part:

> "Their manner of eating and drinking is: Everie man hath a table alone, without tablecloths or napkins, and eateth with two pieces of wood like the men of *China:* they drinke wine of Rice, wherewith they drink themselves drunke, and after their meat use a certaine drinke, which is a pot with hote water, which they drinke as hote as ever they may indure, whether it be Winter or Summer the aforesaid warme water is made with the powder of a certaine hearbe called *Chaa*, which is much esteemed, and is well accounted of among them, and al such as of any countenance or habilitie have the said water kept for them in a secret place, and the gentlemen make it themselves;

Early Dutch East India trading ships were often called "Indiamen," a term that lasted into the 1800s.

and when they will entertaine any of their friends, they give him some of that warme water to drinke: for the pots wherein they sieth it, and wherein the hearbe is kept, with the earthen cups which they drinke it in, they esteeme as much of them as we doe of Diamants, Rubies and other precious stones."[5]

The enterprising Dutch, between 1595 and 1607, sent out several fleets to the Indies. One of them reached Japan and on the way back stopped at Macao to transport the first tea from there to Java. Ruinous competition, however, resulted in the rival fleets being united as the Dutch East India Company. In 1609 the ships of the new company reached the island of Hirado, off the coast of Japan, and in 1610 the Dutch began the transport of tea from Japan and China to Europe via Bantam, in Java. This was an event of great historical importance.

The Englih East India Company soon after established an agency on Hirado in charge of Mr. R. L. Wickham, who achieved the distinction of supplying the first reference to tea by an Englishman. In a letter to the company's agent at Macao, Mr. Wickham, who must have preferred China tea to Japan tea or else was blithely unconscious of the fact that he was proposing to carry coals to Newcastle, said: "I pray you buy for me a pot of the best *chaw*. This is probably the earliest pidgin English for the Chinese *cha*. The original letter, dated June 27, 1615, is in the India Office, London.[6]

At the turn of the seventeenth century, the Dutch had almost complete mastery of the rich spice trade with the Indies. By 1619 they had founded the city of Batavia in Java as a new base for reaching their great Eastern objective—the Spice, or Molucca, Islands. In the meantime, the English East India Company[7] was creeping out to the East. In their early voyages the English had pushed as far as Japan and had established friendly relations at the Chinese court. By 1610-11 they had founded factories in India at Masulipatam and Pettapoli and had settled on the island of Amboyna, in the Spice group, where the Dutch were already established.

The territorial right of the English in the Indian Archipelago was disputed by the Dutch traders, who considered they had prior rights. The contention that developed culminated in 1623 in the "massacre of Amboyna," the immediate effect of which was to force the English company to admit the Dutch claim to a monopoly of the Far Eastern trade and to retire to the mainland of India and the adjoining countries. This is the reason that the first teas used in England in 1657, and thereafter, came from Dutch sources, though they arrived, in compliance with the Navigation Act of 1651, in ships of English registry.

If we disregard two small gifts of tea for the English King in 1664 and 1666, the first importation of tea by the English East India Company was in 1669, when that company brought 143 pounds from Bantam, in Java.

So began an importation into England which in time was to build fortunes and dot the seas with tea ships. Later Charles II rechartered the English company, granting it powers usually enjoyed only by governments. The company then proceeded to build up an Oriental trade, which soon far outstripped its rivals—the Dutch and the Portuguese.

While tea was being carried into Western Europe over water routes, overland caravans by way of the Levant were bringing it to other parts of Europe. The first tea so to arrive was a gift of several chests brought by a Chinese embassy to the Russian court at Moscow in 1618. Eighteen arduous months were required for the journey, and if the Chinese hoped by this present to create a demand for their product, the journey was in vain, for the tea failed to win Russian friends at that time. For nearly a score of years after the arrival at Moscow of the imperial gift of tea, nothing of historical importance appears in connection with the early use of the drink in Europe.

During this period the many early ecclesiastical panegyrics on tea as a wonderful cure-all were not passing unchallenged. The first of the opponents, Dr. Simon Pauli (1603-80), a German physician, published in 1635 a medical tract full of terrifying alarms and claiming that the use of tea hastened the death of all past the age of forty.

The next account praises tea as much as Dr. Pauli condemned it. It is from the journal of Johann Albrecht von Mandelslo, a young German traveler who, in 1633-40, accompanied an embassy from the Duke of Holstein-Gottorp to the Grand Duke of Muscovy and the King of Persia. "At our ordinary meetings every day," he writes, "we took only *thé*, which is commonly used all over the Indies, not only by those of the country but also among the Dutch and English, who take it as a drug. The Persians, instead of *thé*, drink *kahwa* [coffee]."

The earliest reference to the use of tea in Holland appears in a letter dated January 2, 1637, from the "Lords XVII," the name by which the seventeen directors of the Dutch East India Company were popularly known, to the Governor General of Netherlands East India, at Batavia. It reads: "As tea begins to come into use by some of the people, we expect some jars of Chinese as well as Japanese tea with each ship."

That the tea drink was indeed growing in favor in Europe about this time is confirmed by Mandelslo in describing the whipped tea of the Japanese, which he calls *tsia* [matcha]. He says: "The Japanese prepare it quite otherwise than is done in Europe."

Writing in 1638, Adam Olearius, or Oelschlager, secretary of the embassy from the Duke of Holstein-Gottorp to the King of Persia,[8] states that the excellent qualities of tea are well known among the Persians, who "boil it till the water hath a bitterish taste and a blackish colour, and add thereto fennel, aniseed, or cloves and sugar."

Tea Comes to Europe & America

In the year 1638 Vassily Starkoff, the Russian ambassador at the court of the Mogul Khan Altyn, partook of an infusion of tea, but declined a present of a quantity of it for his master, the Tsar Michael Romanoff, founder of the Romanoff dynasty, as something for which the Tsar would have no use. However, if Russia and eastern Europe were still insensible to the advantages of the tea drink, high society at The Hague[9] was beginning, about the year 1640, to adopt it as a fashionable, although an expensive, beverage.

The first tea introduced into Germany came by way of Holland about 1650. By 1657 tea had become a staple article of commerce, quoted at fifteen gulden a handful in the price lists of chemists in Nordhausen.

In Germany, Professor Johann Jakob Waldschmidt of Marburg wrote: "The high and mighty gentlemen who bring upon themselves a hundred thousand pounds of care concerning the confused situation in Europe would do well to drink hot tea water for the maintenance of their health."

There were strenuous adversaries of tea in Germany, however, prominent among whom was the Jesuit, Martino Martini, who claimed that tea was the cause of the dried-up appearance of the Chinese. He exclaimed: "Down with tea! Send it back to the Garaments and Sauromates!"

Responding to a newly aroused interest in the subject, William Ten Rhyne, a Dutch naturalist, wrote of the tea plant in 1640, and in 1641 Dr. Nikolas Dirx (1593-1674), a celebrated Dutch physician, writing under the *nom de plume* of Nikolas Tulp, was one of the first Europeans of his profession to sound the praises of tea.

Dr. Jacob Bontius, a physician and naturalist of Batavia, in Java, still further illumines the subject in one of the quaint dialogues with which he enlivens the *Historiæ Naturalis et Medicæ Indiæ Orientalis*, first published in 1642. This is also included in the collection of Gulielmus Piso, *De Indice Utriusque re Naturali et Medicæ*. To quote:

> ANDREAS DUREAS. You have mentioned the drink of the Chinese called *Thee:* what is your opinion thereof?
> JACOBUS BONTIUS. The Chinese regard this drink almost as something sacred . . . and they are not thought to have fulfilled the duties of hospitality until they have served you with it, just like the Mohammedans with their *caveah* [coffee]. It is of a drying quality, and banishes sleep .... It is beneficial to asthmatic and wheezing patients.

Other famous Dutch physicians of the period, among them Blankaert, Bontekoe, Sylvius, Van Duverden, Bidloo and Pechlin, followed with equally laudatory opinions, as did Father Athanasius Kircher, a learned chemist; Jacob Breynius, a botanist; and Johannes Baptista van Helmont (1577-1644), a famous chemist, physiologist, and visionary. Helmont's pupils were taught that tea had the same effect on the system as blood-letting or laxatives, and should be used instead.

Of the Dutch physicians who wrote in praise of tea at this time, Dr. Cornelis Decker (1648-86), of Alkmaar, otherwise known as Dr. Bontekoe, was easily its most distinguished advocate. He is generally credited with having done more to promote its ensuing general adoption in Europe than anyone else. Bontekoe advised the use of eight to ten cups of tea daily, but found no reason to object to fifty, a hundred, or two hundred cups, as he frequently consumed that quantity himself. History whispers that Dr. Bontekoe may have been retained by the Dutch East India Company to write in praise of tea. At all events, it is recorded that the company made him a handsome honorarium for the impetus given their sales.

The earliest mention of milk used as an ingredient of tea is recorded by the Dutch traveler and author Jean Nieuhoff (1630-72), who accompanied an embassy of the Dutch East India Company to the Chinese Emperor in 1655.[10]

Apothecaries were among the first dealers in tea. In Holland they sold it by the ounce, along with sugar, ginger and spices, but gradually tea found its way into shops for colonial produce, which subsequently developed into grocery shops. Between 1660 and 1680 its use in the Netherlands became general, first in the homes of the gentry, and later in the houses of the middle classes and the poor. As was the case with coffee, history records no official intolerance of tea in Holland.

Russia began regularly to import tea from China by way of the picturesque overland caravan route, through Manchuria and Mongolia, after the signing of the Nerchinsk treaty with China in 1689. The Russian trade with China was confined by this treaty to the town of Kiakhta,[11] on the northern frontier of China, which thus became the sole entry port for the exchange of the products of both countries.

It is likely that the Scandinavian countries first became acquainted with tea through the commercial activities of the Dutch and later through the Danes, who began to take part in the India trade in 1616.

It was after ecclesiastical notices and Dutch medical comment had made the new China drink a leading topic of discussion throughout the capitals of Europe, that tea found its way to France. It is said to have appeared first in Paris in 1635, but Commissioner Delamarre, in his *Traité de Police*, or *Treatise on the Police*, claims it began to be used in Paris in 1636. Alfred Franklin casts doubt on both dates by declaring the earliest mention of tea in Paris to be contained in a letter of March 22, 1648 from Dr. Gui Patin (1601-72), the celebrated French physician and writer. In this letter Patin refers to tea as "the impertinent novelty of the century," and states:

"One of our doctors, named Morisset, who is much more of a braggart than a skilful man . . . caused a thesis on *thé* to be published here. Everybody disapproved of it; there were some of our doctors who burned it, and protests were made to the dean for having approved the thesis. You will see it and laugh at it!"[12]

While Patin was the declared enemy of all innovations, especially in medicine, he was by no means alone in opposing the introduction of tea as a medicine in France. Morisset's dissertation entitled *Does Tea Increase Mentality?* in which he hailed the drink as a "panacea," caused such an uproar in the French medical world that no other physician of the College de France dared to speak in its favor.

According to Father Alexander de Rhodes (1591-1660), the Parisians a few years later, in 1653, were paying high prices for their tea. He writes: "The Dutch bring tea from China to Paris and sell it at thirty francs a pound, though they have paid but eight and ten sous in that country, and it is old and spoiled into the bargain. People must regard it as a precious medicament; it not only does positively cure nervous headache, but it is a sovereign remedy for gravel and gout."

De Rhodes' testimonial to the efficacy of tea as a remedy may have inspired Cardinal Mazarin, the distinguished courtier and prime minister of France, to use it for his gout. We learn of this through another letter of the eminent Dr. Patin, dated April 1, 1657, heaping ridicule on the remedy selected by the illustrious prelate. "Mazarin," sneers the doctor, "takes *thé* as a preventive of gout. Isn't this a powerful remedy for the gout of a favourite!"

In 1657, Chancellor Sequier, who was a devotee of tea, accepted the dedication of a thesis written by the son of the celebrated surgeon Pierre Cressy, extolling his favorite drink. This disgusted Patin, the implacable foe of tea, but a surprise was in store for him; the younger Cressy had made a study of the effect of tea as a treatment for gout, which he advocated so eloquently for four hours that the faculty of the college not only gave up its former hostility to tea, but even smoked it like tobacco.

In 1659 Dr. Denis Jonquet appears to have voiced the general sentiment of the medical profession in Paris by his reference to tea as a divine drink.

A weird recipe for making tea was brought to Europe by the missionary Pere Couplet when he returned from China in 1667. It was as follows:

"To a pint of tea, add the yolks of two fresh eggs; then beat them up with as much fine sugar as is sufficient to sweeten the tea, and stir well together. The water must remain no longer upon the tea than while you can chant the Miserere psalm in leisurely fashion."

Tea Comes to Europe & America

In 1671, Phillipe Sylvestre Dufour published at Lyons his admirable treatise *Concerning the Use of Coffee, Tea, and Chocolate,* and in 1680 Madame de Sévigné, the famous letter-writer to whom we are indebted for preserving so many incidents of historic interest, records that Madame de le Sablière conceived the idea of mixing milk with her tea. This is the earliest record of the use of milk in tea in Europe. Again, in 1684, Madame de Sévigné writes: "The Princess of Tarente took twelve cups of tea daily, and Monsieur le Landgrave forty. He was dying, and this resuscitated him visibly."

By 1685 we find tea in high favor in literary circles, with Pierre Daniel Huet, Bishop of Avranches, celebrating it in a Latin poem of fifty-eight stanzas, under the title *Thea, elegia, and Pierre Petit,* another learned French writer, producing a poem of five hundred and sixty stanzas entitled *Thea Sinensis (Chinese Tea).* Earlier in the century Paul Scarron, the dramatist, had already become its devotee.

Pomet, the Parisian apothecary, emerges from the smoke of this literary bombardment to tell us that he was selling Chinese tea at 70 francs a pound, and Japanese tea from 150 to 200 francs, in 1694. He remarks that its vogue as a drink of the middle and upper classes had suffered considerably because of the introduction of coffee and chocolate.

Interior of a London Coffee House, c.1700, where prepared coffee, tea and chocolate were the beverages of choice for men.

Tea Comes to Europe & America

The first mention of tea in Scandinavian literature occurs in a comedy, *The Lying-in Woman*, written in 1723 by Baron Ludvig Holberg (1684-1754).

The introduction of tea as a drink into England forms a chapter teeming with high adventure, strange peoples, and intriguing events.

While the English had knowledge of tea from Linschoten's *Travels* as early as 1598, and through the agents of the East India Company in the early years of the seventeenth century, its use appears to have been neglected, for there is no mention of it by the early English dramatists, whose works mirror the tastes and humors of their time. It seems extraordinary that the English East India Company should not have discovered and developed the possibilities of tea as early as did their commercial competitors, the Dutch East India Company, who were bringing Chinese, as well as Japanese, tea with every ship in 1637. Yet it certainly can have been known in England to only very few as early as 1641, for in a rare *Treatise on Warm Beer*, published in that year, the author undertakes to chronicle the advantages of the known hot drinks as opposed to cold, and mentions tea only by quoting the Italian Jesuit Father Maffei that "they of China do for the most part drink the strained liquor of an herb called *Chia* hot."

As yet there was no word for "tea" in the English language, so early British authors were wont to employ some approximation of its Chinese name, *cha*. Tea appears as *chia* in *Purchas His Pilgrimes*, in 1625. To quote from this early English collector of travels: "They use much the powder of a certaine herbe called *chia* of which they put as much as a Walnut shell may containe, into a dish of Porcelane, and drink it with hot water." In a footnote, Samuel Purchas observes that *chia* is used "in all entertainments in Iapon [Japan] and China."

In 1637, an English fleet of four ships entered the mouth of the Canton River and, with characteristic aggressiveness, forced their way past the Portuguese, who opposed them at Macao. Upon reaching Canton, they established direct contact with Chinese merchants. There is no record to show that any tea was transported at this time, however, nor upon the occasion of a second visit of the English at Macao, which occurred twenty-seven years later.

Shortly after 1644, English traders established themselves at the port of Amoy, which was their principal Chinese base for nearly a century. Here they picked up from the Fukien dialect the word *t'e* ("tay") for the drink used by the Chinese, and they spelled it *t-e-a*, writing *ea* as a diphthong, having the sound of long *a*.

There is no record of the earliest importation of tea into England. Probably this occurred more or less contemporaneously with its appearance in Holland, France and Germany, sometime about the middle of the seventeenth century. From a broadside by a London coffee house keeper, one Thomas Garway, or Garraway,[13] we learn that previous to the year 1657 the leaf and drink had been used only "as a regalia in high treatments and entertainments, and presents made thereof to princes and grandees." For such use purchasers were compelled to pay £6 to £10 per pound, and to get their supplies abroad, as tea was not as yet sold in Britain. The same broadside tells us that in 1657 the tea leaf and beverage were first publicly sold in England by Thomas Garway, tobacconist and coffee house keeper, at his place in Exchange Alley. This famous coffee house, known to succeeding generations as "Garraway's," was a center for great mercantile transactions. Here men prominent in the commercial life of the metropolis were wont to refresh themselves with ale, punch, brandy, arrack, etc., in addition to tea and coffee.

The tea sold by Garway was reputed to possess remarkable preventive and curative qualities, but there was little general knowledge of it in London; so Garway sought directions for making the beverage from the best-informed merchants and travelers from the East, preparing it accordingly. For the benefit of customers who desired to make the drink in their homes or elsewhere, he offered to sell all comers the prepared leaf at 16s. to 60s. per pound, thus effecting a saving of from 104s. to 140s. a pound. Having established a fair price, he proceeded to herald the quality and virtues of tea in the broadside, which has assumed historical importance as one of the earliest and most effective advertisements for tea.

Garway observes in the quaint advertising copy of the period, that the drink was suited to hot or cold weather, that it was possessed of many medicinal virtues, and promoted wakefulness.

Who of Garway's patrons, having a corpulent body, a weak "stomack," ailing "uriters," or what not, but would daily seek the protection of this panacea from out the purple East, after reading the claims that were made for it in this remarkable broadside? Much editorial credit, indeed, is due Garway for the diligence by which he contrived to boil down into the limits of a single sheet practically all the claims, fantastic or otherwise, that had been made for tea as a medicine in the writings of the Chinese, or of the early Jesuit missionaries in the Far East.

Prominent men in the social and religious life of Britain were much intrigued by the new China drink. A letter from Daniel Sheldon, factor of the English East India Company at Balsore, written in 1659 to another factor for the company at Bandel, urgently requested a sample of tea to send home to his uncle, the illustrious Dr. Gilbert Sheldon, Archbishop of Canterbury. He wrote:

> "I must desire you to procure the *chaw*, if possible. I care not what it cost. 'Tis for a good uncle of mine, Dr. Sheldon, whome some body hath perswaded to studdy the divinity of that herbe, leafe, or what else it is; and I am soe obliged to satisfy his curiosity that I could willingly undertake a viage to Japan or China to doe it."

Tea Comes to Europe & America

There seems to have been some difficulty in securing the tea at Bandel, for Sheldon wrote again: "For God's sake, good or badd, buy the *chaw* if it is to be sold. Pray favour me likewise with advise what 'tis good for, and how to be used." The final outcome is not revealed by the correspondence, but, whatever this may have been, it is not likely that the Archbishop's curiosity long went unsatisfied, as tea had then been on sale in London for several years.

Samuel Pepys (1633-1703),[14] the gossipy English diarist and Secretary to the Admiralty, to whom we are indebted for so many intimate glimpses of the daily life and customs of his time, writes, under date of September 25, 1660: "I did send for a cup of tee (a China drink) of which I never had drank before."[15]

Englishman Samuel Pepys recorded his first cup of "tee" in his diary entry of Sepember 25, 1660.

Just what claims for the virtues of tea were coming to England from the East is made clear by a manuscript now in the British Museum, which was elegantly transcribed in 1686 from a paper of T. Povey, M.P. and Civil Servant, purporting to be a translation of a Chinese encomium and containing much the same arguments employed in the Garway broadside.

The directors of the East India Company apparently found tea valuable for the use of "the Court of Committees," for their books show entries covering several small purchases of from six to eight pounds thus charged and bought from the coffee house keepers.

Seventeenth century records agree in showing that the real introduction of the tea drink into England began in the London coffee houses, where it was served as well as coffee, chocolate and sherbet. Whereas its previous use in England, as Garway so well points out, was limited to rare "treatments" and the occasional entertainment of some grandee, it was now to be enjoyed by all in the coffeehouse. It soon became the talk of the town.

The coffee houses made much of the new beverage. These unique gathering-places, each with its own more or less distinct clientele, whether of business men, professional men or literati, came to be called "coffee houses" instead of "tea houses" because the public sale of coffee as a beverage in England antedated the public sale of tea by a few years.

The coffee houses, forerunners of London's clubhouses of today, were so congenial to

Tea Comes to Europe & America

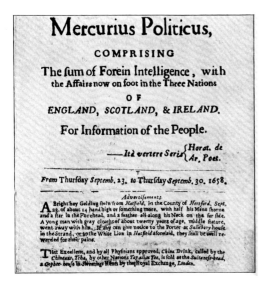

The first advertisement for tea in a London coffee house appeared in September 1658.

the English character that they quickly made a place for themselves that promised to be perpetual. Here every political subject of the day was discussed; and as not only the higher but also the middle classes frequented these new places of entertainment, a knowledge of public affairs was widely diffused.

In 1650 the first English coffee house had been opened by a certain Jew from Lebanon, Jacob by name, at the Sign of the Angel in the Parish of St. Peter of the East, Oxford. "And there," says Anthony Wood (1632-95), the English antiquarian writer, "coffee was by some who delighted in noveltie drank."

Coffee houses soon appeared in various parts of the metropolis as well as throughout the country, and presently they were all of them serving tea, with the other temperance beverages.

The Sultaness Head coffee house was one of the earliest to adopt tea as a part of its entertainment, and on September 30, 1658 its proprietor inserted the first newspaper advertisement of tea, in *Mercurius Politicus*. This advertisement announced: "That Excellent, and by all Physitians approved, *China* drink, called by the *Chineans, Tcha,* by other Nations *Tay alias Tee,* is sold at the Sultaness-head, a *Cophee-house* in *Sweetings* Rents, by the Royal Exchange, *London.*"

About this time tea was everywhere offered and accepted as a wonderful health drink. Quite possibly there may have been a bit of favorable psychology in this, for men have ever been fond of attributing remedial values to their drinks, and tea was soon to be acclaimed "the sovereign drink of pleasure and of health."

Tea, coffee and chocolate all gained a quick popularity in the London coffee houses. We read in Thomas Rugge's *Mercurius Politicus Redivivus* of November 14, 1659: "Theire ware also att this time a Turkish drink to bee sould, almost in evry street, called Coffee, and a nother kind of drink called Tee, and also a drink called Chacolate, which was a very harty drink."

Tea was sold also at Jonathan's, another coffee house, in Exchange Alley. Mrs. Centlivre laid one of the scenes of her play *A Bold Strike for a Wife* at Jonathan's, and while the business of the place is being enacted, she makes the serving lads cry: "Fresh coffee, Gentlemen! Fresh coffee! Bohea tea, Gentlemen!"

Tea Comes to Europe & America

Proportionately as the coffee houses gained vogue and prospered, the taverns became deserted, and the government, faced with a considerable diminution of revenues from wines, found it necessary to make up the deficit by imposing a tax on the liquors dispensed in coffee houses. Furthermore, such places were placed under the same kind of license as that imposed upon taverns and ale houses.

Tea first appeared upon the English statutes in Act XXI, Charles II, 1660, in which an excise duty of eight pence was placed on every gallon of tea, chocolate and sherbet sold. The Act required keepers of coffee houses to take out a license at the Quarter Sessions and provide security for the due payment of the excise duty. Neglect to do this entailed a penalty of five pounds a month.

Excise officers visited the coffee houses at stated intervals to gauge and take account of the number of gallons of each liquid that was made. The plan had many disadvantages and was difficult of execution, as it was necessary for the excise officer to see and measure the taxable drinks before they could be sold. It was customary to infuse an ample supply of tea to outlast the period between inspections and to store it in kegs to be drawn off and heated as required.[16]

In 1669, imports from Holland were prohibited by English law, thus creating a monopoly for the English East India Company.

On account of the scarcity of small change, coffee house keepers and other tradesmen of the seventeenth century put out large numbers of tokens, or trade coins. They were of copper, brass, pewter and even of leather, gilded. They bore the name, address and calling of the issuer, the nominal value of the piece, and some reference to his trade. They were readily redeemed at their face value, were passable in the immediate neighborhood and seldom circulated farther than the next street. The tokens of the Turk's Head alone mentioned tea, although it was sold at all coffee houses.

Tea became a fashionable drink for the ladies of England with the coming of Princess Catherine of Braganza, the Portuguese princess and tea devotee whom Charles II wedded in 1662. She

Catherine of Braganza already had a taste for tea when she arrived from Portugal in 1662 to be the bride of Charles II. She was the first British Queen to drink tea.

was England's first tea-drinking Queen, and it is to her credit that she was able to substitute her favorite temperance drink as the fashionable beverage of the court in place of the ales, wines, and spirits with which the English ladies, as well as gentlemen, "habitually heated or stupefied their brains morning, noon, and night."[17]

With a population that grew from three million at the beginning of the seventeenth century to five million at its close, the England of Queen Catherine's time was, throughout its greater part, "open and untamed," while enjoying the culture handed down from the Elizabethans.

Further impetus was given to tea-drinking as a fashionable entertainment at the court of Charles II when Henry Bennet, Lord Arlington, Secretary of State, and Thomas Butler, Earl of Ossory, returned to London from The Hague in 1666, bringing in their baggage a quantity of tea which their ladies proceeded to serve after the newest and most aristocratic vogue of the Continent. At this time the Netherlands represented the pinnacle of elegance in tea serving, and every home of any consequence had its exclusive tearoom.

At the time that Lord Arlington and Lord Ossory returned, Abbé Raynal (1713-96), a French historian, informs us: "Tea sold in London for near seventy livres [£2.18s.4cl.] a pound, though it cost but three or four [from 2s. 6cl. to 3s. 4cl.] at Batavia." The price was kept up with little variation, regardless of the fact that the high cost prevented its general use. However, its vogue at court gave it added interest to the ladies; and the apothecaries of London hastened to add it to their pharmacies. In 1667 Pepys records in his diary: "Home and found my wife making of tea; a drink which Mr. Pelling, the potticary, tells her is good for her cold and defluxions."

After the attempted suppression of the coffee houses as places of sedition by Charles II, these "penny universities," with their service of a dish of tea or coffee for two-pence (including newspapers and lights) took on new life, and groups of patrons began to favor particular houses. It is easy to trace the transition of a group into a clique that later became a club, continuing for a time to meet at the coffee house, but eventually demanding a house of its own.

There followed the decline of the coffee house and the rise of the pleasure garden. Then "tea grocers" began to sell the leaf to the better-class homes. About the middle of the eighteenth century it came into common use. "Persons of quality," however, continued to pay thirty shillings a pound for Bohea and for green.

Following the coffee houses and chemists' shops, glass-sellers, milliners, silk-mercers and chinaware-dealers began to handle tea. There is even a reference to a "shorthand author" selling tea–his only other trade. As late as 1805 "polite grocers" in the Strand were accustomed to weighing tea in apothecaries' scales.

Tea Comes to Europe & America

One tea firm in the city of London traces its descent from Daniel Rawlinson, friend of Pepys, who in 1650 established himself as owner of the Mitre Tavern. When tea and produce were added, he adopted the Three Sugar Loaves and Crown as his sign. Twinings in the Strand evolved out of Tom's Coffee house, established in 1706. Here for the first-time women came in their sedan chairs to select their blends. Fortnum & Mason, Ltd. dates back to Queen Anne's reign, and the tea business of R. O. Mennell & Co. was founded by Maria Tewk,[18] spinster, at York in 1725.

In 1680 tea was first served in Scotland at Holyrood Palace, Edinburgh, by the Duchess of York, Mary of Modena, who, as the wife of James II, was later Queen of Great Britain and Ireland. The Duke and Duchess were virtual exiles, first at The Hague, where they picked up tea drinking as a social art, and later at Holyrood, where they introduced the novel refreshment to the wonder of their friends and devoted adherents among the Scottish nobility.

Thomas Twining opened Tom's Coffee House in 1706. His tea and coffee shop, The Golden Lyon, opened on The Strand eleven years later. 18th century lithograph titled The Polite Grocers on The Strand.

In 1705 George Smith, a goldsmith of Luckenbooths, Edinburgh, advertised green tea at 16s. and Bohea tea at 30s. a pound. There may have been some association of ideas of value in offering tea for sale with jewelry, but how much tea was sold to the canny Scots at such prices is not recorded. However, by 1724 all classes in Scotland were drinking the beverage.

Some there were who regarded the drink as a highly improper article of diet, expensive, wasteful of time, and likely to render the population weakly and effeminate. Such was Lord President Forbes' conviction in 1744, and it was about this time that an energetic movement was begun all over Scotland to stamp out the "tea menace." Towns, parishes, and counties passed resolutions condemnatory of the Chinese leaf and pointing strongly to the manlier attraction of beer.

Initiating the first of several attacks on tea in England, in 1678, Mr. Henry Sayville wrote to his uncle, Mr. Secretary Coventry of His Majesty's Government, in sharp reproof of certain of his friends "who call for tea, instead of pipes and a bottle after dinner." This he characterized as "a base Indian practice."

The East India Company offices were located on London's Leadenhall Street until the building was razed in 1860.

In 1730 Dr. Thomas Short, a Scottish physician, published *A Dissertation upon Tea*, in which he stated that he refused to take the imaginary good qualities of the beverage on trust. He believed that it threw "some Persons into Vapours" and many other disastrous-sounding ailments.

One of England's several tea controversies flared up about 1745, and we catch its echo in an old copy of the *Female Spectator*, which denounces tea in no uncertain terms as "the bane of housewifery." Arthur Young (1741-1820), the most influential social economist later in the century, described the effects of tea drinking upon the entire national economy as being altogether evil. He was greatly disturbed because of the growing custom "of men making tea an article of their food, almost as much as women, labourers losing their time to come and go to the tea table, farmers' servants even demanding tea for their breakfast!" He went so far as to prophesy that if they continued to waste time and to injure their health by so bad a beverage, "the poor in general will find themselves far more distressed than ever."

Both tea and English prosperity suffered a new attack in 1748, by no less a figure than John Wesley (1703-91), the great preacher, who urged his followers to discontinue the use of tea for both medical and moral reasons. Wesley inveighed against tea drinking as hurtful to both body and soul. Unlike the Buddhist priests of China and Japan who early seized on this non-intoxicating beverage as a weapon with which to attack the alcoholic stimulants in use, he denounced tea in much the same terms he employed against strong drink, calling on his adherents to abstain from its use and apply the money they would thus save to charitable works. It was because of his recovery from a paralytic disorder which, he said, disappeared as the result of leaving off tea that Wesley took this attitude.

We find that during the latter part of his life, however, Wesley became a regular tea drinker again, and it is stated that he even gave tea parties. The Reverend George H. McNeal, Minister of Wesley's Chapel, London, says that when Wesley was at home, all of the Methodist preachers in London gathered at his house for breakfast on Sunday morning before they went to their various appointments, and that at these breakfasts a teapot which held about half a gallon, and had been specially made for him by the famous potter Josiah Wedgwood, was regularly used. It now forms one of the exhibits in the room of the City Road house where Wesley died.

One of the most famous attacks on tea was made in 1756 by Jonas Hanway (1712-86), an apparently amiable and well-disposed London merchant and author. In his *Journal of an Eight Days Journey*, Hanway branded tea as "pernicious to health, obstructing industry, and impoverishing the nation."

The Hanway journal came in the way of Dr. Samuel Johnson (1709-84), who answered it with a degree of alacrity proportioned to his avowed fondness for the beverage of his choice. "Dr. Johnson was a lover of tea to an excess hardly credible," writes Sir John Hawkins, one of his biographers. "Whenever it appeared, he was almost raving, and called for the ingredients which he employed to make the liquor palatable. This in a man whose appearance of bodily strength has been compared to Polyphemus."[19]

Knowing this foible of Johnson's, the reader will more readily appreciate the delight with which the redoubtable doctor sprang to the defense of his favorite beverage. In articles published in the *Literary Magazine* he overwhelmed Hanway with good-humored ridicule, proclaiming himself "a hardened and shameless tea drinker, who has for many years diluted his meals with only the infusion of this fascinating plant; whose kettle has scarcely time to cool; who with tea amuses the evening, with tea solaces the midnights, and with tea welcomes the morning."

The use of tea as a beverage was unknown to the American colonists who, early in the seventeenth century, settled along the Atlantic seaboard. Indeed, at that time it was almost unknown in the mother countries. Although there are no specific records of its earliest use in America, it is more than probable that the custom was brought from Holland, and that Dutch New Amsterdam was the first American colony to drink the beverage, about the middle of the seventeenth century.

We are not left in the least doubt as to the use of tea by the burghers of New Amsterdam, or at least by those who could afford to buy it, for some of their inventories that have been preserved show that tea drinking became as much a social custom in the colony as it did in Holland, and at about the same time.

Tea was known and probably used to a limited extent in the Massachusetts colony as early as 1670: It was first sold at Boston in 1690 by two dealers, Benjamin Harris and Daniel Vernon, who took out licenses to sell tea "in publique" in accordance with the English law requiring every purveyor of tea to have a license for its sale. Apparently, its use in Boston was not uncommon subsequent to that time, for we find Chief Justice Sewall jotting in his diary that he drank it at Mrs. Winthrop's residence in 1709, and he makes no comment to indicate that there was anything unusual in the occurrence.

Bohea, or black tea, then popular in England, was the kind commonly used, but in 1712 Zabdiel Boylston, a Boston apothecary, advertised "Green and Ordinary" teas at retail.

William Penn is generally credited with the introduction of tea into the Quaker colony which he founded on the Delaware in 1682. He also brought to Philadelphia, the "City of Brotherly Love," that other great drink of human brotherhood, coffee. At first, "like tea, coffee was only a drink for the well-to-do, except in sips."[20] As in the other English colonies, too, coffee languished for a time while tea rose in favor, more especially in the home. Following the Stamp Act of 1765,[21] succeeded by the Trade and Revenue Act of 1767, the Pennsylvania colony joined hands with the others in a general boycott on tea, and sales of coffee were increased here as elsewhere in the colonies.

By the middle of the eighteenth century the American colonies had begun to suffer from growing pains. Most of the dispassionate twentieth century historians agree that the Revolutionary War might just as well be charged up to Big Business, represented on the one hand by the East India Company's monopoly of tea and on the other by British and colonial tea merchants. It might have been started by free molasses or free rum, but, as a matter of fact, it was tea.

Two years before the passage of the Stamp Act, Boston merchants had already united in a club to oppose any attempts to make the tax on molasses effective. As John Adams said later, "molasses was an essential ingredient in American independence." Tea was another. In 1765, the Stamp Act, the first measure of the oncoming madness, was passed by Parliament, causing an immediate outburst of protest and resistance from the American colonists, led by Patrick Henry of Virginia. They were, then, simply Englishmen making the usual fuss about being taxed. James Otis said they shouldn't be taxed without the consent of their own assemblies.

Tea Comes to Europe & America

In the trade of Canton, tea had by this time assumed a position of prime importance. Incidentally, the tea shipments of the rival Continental East India companies far exceeded those of the English company. The reason was obvious; most of these shipments were being smuggled into England and America, the high duties offering every incentive to "free trade."

Here it is interesting to note that the American colonists in the eighteenth century were as great consumers of tea as were the Australians in the succeeding centuries; however, they were beginning to prefer the cheaper smuggled tea to that which reached them, duty-paid, from the London tea sales.

The obnoxious Stamp Act was repealed in 1766, too late for any moral effect in America, where the Dutch were scooping in all the trade in sight. There followed in 1767 the ill-fated Townshend duties and their repeal in 1770—all except the three pence per pound on tea—and then the stage was completely set for the act of supreme folly.

In dire financial straits and with a huge surplus of tea on its hands, the East India Company in 1773 complained to Parliament that the colonial tea business was being absorbed by the Dutch because the colonists would no longer buy the duty-paid English article. They suggested the time had come for England to throw overboard the rights of British export merchants and colonial importers in order that the great English East India Company might be saved. Their solution was that they be allowed to export tea on their own account to America, free of the duty which other British export merchants had to pay, and then to sell it through their own agents in America upon payment of the small American duty, which the colonial merchant was refusing to pay as a matter of principle. By this ingenious method two middlemen's services and profits would be abolished, the Dutch interlopers would be confounded, the smuggling of tea would stop, and the colonist would obtain his tea more cheaply than the home consumer in England.

Parliament sanctioned the scheme, and the die was cast. There was probably as much indignation among the British export merchants as among the colonial importers. With the latter, however, this act of favoritism was the one thing needed to turn the scales in favor of the colonial politicians who had lately found the merchant class rather cold to their revolutionary appeals. The most promising business of the New World was being attacked. The colonial merchant was a free-thinking and free-trading individual to whom anything smacking of monopoly was anathema. His livelihood was being taken from him by a most unholy alliance between the Government he had always trusted and the world's greatest monopoly. To arms, to arms!

Having made its adjustments, the East India Company proceeded toward the execution of its plans by appointing special agents to receive the tea on consignment in Boston, New York, Philadelphia and Charleston upon payment of the small American duty.

Already American resentment against the Tea Act, and the various other measures which preceded it, had taken definite form. The assemblies of several of the colonies had adopted resolutions of protest, and these, with a number of petitions, were sent to England, where they either went unheeded or were rejected outright. In the American seaports, there were meetings and demonstrations of various sorts by organizations calling themselves the "Sons of Liberty," and many groups of colonial dames throughout the colonies were inspired to pledge themselves to drink no tea. Five hundred Boston ladies thus pledged themselves, and it is on record that the ladies of Hartford and many other American towns and villages took similar action. In a general way, these agreements were in support of a non-importation movement directed against British goods, but in particular against tea after the passage of the Tea Act. In some parts of the Massachusetts colony it was impossible to purchase tea, even for medicinal purposes, without a permit.

In late summer 1773, consignments of the East India Company's teas were cleared in seven chartered ships bound for Boston, New York, Philadelphia, and Charleston. As a result, there was held not only the famous Boston Tea Party, but three others.

While Philadelphia, the big boy in the colonial family, took the lead in resisting the plans of the parental Government, and the disaffection quickly spread to New York, it was Boston that got the first action. On December 16, 1773, certain citizens of Boston, disguised as Indians, dumped the entire Boston consignment of 340 chests of Chinese black and green tea into Boston harbor.

On December 26, 1773, a tea ship, *Polly*, bound for Philadelphia was halted within sight of the city and sent back to London under threat of burning. The Charleston tea ship, *London*, landed its cargo early in December 1773, but without payment of duty; whereupon the collector seized the tea and stored it in a damp cellar where it quickly spoiled.

In April 1774, the ship *Nancy* finally arrived in the port of New York, followed by the *London*, up from Charleston with 18 chests of tea in a general cargo. The *London's* tea was dumped into the harbor while the *Nancy*, with a full cargo of tea, escaped similar treatment by returning to the safety of England.

In August 1774, a ship bound for Annapolis with a general cargo, including some tea, was sent back to England. In October of the same year, the *Peggy Stewart* arrived at Annapolis with two thousand pounds of tea and, on October 19, she was burned at her anchorage, the torch being applied by her owner.

Six days after this incident, 51 patriotic women of Edenton, North Carolina, led by Penelope Barker, drew up a resolution pledging themselves to boycott all British goods, including tea.[22]

Tea Comes to Europe & America

Three ships, chartered by the English East India Company to carry Chinese green and black teas to Boston merchants, were boarded by "The Sons of Liberty" on the night of December 16, 1773 and their cargos of tea were broken and tossed into Boston Harbor at Griffin's Wharf.

On November 1, 1774, the *Britannia Ball* arrived at Charleston with eight chests of tea, which the owners broke open publicly and dumped overboard. On December 22, 1774, colonists at Greenwich, New Jersey, also disguised as Indians, burned a large consignment of tea stored there.

While the American colonists were registering, through their tea parties, their determination to resist enforcement of the tea tax, the home Government was taking an equally determined stand that its measures against America must be enforced.

The "people" of England had little to do with the War of American Independence. The original cause, as wittily diagnosed by the late Dean Alvord, of the University of Michigan, was *flapperitis exuberans*. The immediate cause was the attempt to perpetuate a tea monopoly distasteful alike to British and American merchants; and so England lost an empire to oblige the East India Company.

Thus, amid the boom of cannon and the roar of musketry, a great republic was born—one that was soon to become the wealthiest consumer-nation in the world, but with a prenatal disinclination for tea.

NOTES

1. In 1559 Giambattista Ramusio, a high government official in Venice, published the last of his three volumes entitled *Navigationi e Viaggi*, which contains the first known reference to tea by a European. Ramusio was quoting a Muslim traveler who told of people of the East drinking tea.

2. Kublai (modern spelling: Qubilai) was the grandson of Chinggis (formerly spelled Genghis) Khan. He made himself Emperor of China and established the Yuan ("original") dynasty in 1271. He lived like a Chinese Emperor, though he preferred to sleep in a yurt on the palace grounds, and his few hundred thousand Mongols ruled the world's most advanced civilization with some ten million Chinese subjects. His greatest success as Emperor was that the Yuan eventually unified the country as it had not been in centuries. Whether Kublai was crueler than the previous emperor is subject to debate. He embraced Chinese ways and loved tea enough to establish an imperial tea garden which I found still existing in the Wuyi Mountains. Why Marco Polo, who for a time served Kublai as governor of Hangzhou in the tea growing province of Zhejiang, never mentions tea, nobody knows. Kublai was succeeded by 12 Khans in succession until 1368, when the Yuan dynasty collapsed in the usual chaos and a new dynasty, the Ming, was proclaimed.

3. Like the Americas, the Orient was enormously alluring to the most brilliant and adventurous members of the recently establish Jesuit order. The first Jesuit to undertake the voyage East was St. Francis Xavier, one of the founders of the Society of Jesus. Those who followed were often men of genius, as eager to learn as to teach, like the justly famous Matteo Ricci who reached China in 1593 and rose to become an advisor and instructor to the Emperor. Ricci's fellow Jesuit, the long-ignored João Rodrigues, was equally remarkable. Rodrigues spent fifty-six years in Japan and China, won the friendship of Japan's preeminent *daimyō* warrior Hideyoshi and his Tokugawa successor, played an active role in the silk trade between China and Japan, and was for many years the most influential European in all Japan. He compiled the first grammar of the Japanese language, then travelled widely throughout China where he conducted official business with the court on behalf of Macao and finally took part in military skirmishes between Ming loyalists and Manchu invaders. In 1604, as an old man back in Portugal, he published a lengthy account of Japanese culture. He goes into detail about the cultivation and manufacture of tea and praises the tea ceremony from personal experience. Alone among European observers, he delves into Asian esthetic values and canons of taste. Surprisingly, Rodrigues had to wait until 1973 for a proper biography by Michael Cooper.

4. Padre Matteo Ricci: *Annua della Cina del 1606 e 1607 del Padre M. Ricci*, collected and published by Padre Nicolas Trigault, Rome (1610) and Spence, Jonathan: *The Memory Palace of Matteo Ricci*, Viking, New York (1984).

Tea Comes to Europe & America

5. Jan Hugo van Linschooten: *Discours of Voyages* (London, 1598), p. 46. Translated into English by the author, from the original Dutch edition, published in 1595-6.

6. This island, located off the Northwest coast of Nagasaki Prefecture, became the port to which Europeans were allowed restricted trade with the Japanese. In 1609 the Tokugawa Shogunate permitted the VOC to trade with Japan after which the Dutch Trading Post was constructed in Hirado under the guidance of Matsura Takanobu, Lord of Hirado. In 1613, the British ship *Clove* became the first British vessel to reach Japan. The Dutch allowed R. L. Wickham, agent for the English East India Company, to reside on Hirado. Wickham was the first Englishman to refer to tea in a letter he penned requesting some tea *(chaw)* from his English colleagues in China be sent to Hirado.

7. The English East India Company was chartered by Queen Elizabeth I, on December 31, 1600, as "The Governor and Merchants of London Trading into the East Indies." This unregulated corporation would help fund Parliament and shape the British Empire until its demise in the 1850s and final dissolution in 1874.

8. Descendants of Chinggis Khan's Mongols ruled Iran for centuries after the Mongol Yuan dynasty collapsed in China. During this period, Persia traded cobalt, the blue pigment used in Ming blue-and-white porcelains, for Chinese luxuries like tea, which the Persian elite adopted long before the elite of India got a first taste. In the early 1900's a canny English diplomat toured Iran offering to replace old China for new. He returned home with a fortune in used Ming ceramics.

9. The Hague, Holland's capital, seat of the royal court and ruling elite who became the first and leading customers for tea imported by the VOC, ie Verenigde Oostindische Compagnia, the Dutch East India Company. By 1637 it had also come into use by the merchant class.

10. This was the first European attempt to establish diplomatic and trade relations with the Qing dynasty which had come to power just ten years previously. Such efforts were to be largely fruitless for almost two hundred years.

11. This "confinement" was the result of a subsequent treaty, the first permitting Russian caravan trade. Russia was slow to take to tea. The Swedish envoy to Moscow reported in 1674 that tea cost thirty kopeks per pound there and was only used against hangovers. The first official Russian caravan entered Beijing in 1699 and for three decades thereafter caravans arrived regularly every three years, the time it took to make the return journey to Moscow and back. Only in 1727 did Russia negotiate a further trade agreement by which a marketplace was established at Kyakhta, a Russian outpost on the border of Mongolia. Chinese merchants promptly built a market of their own, separated from the Russian market by a wooden fence demarcating the border. This outpost was called Maimaicheng or "Trade City." By 1750, half a million pounds of tea were being traded annually at Kyakhta, half of it brick tea destined for the nomads of Siberia. Just fifty years later the volume was six times as much. Getting the tea across Central Asia to market in Russia, on the backs of camels or horses, took between 100 and 200 days of hard travel.

12. Alfred Franklin: *Le Cafe, le The, et le Chocolat, La Vie privée d'autrefois* (Paris, 1893).

Thomas Garraway was England's first tea entrepreneur, selling tea in his London coffee house.

13. Thomas Garraway, England's first tea entrepreneur, in September of 1658 advertised tea for sale at his coffee house. His "notice" (in a periodical announcing the death of Oliver Cromwell) proclaims tea's healthfulness and lists all the claims made by Dutch doctors for tea's health benefits. Doubtlessly Garraway's tea as well as his tea knowledge came from Holland. Coincidentally, that same year London's first chocolate house opened with "an excellent West India drink where you may have it ready at any time and also unmade." Within a short two years after Garraway's advertisement, Cromwell's Puritan Commonwealth collapsed and England's "Merrie Monarch" Charles II returned from exile in Holland and assumed the throne as England's first tea-drinking king. In 1662 he married the Portuguese princess Catherine of Braganza, a fellow tea lover. A liking for tea spread from the Royal Household and soon became fashionable in elite London society.

14. A student of English history has no better friend than Samuel Pepys. As an accomplice, he is the tireless chronicler. To satisfy our curiosity, he partakes in every aspect of life; politics, work, society, health and sex. To deliver to us the pathos of seventeenth century life, he has attended every tribulation visited upon a people destined for greatness; England's Restoration, war, the Great Plague and the Great Fire of London. Throughout all, he does not merely report, but fearlessly reveals his personal experiences, unvarnished and forthright. In retirement, he moved to a country house owned by a friend. Today that house has been encompassed by an ever-growing metropolis. Pepys' due diligence in reporting the new "China drink" is mentioned by Ukers and numerous authors since his day.

15. Pepys wrote his diary in phonetic shorthand. The original, comprising six volumes, is preserved in the Pepysian Library at Magdalene College, Cambridge.

16. This must have been the worst tasting tea any British subject has ever tasted, worse even than the "Able-bodied" tea served throughout the Royal Navy after 1823, when tea was first included as a regulation part of every sailor's daily ration.

17. Agnes Strickland: *Lives of the Queens of England* (London, 1882).

18. Maria Tewk, also spelled Mary Tuke, was a formidable business woman, who started selling tea in York in 1725. She no doubt sold tea smuggled from Holland for the Dutch East India Company (EIC) had her arrested and fined repeatedly for selling tea "without a license." Each time, Mary Tuke paid the fine and went right back to selling tea. Eventually the EIC gave up trying to stop her. She died a spinster in 1752, leaving her business to her nephew and apprentice William Tuke. Two centuries after Mary started it, the business was re-christened R.O. Mennell & Co., having never left the ownership of Tuke descendants. R. O. Mennell is the author of *Tea: An Historical Sketch* (1926), which details the saga of the House of Tuke and its role in British tea history.

Tea Comes to Europe & America

The first London Tea Auction was held at the East India Company's headquarters on Leadenhall Street in 1679. The London Tea Auction, *c.1808, lithograph courtesy of the British Library.*

19. From classical Greek mythology and literature, Polyphemus appeared in Homer's *Odyssey* as a giant man-beast who imprisons and eats several of Odysseus' men. Odysseus gets the giant drunk, and while he sleeps, Odysseus blinds him in his single eye with a fire-hardened wooden spear. He and his men escape the blind Cyclops guarding the cave's entrance by clinging under the bellies of the giant's sheep as they go out to pasture.

20. Ellis Paxson Oberholtzer: *Philadelphia, a History of the City and its People* (Philadelphia, 1912), Vol. I, p. 106.

21. The Stamp Act was passed by the British Parliament on March 22, 1765. The new levy was imposed on all American colonists and required them to pay a tax on every piece of printed paper they used. Ship's papers, legal documents, licenses, newspapers, other publications, and even playing cards were taxed. The money collected by the Stamp Act was to be used to help pay the costs of quartering British troops on the American frontier.

22. This was the first recorded incidence of a political event organized by women on American soil.

The Clipper Ship Taeping.

SHIPS IN AZURE

While the progress of both tea and coffee is associated with the development of ships and shipping, the poetry, romance and high adventure of tea is more definitely interwoven with those glorious days when the East Indiamen and the clipper ships sailed the seven seas.

Before the English East India Company turned its thoughts to tea, Englishmen drank mostly coffee. It is interesting to note that just as America started out to become a nation of tea drinkers, only to boycott it for coffee, so England, earlier in its history the largest coffee consuming nation, became, instead, the world's largest tea consumer. Men and ships brought this about, but particularly such ships as those which graced the coat of arms of the old East India Company—"three ships in azure," they were called—these and the graceful white-winged tea clippers of the era that followed on.

Within fifty years of the opening of the first coffee house in England, there were two thousand coffee houses in the City of London, alone. Toward the close of the seventeenth century, however, the East India Company was much more interested in tea than in coffee. Having lost out to the French and the Dutch on the "little brown berry of Arabia," The Company engaged in so lively a propaganda for tea that, whereas the annual tea imports from 1700 to 1710 averaged 800,000 pounds, in 1721 more than 1,000,000 pounds of tea were brought in; in 1757, some 4,000,000 pounds. And when the coffee house finally succumbed, tea, and not coffee, was firmly entrenched as the national drink of the English people.

While it is often said that the English East India Company owed its birth to pepper, its amazing development was due to tea. Its early adventures in the Far East brought it to China, whose tea was destined later to furnish the means of governing India.

During the hey-day of its prosperity John Company, otherwise the "Honourable East India Company," maintained a monopoly of the tea trade with China, controlled the supply, limited the quantity imported into England, and thus fixed the price. It constituted not only the world's greatest tea monopoly but also the source of inspiration for the first English propaganda on behalf of a beverage. It was so powerful that it precipitated a dietetic revolution in England, changing the British people from a nation of coffee drinkers to a nation of tea drinkers, and all within the space of a few years. It was a formidable rival of states and empires, with power to acquire territory, coin money, command fortresses and troops, form alliances, make war or peace, and exercise both civil and criminal jurisdiction.

The English East India Company was chartered in the closing days of the year 1600. In 1601 Captain James Lancaster made his famous voyage on the company's behalf and established a factory at Bantam in Java. The Dutch had preceded the English in the Indies by four years, although the Dutch East India Company was not chartered until 1602.

There were sixteen rival East India companies of Dutch, French, Danish, Austrian, Swedish, Spanish, and Prussian origin, operating at various times from the continent of Europe, but none of them reached the position of commanding importance occupied by the British East India Company.

At the start the trade with the East was in the hands of the Levant Company,[1] which made huge profits out of the trade with India by way of the overland route through Asia Minor, and when the sea route to the East by way of the Cape of Good Hope had been opened, certain members of the Levant Company were first to see its advantages.

Accordingly, in 1599 a number of members of the company met and discussed the possibilities of developing the sea route to the East, for the Portuguese and Dutch were by then obtaining such a firm foothold that unless something was done immediately it was felt that the opportunity would never return. A petition to Queen Elizabeth was presented, but it was not approved until the last day of 1600, when these gentlemen were given a monopoly of the Indian trade for fifteen years. This in itself was valuable, but still more valuable was an exemption from export duties for the first four voyages, and permission to take out coin of the realm, which ordinarily was prohibited. The corporation was empowered to make by-laws, to export all kinds of goods free of duty, to export foreign coin or bullion, to inflict punishments, and to impose fines, with many other privileges of great pecuniary benefit. It started with a practical monopoly of all the wealth to be found by trade or discovery between Cape Horn in the Western Hemisphere and the Cape of Good Hope in the Eastern Hemisphere. Its charter conferred the sole right of trading with the East Indies. Unauthorized interlopers were liable to forfeiture of ships and cargoes.

At first the fleets of the East India Company traded chiefly in spices. The first East Indiamen penetrated as far as Canton in 1637, but tea does not appear to have appealed to these pioneers, and although Englishmen in China and Japan were drinking it as early as 1615, none was brought home.

Ships in Azure

The East Indiamen of this day were slightly, but not greatly, superior to the average merchant ship of the time. In the matter of size, they were not very imposing, the great majority being of 499 tons burden. The reason for this was the law that ships of five hundred tons or over must carry a chaplain. The Court of Directors, while willing to pay their servants generously and to find rich jobs for their relatives as well as themselves, saw no reason to let any more money go out of the family than was absolutely necessary.

The first direct consignment of tea was rather less than a hundredweight, but it soon became popular and huge quantities were carried by the East Indiamen. These ships carried only the better quality of tea; although, when one compares the conditions of their voyages with the care taken nowadays, there is some doubt as to just what "best quality" meant.

The Dutch and Ostenders were importing large quantities of the cheaper kinds, and a goodly proportion of their imports was immediately smuggled across to England and sold at very much less than the East India Company's prices. At the same time the officers and men of the ships were themselves very prone to smuggling, and at a rather later date it was a standing order of the revenue service that as soon as an East Indiaman dropped her anchor in the Downs, every available cutter or boat was to be told off to watch her and prevent her officers and men from landing the tea that they had bought as a private venture in the East.

Although the East India Company had traded with China since the early days of the eighteenth century, the charter was completely revised in 1773 and the company was given the monopoly of the British trade with China as well as with India. This extension of the regular run was of considerable indirect advantage, for the company had not the docking facilities in the East that it had at Bombay, and the longer run forced it to build bigger and better ships. Both the building and the running were exceedingly wasteful, however, and it has been estimated that the company made only about two-thirds of the profits it might easily have made with a little careful management.

Voyages to India were long enough, but to China they were needlessly protracted. Not only was no effort made to drive the ships as might have been done, but they were kept in Chinese waters for a long time waiting for cargoes. So long was the delay that it was customary to unrig the ships completely and refit them when they were due to sail again.

All this time the East India Company had been nothing more than a corporation of individual merchants, just as it was when founded by Queen Elizabeth. Every merchant had his own ax to grind and his own profits to make, with the Court of Directors maintaining a certain discipline. The company never owned its own ships, but for many years they were supplied by individual directors, who were known as ships' husbands. The company took them up for so many voyages, generally six, and then made them conform to its regulations.

Gradually this privilege of chartering ships for the company got out of the hands of the directors themselves, but every effort was made to keep it a close corporation, and it was very difficult indeed for an unknown man to get his ships accepted.

Very often the ship's husband, after having his tender accepted, would sell the privilege to his captain; sometimes for as much as ten thousand pounds. With the freight money, the generous pay and allowances, and the permission of the East India Company to trade in certain commodities privately and to carry fifty tons outward and twenty tons homeward, such an officer was able to make a large sum every voyage. Also, the captain frequently let his quarters to passengers, with the result that ten thousand pounds profit to himself on a single voyage was not an unknown return.

When this custom had gone on for some time, the command of Indiamen became almost hereditary, and until the Court of Directors stepped in and demanded a certain amount of time at sea and experience, men who had never been to sea before and were scarcely out of their teens took the command of ships.

The fare to India varied, principally according to the rank of the passenger in the company's service; for there were few travelers who did not wear its uniform. A high official would pay anything up to £250, while a young subaltern just gazetted would find that his voyage out cost him barely £100.

Food and wine were liberally supplied, but, curiously enough, the company refused to fit out the cabins, and the first thing to be done after booking a passage was to purchase the necessary furniture from the riverside firms that specialized in its construction; the ship's captain or his officers generally buying this furniture for a song at the end of the voyage and selling at a big profit to homecoming travelers.

So troublesome was the smuggling of tea in the seventeenth century that acts were passed to prohibit its being imported into England from any other part of Europe; later these had to be modified by the provision of licenses whenever the East India Company's supply fell short of the demand, as was constantly happening. In spite of this, however, the company carried more tea away from China than anybody else, the figures in 1766 being 6,000,000 pounds carried by the English company, 4,500,000 by the Dutch, and no other company more than 3,000,000. The company began to get into low water in the middle of the eighteenth century, and in 1772 had to beg the Government to remit the contributions it owed, and in addition to lend it one million pounds. These boons were granted, but at the same time the authorities passed the India Acts, by which more economical management was enforced. Soon afterwards the East India Company was granted the privilege of placing its tea in bond and paying the duty when it was taken out. This made a considerable difference to the trade, for it allowed the sales to be distributed much more evenly throughout the year; though at this time it was estimated that only one-third of the tea drunk in Great Britain paid duty, all the rest being smuggled.[2]

In the beginning, tea could only be procured from China. It was a very precious thing—"a treasure of the world." The English appear to have been slow to appreciate its commercial aspects. While the Dutch were busy promoting its introduction and sale on the Continent, and were selling it to London coffee house keepers, the agents of the English East India Company were singularly neglectful of their opportunities to provide direct importations.

There were, of course, good reasons for their tardiness, the principal one being Dutch supremacy in the Far East. And so it is not until 1664, nearly fifty years after Mr. Wickham's famous personal request for a pot of "chaw," that we find any reference to tea in the company's records, and then it is only to note the purchase of some two pounds two ounces of "good thea" by the Court of Directors for presentation to His Majesty in order that he might "not find himself wholly neglected by the Company." Several authorities aver that Charles II promptly transferred the gift to his Queen Consort, Catherine of Braganza.

In 1666, among several "raretyes" provided by the secretary for His Majesty, twenty-two pounds twelve ounces of thea were purchased at fifty shillings a pound and "for the two cheefe persons that attended His Majesty, thea @ £6.15s."

Meanwhile, it appears that the company's servants occasionally reported to their masters upon the custom of the Chinese in partaking of an infusion of an aromatic plant called "tay," but these masters, being more obsessed with the idea of trading the Orientals English cloth in exchange for sleeve and sewing silks, failed utterly to envision a future when tea would dominate all other trading on the Royal Exchange. It was 1668 before the company's first order for importing tea reached the agent at Bantam.[3] It instructed him "to send home 100 lb. waight of the best tey that you can get."

The company's first importation followed in 1669, when two canisters weighing 143 lb. 8 oz. arrived from Bantam. This was followed in 1670 by four pots weighing 79 lb. 6 oz. Of these two shipments, 132 lb. were found to be damaged and sold at the company's sales for 3s. 2d. per pound. The Court of Committees consumed the remainder.

Thereafter tea was imported year by year (with the exception of the years 1673-7) from Bantam, from Surat, from Ganjam and from Madras. One of the importations, 266 lb. from Bantam, is recorded as having been "part of the present from Tywan [Formosa]," but in general the company's factors bought at Bantam from Chinese junks trading there, and at Surat from the Portuguese ships trading from Macao to Goa and Daman. Nearer than this they could not get in reaching out for the China trade.

In 1678 the company imported so much tea from Bantam that the London market was glutted. Two years later tea was selling in London for thirty shillings a pound and in the American colonies at five to six dollars a pound for the cheapest qualities.

In 1681 the company gave a standing order to its agent in Bantam for "tea to the value of one thousand dollars annually."

Driven out of Java by the Dutch in 1684, the company was forced to turn elsewhere for its supplies of "the divine herb." The first direct shipment from Amoy arrived in London in 1689. Not until 1715 does green tea appear to have taken the fancy of Britishers. Until then it was all Bohea, black tea from the famous hills in southern China where the original Bohea tea was grown.

The close of the seventeenth century had witnessed a number of subsidiary companies in a mad scramble for a share in the lucrative trade of the Far East.

Having created in the East India Company a Frankenstein monster of commerce, the Government found itself hard put to devise ways and means to make the monster give an accounting of its stewardship. The first hundred years had been marked by a series of duties cunningly devised to replenish the royal coffers by exacting adequate customs returns for the extraordinary privileges accorded the gentlemen adventurers trading with the Orient. These duties representing part of the price which the Occident was to pay for its tea, continued to annoy and irritate English traders and English tea drinkers for over two and a half centuries before they were abolished in 1929, only to be reimposed three years later.

At the start, semiprivate adventurers frequently realized larger profits than the parent corporation. The outcome was several companies or corporations operating under special privileges, these in turn being harassed by private adventurers. In 1698 the interlopers set up a new East India Company which was approved by Parliament. An ultimate settlement was brought about by a consolidation, in 1708, of the different interests in "The United Company of Merchants of England trading to the East Indies."

Once it became entrenched in China, the English East India Company protected its monopoly for nearly two centuries; no British subject was allowed to land at Canton without its permission, nor any British ships to trade except under license.

The company ordered its tea put "in chests and not in tubs as usual," in its instructions to the Loyal Blisse, loading at Canton for the season of 1713. Sixty years later the Boston Indians were to find chests much easier to handle than tubs or pots.

By 1718 tea had begun to displace silk as the main staple of the China trade, and in 1721 Fate began to set the stage for the drama in the West. Under the ministry of Sir Robert Walpole the import duty on tea was removed and an excise tax on withdrawals from bond replaced it.

This change of policy was followed by orders prohibiting the importation of tea from all parts of Europe, thus making the East India Company's monopoly complete; so by 1725 we find that tea had become such a sacrosanct thing in England under the *regis* of the East India Company that its adulteration was made punishable by seizure and a fine of a hundred pounds. Still further punishment was added in 1730-1; owners of tea sophistications were fined ten pounds per pound and in 1766 the penalty was increased to include imprisonment.

In 1739 tea led in value all other items in cargoes brought by the ships of the Dutch East India Company to Holland. Smuggling to England and America was on the increase, for the British East India Company's monopoly was inviting the inevitable interference from outsiders. Ten years later, London was made a free port for tea in transit to Ireland and America.

As was to have been expected, the English East India Company survived the War of American Independence, muddled through its financial difficulties and, by means of much helpful legislation from the State, designed to kill off adulterations and defeat smuggling, emerged from its second century more powerful than ever.

The East India Company constructed docks and warehouses, The Docklands, upriver from London in order to accommodate the ever-growing number of ships arriving daily laden with cargo from the East.

The Commutation Act of 1784 repealed the existing duties, amounting to about 119 per cent, and substituted therefor a duty of 12.5 percent computed on the sale prices obtained at the East India Company's quarterly tea sales. These were hedged round with certain restrictions, "that the company might take no advantage of the real monopoly of tea which this act would throw into their hands," but, notwithstanding this supposed protection, a general revolt against the high-handed methods of the company by the thirty thousand wholesale and retail tea dealers of London followed.

Pamphlets and meetings of general protest were the means employed to rouse public opinion against the company toward the close of the century. Again, it was the British people warring against special privilege.

The agitation was designed to force the Government to serve upon the company the three years' notice required by law in the event of a proposed termination of its monopoly. Although it failed of its purpose at this time, the way was prepared for another attack in 1812. The directors relied upon "the wisdom of Parliament and the good sense of the nation in general," to resist these "rash and violent innovations upon the system of the Company." They further contended that open "competition would be ruinous to the public interest; the cost of teas would be enhanced."

The American tea merchants of 1773 had established a dangerous precedent for dealing with monopolies, however, for the War of American Independence had been fought and won by rallying public opinion round a free-trade ideal. Now another war with this young country was about to break out.

The English tea merchants were only too ready to aid and abet the Americans in bringing fresh disaster to the East India Company. They viewed the War of 1812 as a blessing. John Company stood at bay. When the Earl of Buckinghamshire gave an evasive answer, they protested against a "tide of prejudice and popular clamor being permitted to determine public counsels," but this truculent attitude could not avert the blow. In 1813 the company's monopoly to India was ended, though the China monopoly was permitted to continue for another twenty years.

Undoubtedly, the attitude of the company toward the American colonist was, in large measure, responsible for its ultimate undoing. After all, the colonists were Englishmen, and many of their fellow countrymen at home sympathized with their aspirations.

Following the company's refusal to consider seriously the cultivation of tea in India, because it was fearful of the effect upon its only remaining monopoly, the China trade, came the discovery of indigenous tea in Assam in 1823.[4] Ten years later the company again faced the same jealous outcry against a continuance of its special privilege, and in 1834 it was forced to yield to the agitation for the complete abolition of its trading monopoly.

Meanwhile the tea of China had furnished the means of governing India; or perhaps it would be fairer to say the export of tea and the import of opium, for the East India Company originally organized and financed the cultivation, shipment and distribution of opium to China.[5] As is recognized, it was largely the opium traffic that caused the wars between China and Great Britain in 1840 and 1855.

The profits which had accrued to "a handful of adventurers from an island in the Atlantic," as Macaulay described the company in the House of Commons, had made possible "the subjugation of a vast country divided from the place of their birth by half the globe." Wherefore the company was permitted to continue its administrative functions in India until the Indian mutiny caused the transfer of the Indian administration to the crown, August 2, 1858. Thus ended, after 258 years of glorious adventures, the greatest of all monopolies.

It was at Mr. Thomas Smythe's house in Philpot Lane, the city mansion of its first governor, that there was started the business that was to shape the destinies of empires. John Company had several homes afterwards, all of them landmarks. The third and last building, reconstructed after plans of Richard Jupp in 1796-9, in Leadenhall Street, was one of the show places of London. It contained the famous salesroom.

John Company employed nearly four thousand men in its warehouses, and, before the trade with India closed, kept more than four hundred clerks to transact the business of this greatest tea company that the world has ever seen.

The military department superintended the recruiting and supplying of the Indian army. There was a shipping department, a master attendant's office, an auditor's office, an examiner's office, an accountant's office, a transfer office and a treasury. The buying office governed the fourteen warehouses, and so controlled the home market, having often in store some fifty million pounds weight of tea; 1,200,000 lb. were sometimes sold in one day at the annual tea sales, which were described as "bear-garden scenes."[6]

The quaint conservatism of the company may be noted from the directors' custom of signing their letters "Your loving friends." This has been pointed to as evidence of the splendid relations existing between the company and its servants, but when, as frequently happened, the salutation closed a letter of admonishment or stinging rebuke, it probably was looked upon by the recipient as cold politeness, a conventional gesture.

Like the leaders of many successful commercial enterprises, the directors of the East India

Company owed their success to their ability to surround themselves with people cleverer than themselves. Many of those whose names are written high on the rolls of England's great were numbered among the servants of John Company. Aside from the generals and the captains who served the company in Java, India, China, and other stations overseas the company drew to itself at home many of the brilliant minds of the age.

To mention only a few of these, there were: John Hoole (1727-1803), the dramatist and translator, accountant and auditor for the East India Company; James Cobb (1756-1813), also a dramatist; Charles Lamb (1775-1834), poet, essayist, humorist and critic, author of the *Essays of Elia*, who was for the greater part of his life a clerk in the office of the East India Company; James Mill (1773-1836), the journalist, meta physician, historian and political economist, of the company's department of examiners; his son, John Stuart Mill (1806-73), the philosopher and political economist; Thomas Love Peacock (1785-1866), satirical poet and novelist; and a score of lesser-known but still distinguished men of letters and clerics.

John Company was "a corporation of men with long heads and deep purposes." Macaulay told Parliament in 1833 that it was a mistake to suppose that the company was merely a commercial body till the middle of the eighteenth century. Commerce was its object, but, like its Dutch and French rivals, it was invested with political functions as well. It was at first a great trader and a petty prince; then it became a great nabob, sovereign of all India.

The company's honor roll included the names of many merchants having the sentiments and abilities of great statesmen. "The East India Company has left its mark on the world," said Sir Alfred Lyall in 1890. "It accomplished a work such as in the whole history of the human race no other trading company ever attempted and such as none surely is likely to attempt in the years to come," said *The Times* in 1873.

In its valedictory petition to Parliament in 1858, written by John Stuart Mill, the East India Company solemnly reminded the nation that the foundations of the British Empire in the East "were laid by your petitioners at that time neither aided nor controlled by Parliament, at the same period at which a succession of administrations under the control of Parliament were losing to the Crown of Great Britain another great empire on the opposite side of the Atlantic."

This was eloquent and forceful, but none the less futile. There was pathos in it, too, for it seemed to be calling upon posterity to witness that John Company must not be blamed for the loss of that Western Empire, and even if it were, not to forget that Britain's magnificent Empire of the East had been acquired for her by John Company at its own expense, and that for a century the Indian possessions had been governed and defended from the resources of those possessions without the smallest cost to the British Exchequer.

Ships in Azure

As the tea trade grew in importance after the abolition of the monopoly of the East India Company, merchants began to demand more rapid transit for each new season's teas. The slow and stately East Indiamen were becoming obsolete. These frigate-built ships were jocularly known as "tea waggons."

Although tea became an outcast from America's trade during the struggle which preceded the American Revolution, two unseen influences conspired to establish an entirely new tea trade in the United States, once the war was ended. One was a natural, inherited taste of the former Dutch and English colonists for tea. The other was the fact, soon learned by shipmasters in the new commerce which sprang up between America and the Orient, that tea was the only commodity obtainable at Canton in sufficient quantities to fill cargoes.

Cantonese warehouses, or "chops," were filled with tea chests awaiting pick up by the East India Company's "tea waggons."

John Ledyard was the first to envision an American trade with China, carrying furs in exchange for teas, silks, and spices. Robert Morris, of Philadelphia, was the first to make his dream possible, by outfitting the *Empress of China* for the purpose in 1784. The trip was a great success. Peter Schermerhorn and John Vanderbilt helped in another venture. Trading furs made it possible to keep specie at home among the bankrupt colonies, where it was badly needed. The new-born tea trade soon became a gold rush.

John Jacob Astor (1763-1848) was early in the trade and stayed in it for more than twenty-five years. Stephen Girard (1750-1831) was prominent among the Philadelphia merchants in the trade. Astor and Girard made great fortunes in tea and were looked up to as financial giants. Thomas Handasyd Perkins (1764-1854) of Boston was another. These men became millionaires in addition to developing profitable trade relations for the well-nigh bankrupt states.

In America, a type of schooner had evolved from the swift privateers produced in Baltimore for the War of 1812, and these became known as Baltimore clippers.[7] Sometimes they were rigged as hermaphrodite brigs, but they never carried more than two masts, whereas the sailing vessel which introduced the age of the clipper ships was three masted.

Ships in Azure

The Empress of China *became the first American ship to trade directly with China in 1784 when it delivered a cargo of New England ginseng in exchange for Chinese tea at Canton. It was a joint venture of Philadelphians and New Yorkers, organized by Philadelphian financier Robert Morris and captained by Philadelphian John Green. A financial success, the voyage inspired imitators, which helped establish Philadelphia as a major center for U.S. trade with China.*

In 1816 the famous Black Ball Line of square-rigged packet ships appeared on the run from New York to Liverpool carrying passengers, mails, and cargo. Competition increased and with the opening of the Erie Canal, in 1825, New York and New England shipbuilders were besieged with orders for fast ships to sail the seven seas.

In 1832 Isaac McKim, a Baltimore merchant, conceived the idea of building for the China trade a three-masted, full-rigged vessel along the lines of the fast Baltimore clippers. She was built by Kennard and Williamson of Fells Point and named the *Ann McKim,* after the owner's wife. Being a kind of hobby with him, she was fitted with the most expensive Spanish mahogany hatches and brass fittings, including twelve brass guns. She was 493 tons register, 143 feet long and 31 feet wide. Although she proved to be one of the finest and fastest ships on the China run, her carrying capacity was comparatively small for her length and her crew requirements.

Upon the death of Isaac McKim, in 1837, the *Ann McKim* was purchased by Howland and Aspinwall, the pioneer New York tea merchants, who afterwards introduced the *Rainbow,* the first of the extreme American clippers. Later the *Ann McKim* was sold to the Chilean Government. She caused a sensation when she was first put into the China trade, despite the complacency and skepticism of maritime circles in the early thirties. It was beginning to be realized that tea was a cargo that was best handled quickly, while travelers on business were also realizing that time was money. Accordingly, there was every incentive for improving upon the little *Ann McKim* by building the famous *Rainbow,* which in turn was followed by a host of other American clippers. The reign of the clipper ship furnishes the most romantic chapter in the history of America's merchant marine.

With the dawning of the new era in naval architecture the blunt, full-bodied ship gave way to a radical departure in design. The "cod's head and mackerel tail" of old tradition evolved into a thing of beauty, grace and speed. The stem was carried forward in a curve, lengthening the bow above water; the water-line was concave before it became convex at both the bow and the stern, while the masts shot further skyward, carrying tier upon tier of sail.

In 1841, John Willis Griffiths (1809-82), "a grey-eyed, dreamy-browed fellow," was employed as a draughtsman by the shipbuilding firm of Smith & Dimon. It was his genius that revolutionized the science of marine and naval architecture by the introduction of the first extreme clipper-ship model.

Griffiths proposed the clipper ship in 1841 and designed the *Rainbow* in 1843. She was of 750 tons registry and was launched from the Smith & Dimon yards, New York, in 1845. One observer declared her bow had been turned outside in and that "her whole form was contrary to the laws of nature." Opinion was divided as to whether she would float or sink.

She exceeded all expectations however. Her maiden voyage to China started in February and she was back in New York in September, having paid her cost, $45,000, and her owners, Howland and Aspinwall, an equal sum in profit. On her second voyage, she was so fast that she herself brought back to New York the news of her arrival in Canton. She had made the round trip faster than any other ship could sail one way—ninety-two days out and eighty-eight back. Her commander, Captain John Ladd, called her the fastest ship in the world, and certainly she was one of the smartest. Although she was lost on her fifth voyage, her performance had proved the superiority of the clipper type. There was a second *Rainbow* after the Civil War.

Griffiths' second clipper, the *Sea Witch*, 890 tons, built for Howland and Aspinwall in 1846, was for three years considered the fastest ship that sailed the seas. She made Hong Kong in one hundred and four days and returned to New York from Canton in eighty-one days. Later she bettered the run from Canton to New York by four days, making 358 miles in one day's run. There was also a later ship called the *Sea Witch*.

Almost as soon as they had begun to send their ships overseas, Americans had appreciated the value of the China trade, and several New England merchants had made fortunes in it. Their competition was not regarded very seriously by the British, who had such a huge preponderance in numbers and were backed by a monopoly that appeared to assure them a comfortable profit for all time. After the first China War had been fought, however, and the trade to China greatly increased, American merchants brought out a regular fleet of clippers and captured such a large proportion of the trade that the British were forced to follow their lead.

Meanwhile, in 1844, A. A. Low & Brother, the New York tea merchants, had contracted with Brown & Bell to build the *Houqua*, named in honor of a Cantonese hong merchant.

In 1846 Alexander Hall & Co., of Aberdeen, built the clipper schooner *Torrington* for Jardine, Matheson & Co., to compete with the American opium clippers in the Chinese coast trade. The *Torrington* was rigged as a two-masted schooner, and differed from the American clipper in many points of construction. She succeeded so well that she was soon followed by others in this particular line, and the system of construction spread to the ships that carried tea home to England. The repeal of the Navigation Laws, which limited trade between Great Britain and

Ships in Azure

New York tea merchants A. A. Low & Brother commissioned Brown & Bell to build the Houqua, *named in honor of a Cantonese hong merchant, in 1844.*

her colonies to British ships, permitted American ships to carry cargoes of China tea straight to England, and the competition between the two flags became keener than ever.

In 1847 A. A. Low & Brother brought out the *Samuel Russell*, 940 tons, built by Brown & Bell. The British competitors were the *Stornoway, Torrington* and, later, *Lord of the Isles*, the last-named the first tea clipper to be built of iron. She made a remarkable run of eighty-seven days from Shanghai to London during the northeast monsoon in 1855.

The *British Challenger,* in 1863, was the first vessel of any nationality to load tea at Hankow. Captain Thomas Macey paid the American tug *Firecracker* a thousand pounds to tow his ship up the Yangtze to Hankow. Although considered a dangerous experiment, Captain Macey's enterprise paid, and his example was soon followed by other China captains. Though the chief difficulty was the navigation of the Yangtze, the traders had to keep their armory in readiness for any eventuality. Basil Lubbock declares that two of the missionaries taken up river by the *Challenger* were actually eaten by Chinese cannibals. Captain Macey loaded a thousand tons of tea in June 1863, at £9 per ton, and made the run home in a hundred and twenty-eight days.[8]

A. A. Low & Brother's fleet had added to it later the *N. B. Palmer*, the *Great Republic* and the *Yokohama*. Of the last a story relates that once when she was loading in Japan, a Scottish vessel named *Caller Ou*, loading at the same time, got away two days ahead of her. Captain Berry of the *Yokohama*, fearing that he would have hard work overhauling the Scot, beating down the China Sea against the southwest monsoon then blowing, decided to try the longer way home round Cape Horn. He was favored by fair winds, reached New York, unloaded, took on an outward cargo, and set sail again. On passing out of the harbor at Sandy Hook, he met the *Caller Ou* coming in, to the profound astonishment of the Scottish captain.

The *David Brown*, a handsome ship, built by Roosevelt & Joyce in 1853, made the voyage to San Francisco in ninety-eight days. The *Romance of the Seas* sailed from Boston two days later, but caught up with the *David Brown* off the Brazilian coast. They kept close company, finally passing through the Golden Gate side by side. After discharging their cargoes, they again put out to sea together, this time bound for Hong Kong. While they did not see each other during the forty-five-day trip they anchored in Hong Kong on the same day, less than six minutes apart. The log of the *Romance of the Seas* records that skysails and stunsails were not taken in until Hong Kong was reached.

The *Benefactor*, built by Roosevelt & Joyce, was the barque, one hundred tons less than the *Houqua*, which brought the first cargo of tea from Japan to the United States.

The *Maury*, a 600-ton clipper barquentine, was named for Lieutenant Maury, U.S.N., but renamed the *Benefactress* when Maury showed Southern leanings at the outbreak of the Civil War. In 1856, sailing against the iron-built *Lord of the Isles* from Foochow to London, both carrying new teas with a premium of £1 per ton on the first ship home, the Maury reached the Downs the same morning as her rival, which had left Foochow four days ahead of her. They passed Gravesend within ten minutes of each other, but the *Lord of the Isles*, having the faster tug, made her dock first and won the prize.

Several other New York firms engaged in the China trade owned their own ships and sometimes the cargoes as well. Among these firms should be mentioned Grinnell, Minturn & Co., whose most celebrated ships were the *Flying Cloud, North Wind, Sea Serpent, Sweepstakes,* and *Sovereign of the Seas;* Goodhue & Co., who owned the *Mandarin;* Howland and Aspinwall, greatest of the merchant houses, who owned the *Ann McKim, Natchez, Rainbow,* and *Sea Witch;* N. L. & G. Griswold, who owned the *George Griswold, Helena, Ariel, Panama, Tarolinta,* and *Challenge.*

The *Challenge*, 2,006 tons, built in 1851, was the second-largest clipper ship; *Trade Wind*, built by Jacob Bell, New York, for W. Platt & Son, Philadelphia, exceeding her by twenty-four tons. The *Challenge* was at first commanded by "Bully" Waterman, whose exploits have furnished much colorful copy for nautical writers and abundant small talk for retired skippers. Known as "the finest and most costly merchant ship in the world," she was lost off the coast of Brazil after many years in the China tea trade.

The first American ship to carry a cargo of tea from China to London after the repeal of the Navigation Laws was the clipper *Oriental*, 1,003 tons, built for A. A. Low & Brother, New York, by Jacob Bell in 1849. She was 185 feet long and 36 feet in breadth. Her maiden trip to Hong Kong by the eastern passages consumed a hundred and nine days. She returned to New York with a cargo of tea in eighty-one days. On her second voyage, she made Hong Kong in eighty-one days. Then she was chartered by Russell & Co. to carry tea to London at £6 per ton of 4,0 cubic feet, with British ships begging for London cargoes at £3. 10s. per ton of 50 cubic feet. The *Oriental* delivered her 1,600 tons of tea in London in 1850, being ninety-seven days out of Hong Kong—a feat of speed never before equaled. Her first cost was $70,000; her freight on this one shipment was worth $48,000. On her voyage of 367 days from New York through Far Eastern seas to London she had sailed 67,000 miles, logging about 183 miles a day.

Other California clipper ships that followed in the wake of the *Oriental* to London, causing the English ship owners to lose the London tea trade almost entirely to American ships, were the *Surprise*, *White Squall*, *Sea Serpent*, *Nightingale*, *Argonaut* and *Challenge*. The American clippers were able to command twice the price per ton asked by British ships.

The competition which followed the repeal of England's Navigation Laws produced those famous China clippers, which will always live in the romance of the sea. The discovery of gold in California turned the attention of Americans very largely to their own coasts, only a few of their ships going across the Pacific to China for a return cargo of tea, but the British shipping companies built against one another in competition that was just as keen as it had been against the Americans.

All through the fifties and the sixties the type of ship continued to improve, and they became the aristocrats of the ocean, just as the East Indiamen had been in their day. The annual race home with the first of the new season's tea, for a prize of a heavy bonus and, as a rule, a very big stake, became an annual event. The golden age of the tea clippers spanned a generation, beginning in 1843 and ending with the opening of the Suez Canal in 1869.

The appearance of the tea clipper *Stag Hound,* in 1850, caused a sensation and served to focus attention on Donald McKay (1810-80), her designer. "While Donald McKay did not originate the clipper ship," says Richard C. McKay, "he was the man who made it famous. His advance

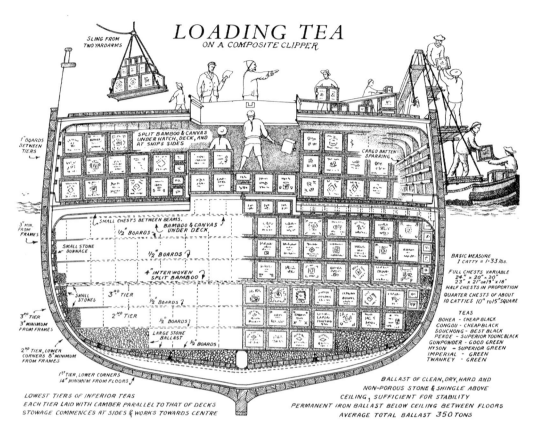

production of a vessel of the extreme clipper class proved a notable contribution to America's prestige as a maritime nation." Shipping men hailed the *Stag Hound* as being pretty near perfection of the clipper-ship type. She was 1,534 tons, at that time the largest merchant ship ever built. She made the run from Canton to New York in eighty-five days. In 1861 she was lost by fire off Pernambuco.

In 1851 Donald McKay's second extreme clipper, the *Flying Cloud,* 1,782 tons, was launched. Though built for Enoch Train & Co., Boston, she was sold while yet on the stocks to Grinnell, Minturn & Co., of New York. She accomplished the run round the Horn to San Francisco in eighty-nine days, twenty-one hours. Three years later she excelled her own record by thirteen hours. These sailing records have never been equaled. The launching of the *Flying Cloud* is said to have inspired Longfellow's poem, *The Building of the Ship*, with its oft quoted line: "Sail on, O Union, strong and great!" She was named by George Francis Train (1829-1904), the American financier and author, junior partner in the firm of Enoch Train & Co.

Like many of the early California clippers the *Flying Cloud* had to cross the Pacific to China to get a cargo home. She made Honolulu in twelve days. One day, under skysails and stunsails, she covered 374 miles. She loaded tea at Macao and returned to New York in ninety-six days, being beaten by the *N. B. Palmer* by ten days, although the latter was three days later in starting. Later she had her revenge, for she beat the *N. B. Palmer* in the San Francisco race of 1852. There were other exciting races with the *Hornet* and the *Archer,* after which, in 1859, she was sold to enter the London-China run. She carried her first load of tea from Foochow to London in one hundred and twenty-three days.

Donald McKay also produced the *Staffordshire* and the *Flying Fish* in 1851. Both were California clippers of the extreme type. The former was wrecked off Cape Sable in 1854, the latter was wrecked in 1858 while coming out of Foochow with a cargo of tea.

The British began building tea clippers in earnest with the *Falcon*, a 937-ton wooden ship produced in 1859 by Robert Steele & Co., Greenock, for Shaw, Maxton & Co. During the next ten years, no less than twenty-six wooden and composite clippers were turned out by British shipyards, some of which became famous.

The *Fiery Cross*, 880 tons (second ship of that name), was built by Chaloner & Co., of Liverpool, and launched in 1860. She was owned by J. Campbell. Her commander, Captain Robinson, was considered "a hard man to beat in the tricky China seas." She won four of the exciting tea races of the sixties. When her racing days were over she was sold to the Norwegians. Subsequently she caught fire and sank in one of the creeks of the Medway at Sheerness.

The *Taeping,* built by Robert Steele & Co., Greenock, and launched in 1863, was designed to beat the *Fiery Cross,* which had won the ten shillings per ton premium awarded to the first arrival in the 1861-2 seasons. The wooden *Serica* also from the Steele shipyards and launched in the same year, 1863, and the composite *Taeping* had several tussles. *Serica* had the great good luck to win by five days her first tea race with the *Fiery Cross* from Foochow. The *Taeping* did not really distinguish herself, however, until 1866, when she won the Great Tea Race, as she did again in 1867 and 1868. The *Taeping* was finally wrecked on Ladds Reef on her way from Amoy to New York; her mate's boat with six men was picked up three days after. The *Serica* was wrecked in 1869.

The *Ariel*, 853 tons, built by Robert Steele & Co., Greenock, and launched in 1864, was commanded by Captain John Keay, who had previously sailed the *Ellen Rodgers* and the *Falcon* with great success. She was "the ideal tea clipper, the fastest thing the wind ever drove through the water," in the opinion of Captain Andrew Shewan, late master of the *Norman Court*. Lubbock said of her: "Like all the fairy-like Steele clippers she was a ticklish jade to handle, and it took a master to get the best of her." Hawthorne Daniel, in *The Clipper Ship*,[9] agrees that: *"Ariel* was too fine astern to make her safe in a following sea. She was sharp at the bow, as well, and in heavy weather fairly drowned her crew. But that was a failing of many British-built ships as well as of more than a few Americans. Speed was considered as being so important in the construction of these ships that seaworthiness was sometimes scamped to obtain it."

In the Great Tea Race of 1866, *Ariel* was the winner at the Downs, but, for want of tidal water, had to wait in the Thames, docking twenty minutes later than her rival, *Taeping*. In 1872 *Ariel* left London for Sydney and was never heard of again. Of the four ships named *Ariel*, the one here mentioned, built in England in 1865, was the only one important in tea history.

The Great Race of 1866 pitted the clipper Ariel *against the* Taeping.

The famous tea clipper *Sir Lancelot*, 886 tons, was a sister ship of the beautiful *Ariel*, launched, like her, at the Steele shipyards in 1864. Her figurehead was a knight in mail armor, his visor open and his right hand drawing a sword. She loaded just under 1,500 tons of tea, and was the first ship to load tea at Hankow after the famous *Challenger*, being chartered by Jardine, Matheson & Co. at £7 per ton. This was in 1866. *Sir Lancelot* was third in the tea race of 1868, making the run from Foochow to London in ninety-eight days. She was the winner of the 1869 tea race from Foochow to London in eighty-nine days, with an added record for a day's run of 354 miles. *Sir Lancelot* was subsequently sold to an Indian merchant, and foundered in a cyclone in the Bay of Bengal in 1895.

The *Thermopylae*, 947 tons, built by Walter Hood, Aberdeen, and launched in 1868, marked a distinct advance in British tea clippers. She was designed by Bernard Weymouth, whose early tea clipper *Leander* was fast, but wet. The *Thermopylae* was built to give a good account of herself in a blow as well as in light airs. "The best all-around ship of the tea clipper fleet," Captain Shewan called her. She was the first British clipper to bear pressing in rough weather. Twice she made the run from London to Melbourne in sixty-three days. In the 1869 tea race from Foochow she lost to *Sir Lancelot* by three days. Her biggest tea cargo was 1,429,000 lb. Later she was sold into the transpacific trade and after that to the Portuguese government, which subsequently sank her off Lisbon in 1907.

The great rival of the *Thermopylae* was the *Cutty Sark*, 921 tons, probably the best-advertised of all British tea clippers. The *Cutty Sark* was a composite ship designed by Hercules Linton to beat *Thermopylae*, and built by Scott & Co., of Greenock, to the order of Captain John Willis, the London ship-owner known as "Old Whitchat." She was launched in 1868 and from 1870 to 1877 made a number of passages for tea, none of them sensational. After that she went on a series of wandering voyages, stopping anywhere a cargo offered. She was beset with all kinds of tragic happenings and romantic adventures until she came under the command of Captain Woodget, when she settled down to a dignified middle age in the Australian wool trade. She, too, later sailed under the Portuguese flag and again started in quest of strange adventures, which ended in 1922 when she was restored to the British nation to be used as a stationary training ship at Falmouth.

Unfortunately, *Thermopylae* and *Cutty Sark* never had a chance of testing their powers properly, for on the only occasion on which a race could be arranged, the *Cutty Sark* lost first her rudder and then the jury rudder that was rigged. She was only a few days behind her rival, however, so that there was little doubt that she would have won had things gone well with her.

The *Blackadder*, an iron clipper ship, designed for the China trade, had a disastrous maiden voyage in 1870, owing to defects in construction. She did not meet with favor at the hands of the tea shippers. She was followed by a most persistent hoodoo through the seventies and eighties, but later gave a better account of herself. Both she and her sister ship, the *Halloween*, however, were built too late, for the Suez Canal was practically completed and Alfred Holt, the Liverpool ship owner, had led the movement that transferred the carriage of tea from sail to steam. The later clipper ships saw the greater part of their service in the Australian trade.

The eclipse of the sailing ship was rapid and dramatic. The opening of the Suez Canal in 1869 gave steamships an advantage over the old windjammers that they had never possessed when forced to watch every pound of coal. Alfred Holt, who had started operations to the west coast of Africa with a single second-hand steamer, saw his opportunity and immediately built with the idea of high speed and economy. Within a few years his Blue Funnel liners had captured the cream of the tea trade.

Other companies followed, some successful and some not, and, although the sailing ships struggled on for some years more, the best gradually drifted into the Australian trade, where gold-seekers and wool cargoes gave them their opportunity. The days of racing home with the new season's tea were over. The steamship-owner weighed comparative cost carefully, and with his bigger cargo capacity and a regular schedule was able to maintain a profitable business without running undue risks. In the early eighties, an attempt was made to revive the craze for speed in a famous steamer known as the *Stirling Castle*, a 5,000-ton ship with a speed of nineteen knots, which reduced the time between China and London to thirty days, or about one-third the clipper-ship time. The *Glenogle* did it in forty days. It was soon found, however, that the expenses ran away with the profits, and the trade reverted to the regular cargo steamers.

The interest and excitement among landsmen during the clipper-ship days has been rivalled only by the English Derby. The tea trade was then the highest class of mercantile pursuit, and during the tea season the cynosure of all eyes was the dashing "tea clipper." Speeding under her enormous spread of snow-white canvas from far-away Cathay to her British or American home port, she was freighted with the choicest of the new season's pickings, meaning a handsome profit to the consignees of the first cargo to arrive. The best sailing masters, the finest seamen, and swiftest vessels afloat were represented in the tea fleet.

The racing of the tea ships was at that time the all-absorbing topic of the hour on Change, at the club, or by the fireside. The winner gained something more substantial than mere fame—not infrequently a fortune was the prize.

In Mincing Lane, the telegrams recording the hours at which the tea ships passed certain points were read with as much avidity as present-day stock-ticker tapes; and when the news came from Start Point that the clippers were beating up the English Channel, the excitement became intense. Before the days of the telegraph, when news travelled slowly, the arrival of the tea clippers had in it even more of mystery and of thrill.

Sometimes the crew of the winning ship received £500 from the owners of the cargo, for the first tea put on the market realized from three pence to six pence a pound more than teas on the slower ships. Swarms of sampling clerks would descend upon the docks to draw samples for brokers and wholesalers as soon as the news came that the racers had passed Gravesend. Some spent the night at nearby hotels; others slept at the docks. By 9 a.m., the samples were being tasted in Mincing Lane. Then bids were made by the large dealers; duty was paid on the gross weight; and by the following morning the new season's Congous would be on sale in Liverpool and Manchester.

An interesting reminder of clipper-ship days is still to be seen in the office of W. J. & H. Thompson, the Mincing Lane tea brokers. It is a wind-clock which hangs on the wall of the sales-room where it was installed to keep the office informed as to the direction of the wind; for, in the days of sail, adverse winds could compel the tea clippers to lie out in the Downs a week or more.[10] The arrow hand of this clock was connected with a weathervane on the roof of the building. A south-westerly wind was the kind of "blow" calculated to bring the clippers flying up the Channel, but a north-easterly wind meant exasperating delay. While a northeaster was not so unwelcome to overworked clerks, for whom it spelled respite from their labors, the keener spirits were all for the winds that brought the sampling of the new season's teas more quickly to hand. With a move of the wind-clock's hand from northeast to southwest, men on horseback would ride from the city to Tooting or Balham—then outlying villages of London, eight miles away—to inform merchants living there of the probable arrival of the tea ships.

The Great Tea Race of 1866 is still a favorite topic of discussion in Mincing Lane. This most exciting of all the tea races started on May 28, 1866, from the Pagoda Anchorage below Foochow, and ended ninety-nine days later, in the London Docks. Basil Lubbock tells the story best in his *China Clippers*.

There were eleven first-class tea clippers in the race. Prominent among them were: *Ariel*, 852 tons, Captain Keay, the favorite in the betting; *Taeping*, 767 tons, Captain McKinnon; *Serica*, 708 tons, Captain Innes; *Fiery Cross,* 695 tons, Captain Robinson; and *Taitsing*, 815 tons, Captain Nutsford. The leaders each carried over a million pounds of tea.

Ariel finished loading first but, getting off to a bad start, had to anchor before the tide had fallen. She was soon passed by *Fiery Cross,* which got to sea first and quickly piled up a day's lead. *Taeping* and *Serica* crossed the bar together.

Ariel almost made up her twenty-four-hour loss at the Cape, which she rounded about two hours behind *Fiery Cross* on July 15. *Taeping* followed twelve hours later. In the passage up the Atlantic all five ships got closer and closer to one another without knowing it. At St. Helena, on August 4, the order was *Taeping, Fiery Cross, Serica, Ariel* and *Taitsing*.

In the doldrums, *Fiery Cross* was becalmed for twenty-four hours, and this, her captain declared, cost him the race. *Ariel* had better luck, having good winds, and took the lead. She was the first to pick up Bishop and St. Agnes lights. In the race up the Channel, *Ariel* and *Taeping* were neck and neck. At the Downs they were only ten minutes apart, in a race across three-quarters of the globe. The times of the five ships at the Downs were as follows:

> *Ariel*, at 8 a.m., Sept. 6 . . . . 99 days out
> *Taeping*, at 8.10 a.m., Sept. 6 . . . . 99 days out
> *Serica*, at noon, Sept. 6 . . . . 99 days out
> *Fiery Cross*, during the night, Sept. 7 . . . . . 101 days out
> *Taitsing*, forenoon, Sept. 9 . . . . 101 days out

However, the race wasn't finished until the sample boxes of tea were tossed ashore at the London Docks. The excitement in Mincing Lane was intense. The progress of the contending ships up the Channel was flashed from each headland. The owners of the two leaders were so scared of losing the ten shillings extra per ton on a quibble as to which ship really won that they privately agreed to divide the premium, to be claimed by the first ship in dock. Of course, the captains knew nothing of this and stuck it out nobly to a grueling finish.

At the end, it was largely a battle of tugs. *Taeping* got the first tug and, to avoid the possibility of *Ariel* getting a faster one, her captain engaged the next tug also, so that it was several hours before *Ariel* got one. At Gravesend, *Taeping* was fifty-five minutes ahead. Even so, Captain

Ships in Azure

Keay's ship reached her Blackwall and East India Dock entrance first, at 9 p.m., but, because of the tide, it was 10:23 p.m. before *Ariel* hove to inside the dock gates.

Meanwhile *Taeping* had preceded *Ariel* up the river, but Captain McKinnon did not reach his berth until 10 p.m., as *Taeping* had much farther to go to reach the entrance of London Docks. "Drawing less water than *Ariel*, "says Captain Keay in his log, "also, the dock having two gates they got her inside the outer gate, shut it, and allowed the lock to fill from the dock; then they opened the inner gate so she [*Taeping*] docked some 20 minutes before us."

A more unsatisfactory finish could hardly be imagined. It was poor consolation to divide the stakes. Shipping men generally agreed that after such an exhibition of racing seamanship the race should have finished when the leading ship took her pilot. Captain Edward T. Miles, now retired in Australia, and a member of the crew of the *Ariel* in this memorable race, recently wrote me:

> "On the merits of the race under sail all honour is with the *Ariel* for we were fully five miles to windward of the *Taeping*" when the tug boat hove in sight, and, without the assistance of steam, must have won the race."

Serica reached the West India Dock at 11.30 p.m., just as the gates were closing; thus, *Ariel*, *Taeping*, and *Serica*, after crossing the bar at Foochow on the same tide, all docked in the Thames on the same tide, ninety-nine days later.

Though the palmy days of sail are no more and the racehorses of the sea have disappeared, they live again in the histories of Clark, Lubbock, Shewan, McKay and Daniel, and in the sea romances of Melville, Dana, Conrad and McFee. America's participation in the golden age of the clipper ships extended a little over a decade; then the Civil War gave Great Britain her chance and she, too, had her decade in the sun; but Suez and the era of steam ended that.

As to records, Basil Lubbock has tabulated all the day's runs of four hundred miles or over by sailing vessels. There are eight, to which Professor Samuel Eliot Morison of Harvard has added two. These ten phenomenal runs were all made by five ships in the years 1853-6; four of these ships, the *Sovereign of the Seas, James Baines, Donald McKay,* and *Lightning,* were designed and built by Donald McKay in Boston, and the fifth, *Red Jacket,* was designed by Samuel A. Pook of Boston and built in Rockland, Maine. Most of these runs were made under the British flag in the Australian trade.

The tea clippers were beautiful ships, splendidly designed and substantially built, with small deck-houses and ample deck-space for fast working. Invariably they looked like model sailing yachts, with their black or green hulls, golden scrollwork, all brasswork polished, decks holystoned, and gear well found. One curious feature was their loose ballast. They carried from two hundred to three hundred tons of shingle (coarse, round, seashore stones), which was adjusted to the keelson and evenly placed along the bottom of the ship, serving as a bed for the tea chests. They generally carried a crew of thirty, and their skippers were men of extreme ability, not afraid to "let her rip," never troubling to snug down at night, always keen to make the fastest possible voyage between ports.

These ships were what shipping men called very "tender." They could not be shifted about easily, once they were unloaded. They stood up tall, carried a great deal of mast and rigging; were, in fact, full-rigged ships—that is, provided with three masts, each mounting square sails. The early tea clippers were built of wood. The ships built at the close of the fifties and in the early sixties were nearly all composite—with iron frames and wooden sides, copper-sheathed. At the end of the sixties the clipper ship was built of iron right through; still later shipbuilders advanced to steel. "The introduction of iron," says Lubbock, "contributed more than anything else to the supremacy of the British merchant marine. It killed off the competition of our American cousins."

The sight of a clipper ship being towed into her berth at New York is a treasured memory of few present-day New Yorkers, but Mr. W. G. Low says he recalls seeing the *N. B. Palmer* being docked at the Pierrepont Stores on the Brooklyn side:

> "Spic and span, her newly-painted black hull decorated with a narrow gold stripe running its full length, yards squared with snowy sails neatly furled and having black crossbands to hold them in place—she was indeed a never-to-be-forgotten picture. At the top of her mainmast floated her red, yellow, and white house flag, while a brand-new U. S. ensign provided a brilliant flash of colour for her mizzen gaff. In the glow of the setting sun she was not only a thing of beauty, but so tall, so stately, so handsome as to make her surroundings seem a little shabby."

The late Captain Andrew Shewan brought together some delightful reminiscences in his *The Great Days of Sail*. Loading tea at the Pagoda Anchorage, Foochow, as described by Captain Shewan, was a picturesque scene. The opening of the market was peculiar to the Foochow tea trade. In the city of Foochow, after early May, when the first-crop pickings arrived, the Chinese merchants were slow to make up their minds to sell at prices acceptable to the foreign buyers. Weeks were spent in haggling, and finally, when the price had been lowered sufficiently and one of the more important foreign firms was tempted to close, the market was open and the rush began. Speed was the order of the day. Forty-eight hours were required to weigh and label the tea chests. Then each hong hurried its chops by lighter to the Pagoda Anchorage, twelve miles below the city, where three or four clippers with good records were chosen as "going ships." As a rule, each clipper in the running had already shipped a "ground chop"—that is, a sufficient number of chests of tea of inferior quality, carried at a slightly lower rate of freight than the new teas, to cover the shingle ballast and so provide added protection to the new-crop chops.[11]

After weeks of idling while waiting for the market to open, suddenly and as likely as not in the night, a blowing of conch shells and much hullabaloo would announce the coming of the first tea chops. The method followed was for the men on the lighters to chant in a long-drawn-out wail the Chinese name of the hong that owned the tea. Thus, Jardine Matheson's employees would wail out unendingly in mournful cadence: "Ee-wo! Ee-wo!" those of Turner and Company would snap back a discordant "Wha-kee! Whakee!" and others in like manner through a whole gamut of barks and whines. Captain Shewan says:

> "Who it was that replied to them and directed them to their destinations I cannot say; certainly, it was not members of the clippers' companies. I believe when they were expected, Chinese rivermen were stationed in anchored boats in readiness to direct them. When day dawned, hopes and fears would be set at rest. Round each of the two or three favorite ships some half-dozen or so lighters would be gathered. The rest of the fleet were out of luck and had to exercise patience. Yet they had not long to wait. In about forty-eight hours the 'Blue Peter'[12] would be flying from the trucks of one or more of the fortunate ones, and the 'tea-chops' would transfer their attentions to the ship next in turn."

For a good description of a tea clipper scudding before a gale Captain Shewan quotes from the diary of Mr. Frank Logan, a passenger in the *Norman Court* to Sydney in 1879, the ship being at the time south of Cape Leeuwin:

> "May 25th, 1879. – A very stormy day, a heavy gale blowing; ship under reefed topsails, rolling and labouring in a mountainous sea.... Mr. Doughty and I were watching the sea over the stern-rail for some time. It was a grand sight: the high seas rolling along, following the ship. Their crests would break with a roar just as they got near us. We would be on the point of making a bolt from our vantage place, imagining that nothing could stop them tumbling on board and engulfing the poor little *Norman Court*.... But lo and behold! her stern would rise in the air and she would be carried along on the top of the wave, with her bow pointing down into the valley, whilst another huge mountain would again be towering above her. 'By Jove!' we would say to one another, 'this one is a terror and will be aboard us for a certainty,' but our brave little ship rode out the gale like a cork."

Captain Shewan gives his version of an amusing and oft quoted tea race incident of 1885. The Jardine flyer, *Cairngorm,* Captain Ryrie, and the *Lammermuir* with Captain Andrew Shewan, Sr., in command, were racing to London for a prize of two hundred pounds, and found themselves together in the Java Sea, in the region of the northwest monsoon, south of the line, sailing close-hauled on the starboard tack, neither making more than two or three knots.

"This was the *Lammermuir's* strong point of sailing," says Captain Shewan, "and the Aberdeen clipper's weak one. Like many extremely sharp ships with slightly hollow lines, she became a trifle sluggish in light winds. Thus, the rather full-bowed *Lammermuir* gradually gained on her, coming up on the lee quarter. The two captains being good friends, Ryrie hung out a white table-cloth, signifying 'Come on board to dinner,' and Shewan, nothing loath, lowered his gig and was pulled over to the *Cairngorm*.

"The mate of the *Lammermuir* at the time was one Francis Moore, a native of Schleswig-Holstein, who had served John Willis almost from boyhood. He had been with my father since 1853, first as second, afterwards as chief mate. He was a first-class seaman and remained in the Willis's employ until about 1878, becoming master of the *Merse* in 1860 and successively commanding the *Whiteadder*, *Blackadder* and *Cutty Sark*. Moore was very proud of the *Lammermuir*, and saw a chance to execute a maneuver that would redound to her credit for all time. This was 'to go through the lee,' as the phrase went, of the crack tea clipper of the day and sail round her; than which nothing could be more irritating to a proud rival.

"Thus while the two captains were below at dinner the *Lammermuir* had so far forereached on the *Cairngorn* that Moore was able to put his helm down, come about on the port tack and stand across the bows of the other. Then, on the weather beam of the *Cairngorm*, he tacked once more and resumed his course. The report of the officer of the watch to Captain Ryrie at the dinner table that the *Lammermuir* was crossing the bows brought the two captains on deck. After the first gasp of surprise, Ryrie was furious. 'Well, I'm jiggered!' he gasped, 'look at the perishing Dutchman! By the powers! I'll dress him down when I get him ashore.' "I do not know whether he had his wish, but at least it was certain he was never able to obliterate the memory of the fact that the *Lammermuir* once sailed round the redoubtable *Cairngorm*."[13]

NOTES

1. Like the British East India Company, the Levant Company was chartered by Queen Elizabeth I. Unlike the East India Company, the Levant Company had no colonial aspirations. Founded in 1592 for the purpose of maintaining trade and diplomatic alliances with the Ottoman Empire, the company focused on establishing trade centers in Aleppo, Constantinople, Alexandria and Smyrna. The company dealt with coffee rather than tea.

2. Charles Lamb, the great English essayist who earned his living as a lowly East India Company clerk, voiced the sentiments of the nation, if not of his superiors, with his comment "I like a smuggler. He is the only honest thief. He robs nothing but the revenue, an abstraction I never cared greatly about." Eighteenth century "free traders" created a black market which carried tea to every door in Britain, delivering tea that could cost laborers a week's wages at a third that amount. At a time when inland communications were unimaginably bad, when most roads were tracks, dangerous at night and unusable part of the year, when most of the populace was illiterate, smugglers undertook a nation-wide sales campaign of an expensive novelty and succeeded in helping Britain become a tea consuming society. As in contemporary drug smuggling, enormous fortunes were made. Smuggling was carried on from 1680, the first year tea was taxed, until 1784, the year the tax was repealed. In the meantime, it was wise to know nothing about it.

> *Four and twenty ponies*
> *Trotting through the dark;*
> *Brandy for the parson,*
> *'Baccy for the clerk.*
> *Laces for a lady,*
> *Letters for a spy,*
> *And watch the wall, my darling,*
> *While the gentlemen go by.*

Studies since Ukers' time are not in unanimous agreement as to the exact quantity of tea smuggled, an assessment made inherently elusive due to the difficulty in obtaining reliable figures, that the tax was recorded and levied in different ways during this period (import duty vs. excise tax), the rate itself frequently changed, and the taxes were not applied consistently across all tea types.

Eden Committee investigations concluded that "…tea was the staple as it were, of smuggling…" and knowledgeable contemporaries such as Richard Twining concurred in his 1784 *Observations on the Tea and Window Act and on the Tea Trade,* assigning the main cause as the exorbitant tea taxes, for a time at 119%. He proposed that at least one-half to two-thirds of all imported tea was contraband. Modern scholars cite that for every one pound of tea coming into England through legal channels, an *additional* 1.4 pounds more was being smuggled in.

3. Bantam was a port in Java where in 1596 the Dutch established an outpost. By 1602 more than 65 Dutch ships had visited and returned home laden with spices and other goods, including "Bantam" roosters and hens. In 1608 they took the first tea to Europe after purchasing it from Chinese in whose Fujian dialect it was not *cha* but *tay*. English traders were allowed to reside in Bantam until they were driven out in 1684. Bantam for a time became the capital of Batavia or the Dutch East Indies, today's Indonesia.

4. Tea had been known for centuries to the indigenous peoples of Assam, where wild tea grew abundantly. An East India Company adventurer named Robert Bruce became the first European to discover this. Well after Bruce died, his brother Charles sent specimens to Company officials in Calcutta in 1832, only to be ignored. Two years later Bruce sent actual plants, seeds and manufactured tea. This time another Company man, Captain A. Charlton, also submitted similar samples of Assam tea and Company officials reported home: "We have no hesitation in declaring this discovery …to be far the most important and valuable that has ever been made on matters connected with the agricultural or commercial resources of the Empire." How very right they were: Between 1890 and 1914, only African gold and diamond mines were more profitable than Indian tea estates.

5. China required silver in exchange for its tea and John Company devised a round-about way to pay with opium. This required enormous hypocrisy. The Company grew opium in India, chiefly in Bihar state, and sold the crop at yearly auctions in Calcutta. It disclaimed any further responsibility for its product once it was sold to what were called "country firms," British and Parsee outfits like Jardine, Matheson & Co which traded goods from India with China by arrangement with the East India Company. The Company required the country firms to sell their opium for silver, which the traders were happy to bank with the Company's agents in Canton to apply against their bills in London or Calcutta. This enabled The Company to collect silver in payment for its opium in China only to turn around and use the same silver to pay for its tea. The silver circulated but stayed where it was. As England bought more tea, The Company grew more opium—a few hundred chests per year in 1770 swelled to over 100,000 in 1870. The tea drunk at Temperance meetings in England was purchased at the price of drug addiction in China. Of the two John Company products, one went down the drain at home while another went up in smoke abroad.

6. Bear Garden was a euphemistic name for a venue for the spectator blood sport called "Bear Baiting," which was introduced in thirteenth century England and became a popular pastime enjoyed by Kings (Henry II & VIII), Queens (Elizabeth I), and Tsars (Nicholas I) as well as the public, often on Sundays. An amphitheater of banked seating for up to 1,000 people surrounded a pit walled in stone, where the unlucky bear—or often bull—would be chained by the neck or hind leg to a post in the pit. Masters loosed specially trained dogs in the hopes of gaining from the scores of wagers placed to which dogs survived. The scene was as civilized as one might expect. Not until 1835 was Bear Baiting finally prohibited for its cruelty by an act of Parliament. The English Bulldog was specially bred for these events; these attack animals are the ancestors of the American Pit Bull breed.

Ships in Azure

7. *Rainbow,* the first "extreme" clipper, was launched in New York in 1845. Her maiden voyage was to China and she made the round trip in under eight months, repaying her cost of forty-five thousand dollars and earning an equal amount in profit. Her second round-trip was faster than any other ship could sail one way—ninety-two days out and back in eighty-eight. The master, though not the originator, of clipper ship design was the Scottish-American Donald MacKay whose ships set sailing records that have never been equaled. Clippers were faster ships because they were slimmer and carried acres more sail. They could sail from China to London or New York without needing to put ashore anywhere for water or stores, a feat previously impossible. Design was one factor but equally crucial were the officers and crew who had not only to force their vessel to the limit and keep her at that pitch for three months or more but—equally demanding—maintain sails, spars and rigging in racing trim. Steam and the Suez Canal ended the great days of sail.

8. Basil Lubbock: Sail: *The Romance of the Clipper Ships* (London: The Blue Peter Publishing Co., Ltd.; 1927), p. 89.

9. New York: Dodd, Mead & Co.; 1928.

10. Memorabilia of by-gone days in the tea trade are regularly discarded and untraceable. Ukers copyrighted the "Picture Tea Map of the World" which he used as end-papers for his *All About Tea.* Twinings acquired a mural-scale ten by twenty-foot blow-up of this map and displayed it in its famous shop on London's Strand until the 1990's. It is now in the possession of the G.S. Haly Company.

11. A chop of tea means a certain number of chests of tea, all bearing the same brand. The word *chop* is hardly used now. The word got a permanent footing in the "Pigeon English" of the Chinese ports where chop houses were customs stations on the Canton River, so called from the chops, or seals, used there. A chop boat was a small cargo boat used to move tea between warehouses and East India Company ships.

12. A blue flag with a white square in the center, raised by a ship about to leave port.

13. Andrew Shewan: *The Great Days of Sail* (London: Heath Cranton, Ltd; 1926).

Plucking shade-grown green tea in Japan, c.1890.

HOW TEA GROWS AND HOW IT IS MANUFACTURED

The original methods of tea cultivation and manufacture were developed in China. All other countries now producing tea commercially had to go to the Chinese, either directly or indirectly, to learn the secrets of its production; but these other countries have improved upon what they learned by the application of scientific agricultural methods and the use of labor-saving machinery.

In China, tea seeds are planted on steep slopes and on patches not needed for other crops.[1] The result of indifferent treatment has been the production of bushes much smaller in size and of lower yield than those grown in India, Ceylon, and Java.

The tea pioneers in Java and India at first imported Chinamen and Chinese plants, and the methods of China, in both field and factory, were followed. Later the ways of the Chinese were modified and in certain cases abandoned. The China plant was replaced by the Assam indigenous variety, the bushes were pruned and plucked in a new manner, and machinery was introduced into the factory.

Present-day methods of tea management by Europeans are almost the opposite of those in China. For planting, the best available land is chosen; the seed first is put out in nurseries, the plants are selected, and then replanted. The bush is carefully pruned to give it a shape conducive to high yield, and the leaf is plucked with a view to encouraging later flushes (young leaf shoots).

Such differences as exist between the methods employed in Java, Sumatra, Ceylon and India, have come about because of climatic and topographical differences. Broadly speaking, the methods in the newer tea countries are similar.[2]

Cultivation & Manufacturing

Tamil women picking tea in a garden near Galle in Ceylon, c.1900.

In China, there has been little change in methods of cultivation and preparation for over five hundred years. The Chinese farmer still treats the tea bush as a supplementary cultivation to his general farming, and centuries-old methods of tea firing obtain. Sporadic efforts have been made to introduce modern processes from India and Ceylon, but there are comparatively few foreign tea making machines in China.[3]

Japan, on the other hand, has learned much about tea cultivation from Java and British India and has developed a distinctive type of tea making machinery. Formosa, likewise, has adopted from other countries' improved cultivation and manufacturing methods.

Large-scale growers of today bring to tea cultivation the same sort of scientific knowledge and intensive care that commercial growers bring to fruits and cereal crops. Every effort is made to assure efficiency. Experimental stations in Java, India, Japan, Sumatra and Ceylon are working constantly to improve methods and products, as well as to develop types of bush that will resist disease, pests and unfavorable climatic conditions.

Tea is an evergreen and will grow in almost any climate so long as no severe drought is felt. Tea will grow in the cool, humid south of England, and it also grows in Ranchi, India, where the temperature in May reaches 115° F. and the humidity falls at times to 17 percent. Tea flourishes, however, and yields best in a tropical or subtropical climate. With a continuous hot, wet climate, like that of Ceylon or Java, tea flushes, or throws out fresh shoots, throughout the year. In northeastern India, where the monsoon ceases in October and the weather becomes cold and dry till April, the bush shuts up and gives no leaf worth gathering from December to March. The climate of China is cooler and dryer than that of India, and much smaller crops are obtained. Japan is so cold in the winter that the bushes cease flushing in spite of the rains.

Cultivation & Manufacturing

Humidity is an important factor in forcing leaf. A dry atmosphere is against crop, but humidity, especially with temperatures of about 85° F., makes the bush flush.

A cool climate produces slow growth and makes for quality, as is shown in the high-grown Ceylon teas, the Darjeeling teas, the early Assams and autumnal Dooars. Frosts, however, blacken the tea leaf on the bush.

In India, tea is cultivated in numerous, but often widely separated, hill districts at altitudes from 1,000 to 7,000 feet. Ceylon teas are grown from approximately sea-level up to 7,000 feet, the greater part of the cultivation lying at about 3,000 feet. Java tea is grown mainly at about 1,000 feet, although the Pengalengan tea is planted at more than 5,000 feet. In Sumatra, the elevations run from 1,200 to 3,500.

In China, the best black teas are produced in Anhwei Province at about 3,000 feet.[4] The most celebrated green teas are grown in the province of Kiangsi at 4,000 feet above sea-level. The finest teas of Japan are produced inland on mountain slopes along streams. Approximately half of the export teas, however, are grown much nearer sea level in the mountainous coast prefecture of Shizuoka. In Formosa, most of the tea acreage is located on plateau at an elevation of 250 to 1,000 feet, but some of the most famous oolongs are raised on broken foothill lands that range from sea-level to 300 feet.

The aboriginal tribes of Siam, Burma and the bordering Chinese province of Yunnan are credited by scientists with having been the first to gather and use the leaves of the *miang,* or wild tea tree, found growing on their native hills.[5] From the wild tea leaves they still make up small bundles of steamed and fermented tea for chewing. In early times, they made a medicinal drink by boiling the raw green leaf. It was this beginning that suggested to the Chinese the cultivation of the leaf and its preparation by drying, in order that it might be available throughout the year as an addition to their *materia medica;* and from the Chinese, at a much later time, the countries to the south learned to preserve leaf tea for use as a beverage, though on a limited scale.

Today the native *miang* is still the only tea produced in Siam. It is all consumed locally. The young trees are not picked until they reach a height of six or seven feet, and they grow to an average of twenty to thirty feet. The picked leaves are tied in small bundles called *kams,* which remain intact during the manufacturing process.

The preparation of *miang* consists in steaming the leaves for two hours, tightly pressing the cooled *kams* into a container, such as a basket or an internode of bamboo, and allowing them to ferment for about a month; then the product is ready for use. Tea in these packs will keep for about a year. Occasionally *miang* in bamboo joints is buried in the ground to preserve it, but this is only done when there is a supply beyond the market demands.

In Burma the natives manufacture their tea in the *miang* manner, only here it becomes *letpet* or pickled tea.

In addition to the Big Six countries (India, Ceylon, Netherlands Indies, China, Japan, and Formosa) tea is being cultivated commercially in French Indo-China, the Malay States, Iran (Persia), Natal, Nyasaland, Portuguese East Africa, Uganda and Kenya, Tanganyika, and Russian Transcaucasia.

Tea usually is grown from seed in nursery beds.[6] The young plants are transplanted to the prepared tea fields when they are six to eight inches high, usually in six months' time. They are set out in rows, three to six feet apart. In two years, they reach a height of from four to six feet. Then they are cut down to something less than a foot. By the end of the third year they are ready for plucking.

Japanese and Formosan tea growers do not set out nurseries, but propagate their tea bushes by planting the seeds directly where they are to be grown or by layering—that is, transplanting rooted branches. Weeding, cultivation between the rows and pruning go on regularly at different periods for twenty-five to fifty years, the average life of a tea bush. When in full bearing—about the tenth year—a single bush will yield as much as a quarter of a pound of leaf in its seasonal flushes.

After several prunings, designed to encourage the bush to produce leaves in successive flushes instead of wood, it assumes a shape like that of a champagne glass. In some countries, like southern India, Ceylon, Java, and Sumatra, plucking is continuous throughout the year; in northern India it extends from June to December, in Formosa from April to November, in Japan from May to October, in China, for Congou or black teas, from April to October, and for China greens from June to December.

The leaves are plucked by native women who strip them into cloth bags or bamboo baskets at their sides, or toss them deftly over their shoulders into baskets hung upon their backs by thongs passing over their foreheads. In fine plucking, the leaf bud and the two next leaves are gathered; in medium plucking the third leaf is also taken; in coarse plucking four or more leaves. The bud represents the finest tea, the leaf next to it being not so fine, and the others are coarser as they go down the branch. In Ceylon, a tea plucker, using both hands, plucks about 30,000 shoots a day. Approximately 3,200 shoots are required to make one pound of manufactured tea.

After plucking, if black or fermented tea is desired, the leaves are withered. This is the first manufacturing process, the object of which is to develop the fermenting principle. In tea factories, the tea is withered on wire or hessian cloth racks or *tats,* in withering lofts or separate houses.

Cultivation & Manufacturing

The second process in the manufacture of black tea is rolling by hand or by machine. The object of rolling is to break open the cells of the leaf in which the tea juices are stored. This must be done without tearing the leaf.

The third process is fermentation, if fermented or black tea is to be made.[7] As soon as the juices produced are exposed to the air, oxidization starts. In making black tea the leaf is fermented on tile or cement floors, or on zinc, glass, cement, or tiled withering tables. In this process the leaf assumes a bright copper color.

Weighing freshly-picked tea leaves in a Ceylon tea garden, c.1880.

If green tea is desired, fermentation is stopped by panning or steaming soon after plucking. In Ceylon and India the freshly plucked leaf is steamed in revolving perforated cylinders. In China, Japan, and Formosa, where hand manufacture is more common, the leaves are tossed about by hand in an iron vessel shaped like a big washbasin and built into a charcoal stove. As soon as they become soft they are taken out, steaming hot, and rolled by hand on a bamboo mat or paper tray, only to be returned to the pan again in a few minutes, the steaming and rolling continuing alternately until the leaves begin to "crisp," when they are put into trays and thoroughly dried over slow charcoal fires. In Japan, much of this work is also done by modern machinery.

In the manufacture of oolong tea, the leaf is given a light wither to permit a slight ferment, after which it is panned and rolled by hand and then fired in hour-glass-shaped bamboo baskets over charcoal fires.

Thus, we see that the difference between green and black tea is the result of manipulation. Both may be produced from leaves plucked from the same bush.

The fourth manufacturing process for black tea is drying or firing, which may be done in baskets over charcoal fires or in tea firing machines. In India, the leaf is given two firings, in Ceylon only one. In the machine firing process the hot air may be driven through the leaves by a force fan or drawn through by an exhaust fan.

The fifth and last process before packing for shipment is sifting and sorting. In the tea factories of India, Ceylon and Java this is usually done by tray machines in which a number of sieves of different-sized meshes are arranged one above the other, having a common motion. The meshes of tea sifters yield the following commercial varieties: Broken Orange Pekoe, consisting of the terminal buds with portions of the finest leaf that have been broken off in the manufacturing process; Orange Pekoe, consisting of some terminal buds and the finest leaves; Pekoe and Pekoe Souchong, consisting of coarser leaves; Pekoe dust or fine broken tea, consisting of the fine powdery fragments; and fannings, consisting of flaky scraps of the leaves.

NOTES

1. China herself, like her tea industry, lay in ruins in Ukers' day. He never visited civil war-torn China but absorbed all he could learn from contemporary Japanese, Taiwanese and American tea colleagues. With the rise of India, Ceylon and Japanese teas, China's tea exports peaked in 1886 and went into a decline lasting most of the twentieth century. Farmers reverted to growing tea for family and locals with little hope of profit. Productivity figures for 2013, by contrast, show China with the greatest total with nearly 2 million metric tonnes (one tonne equals 2200 lbs.), followed by India with 1.2 million and Kenya with 432,400. Kenya, Sri Lanka and India export more tea than China, however.

2. Ukers' view of tea production in China shows him the product of his imperialistic, modernizing, "scientific" age. The countries he praises by way of comparison are, except for Japan, colonies of the British and Dutch employing "improved cultivation and manufacturing methods…," "large scale growers…," and "…the same sort of scientific knowledge…that commercial growers bring to fruit and cereal crops." Colonial tea is produced by plantation labor and industry; it is not the organic, artisanal product of old China.

3. Almost all the tea production in China has been transformed since Mao's founding of the People's Republic in 1949. This is largely the result of Dr. Chen Zong-mao and his colleagues at China's Tea Research Institute in Hangzhou who have introduced scientific understanding and industrial procedures to the ancient craft. Let it not be forgotten, however, that until the mid-twentieth century all the tea in China was organic and largely handmade. This is true of comparatively little China tea today, but anybody who tastes a traditionally made Biluochun, Longjing or Oolong or even a Keemun Hao Ya can see the unmistakable value of what has been lost. The ancient

Cultivation & Manufacturing

artisanal craft has been transformed into an industrialized agribusiness.

4. Keemun (*Qimen*) takes its name from Qimen County in Anhui province. Keemun reigned supreme as China's finest black tea in Ukers' day. Only after the Japanese invasion did China begin production of Yunnan black tea in 1938. Today Yunnan black (*Dianhong*) ranks with Keemun as a *grand seigneur* among China's numerous but lesser breeds of black tea.

5. The Assamese must be included amongst the tribes that first used tea in these areas where Camellia sinensis originated. For these peoples, tea was sometimes a medicine but primarily a food. Lepet, the fermented tea leaf Ukers describes, makes a memorable salad. *Lahpet thoke*, with its pickled regional variations, is Myanmar's national dish.

6. Today tea plants are generally "cloned," the procedure Ukers calls "layering," so that an entire area can be planted in identical specimens of a "mother bush" selected for yield and hardiness. The procedures following are as Ukers describes. For black tea, pruning is all important. By cutting the plant back repeatedly a flat "plucking table" is created, forcing all the plant's energy into production of leaf rather than woody stem.

7. Fermentation, properly speaking, produces alcohol as in wine or beer. Thus, it is not accurate to say tea leaf is "fermented" by simple exposure to air after it has been injured and squeezed by "rolling." The microbial process of fermentation is a wholly different one from tea's enzymatic oxidation. Nevertheless, Ukers' time-honored term "fermentation" is often still used to describe the transformation of green leaf to brown. The Chinese technical term is *fajiao,* which translates "controlled change." In English "oxidation" is the preferred term today and oxidation is an accurate descriptive but not a complete explanation. Rolled leaf turns from green to brown in less than an hour due to oxidation, to be sure, but this does not account for the complex chemical reactions occurring inside the leaf, a divine alchemy for which we have no adequate name.

In 1930, London's Lyons tea shops outfitted their servers, called nippies, *in up-to-date frocks that left every dowdy remembrance of Victorian frilliness far behind.*

TEA MANNERS & CUSTOMS

Throughout the earlier centuries of its use, the tea drink was taken as a medicine. Its Chinese and Japanese advocates regarded it as a remedy for every human ailment. The oldest Chinese manner of making tea was to boil the green leaves in a kettle. The first improvement was to toast the leaves, pound them into tiny pieces, put them in a chinaware pot, pour boiling water over them and add onion, ginger and orange.

The Chinese do not use teapots as a rule, but simply infuse the tea with water much below the boiling-point in the cups from which it is drunk, without milk or sugar. The tea leaves are placed in cups (not unlike our bouillon cups, but without handles), which are then filled with hot water and covered. The covers, which resemble inverted saucers, are used to strain off the tea. The covered cup is raised to the mouth and the lid or cover is raised by the forefinger just enough to permit the liquid to flow into the mouth as the cup is tilted.[1]

Tea is drunk in China by high and low, upon all occasions and at all hours of the day and night. It is presented on receiving visits, making purchases, transacting business, and at all ceremonies. It is invariably offered when one enters a Chinese house. A covered cup, with freshly infused tea, is placed before each guest. The request to take more is generally construed as a polite hint that the interview should end.

Well-to-do Chinese drink black tea, but not usually new tea. They keep it in sealed earthen jars for a couple of years before using it, to moderate the pungent quality which new tea possesses.[2]

Certain classes follow the oldest manner of tea drinking by preparing brick tea. In this method, powdered tea is boiled with rice cakes into a thick, syrupy substance, the bitter taste being removed by adding ginger.

In the cities tea houses, or *kwans*, flourish. They are the equivalent of the Continental cafés and are the only convenient places of public resort. Of the four hundred tea houses in Shanghai, almost all have fixed clienteles. Certain groups of customers have their favorite hours for drinking tea. They may bring their own tea and, for one cash, sit all day at the tables and have as much hot water as they please.

When tea is taken at a teahouse, the practice is to use two cups: a large one for brewing that will hold about a half-pint, and a thimble cup, smaller than a demitasse, from which the beverage is drunk. The larger cup has a saucer, which is placed bottom-side-up over it. This saucer is provided with a notch for pouring the tea into the smaller cup.

In modern homes and in business offices the beverage is made in teapots and is poured into individual cups having neither saucers nor handles. Along the seaboard, however, where foreign influence is strongest, the cups have handles and are placed in saucers, after the Western manner.

Station platform hot water heaters for tea are familiar sights on Chinese railways. A galvanized-iron canopy offers protection from the sun, and beneath it the concessionaire has his charcoal braziers gently burning, keeping hot his kettles filled with water or his single copper cauldron. Passengers usually supply their own tea, teapots, and cups. A copper cash pays for the

The Japanese Tea Ceremony, once a male ritual, became a feminine discipline during the Meiji Period. Photo c. 1920.

hot water. For those who have not their own utensils the hot-water vender supplies them. They are carried on by the train to the next station, where the vender at that station recovers them and returns them by train boy or as service to another traveler—all very like the English custom.

Tea drinking reached its supreme distinction in Japan, under the distinguished patronage of the former Shogun Yoshimasa (1443-73).[3] In Kyoto, the visitor may inspect Yoshimasa's Ginkaku-ji, or Silver Pavilion, which housed the first tea room. Here Yoshimasa spent the evening of his life in retirement, practicing the rites of the *Chanoyu* (literally, hot-water tea), or Tea Ceremony, for which Shuko, the first great tea master, prepared a code of rules. Also in Kyoto one may inspect the Kinkaku-ji, or Golden Pavilion, of Yoshimitsu, who had a passion for the Tea Ceremony.

In the fifteenth century, Japan ennobled tea into a religion of aestheticism–teaism.[4] Teaism is a cult founded on the worship of the beautiful. Love of nature and simplicity of materials are its keynotes. It includes purity, harmony, mutual forbearance. After being given a ritual, tea became a temple ceremony in Japan. Later it became the concomitant of polite social intercourse.

The Japanese *chajins,* or tea masters, invested the serving of tea with a ceremony whose spirit still persists in present-day Japan and in the afternoon tea functions of Europe and America.

In the best practice of *Chanoyu* not more than four guests were invited to the Tea Ceremony in a tea room specially built and designed to accommodate four and a half mats. Before entering the room the guests washed their hands and faces and left their sandals outside the sliding panel, two feet square, which gave ingress to the *chashitsu* and was purposely low, to inculcate humility. Once inside, the guests spent some time in admiring the *kakemono*[5] and the arrangement of flowers while the host collected his utensils. Upon his return the ceremony began. It is an intricate performance in which powdered tea [matcha] is whipped into a light-green froth, served in lacquered bowls and looking very like pea soup. It is, indeed, a tea soup, and not a tea infusion as we understand the tea drink.

I attended a school in Kyoto where the Tea Ceremony may be observed. It is very like the original *Chanoyu*. First the tea utensils were arranged and cleaned with much ceremony, in the prescribed manner, by the young Japanese lady selected to serve my party, who were seated cross-legged on the mats watching her, no word being spoken. After placing a spoonful of the finely powdered tea in the special tea bowl, she poured over it a dipperful of boiling hot water from a kettle simmering over a charcoal fire box.

The mixture was then stirred with a small bamboo whip, suggesting nothing so much as a shaving-brush. Every movement had a meaning all its own; but, then, nearly everything is symbolical in Japan. Every detail of the preparation and service of the tea is as written down

Tea Manners & Customs

The six positions of tea drinking in Chanoyu.

in the ritual provided by the high priest of *Chanoyu,* Sen-no Rikyu, four hundred years ago.[6]

When it is once prepared, the tea drinker is expected to carry out the traditional manner of receiving the dish of tea from the hands of the serving maid with great solemnity, raising it to his lips with both hands in very dignified fashion. The guest may slowly take several sips, but he must be careful to leave a small sip in the howl at the end. As he tosses off this final sip, he is expected to throw back his head and drain the divine nectar into his gullet with a distinct sucking noise, which is supposed to attest his pleased satisfaction and great delight with the draught.

As originally practiced,[7] when the chief guest drank, the tea bowl was passed to the next person, who in turn passed it round until it reached the host, who drank last. Sometimes a cloth or napkin was provided for handling the bowl. This was used not only for holding it, but also for wiping the cup after each person had drunk. The bowl was held in the palm of the left hand, supported by the thumb and fingers of the right. A glance at the illustration on this page will show better than words the prescribed mode of holding the *chawan,* or tea bowl. (1) The guest takes the bowl; (2) raises it to the level of his forehead; (3) lowers it; (4) drinks; (5) lowers it again; (6) returns to the same position as (1). During the last four positions the bowl is given half a turn toward the right, gradually bringing the side which was originally next to the guest round to the opposite position.[8]

When the host had finished drinking, it was the proper thing for him to apologize for the tea, saying what poor stuff it was, and so on. After that, the empty bowl was passed round for the guests to admire, as it was often a piece of great antiquity or of historical interest. With this the ceremony closed, and after further washing of cups and pots, the guests took their leave, the host kneeling at the door of the tea room as they passed out, and receiving their compliments and farewells with many bows and obeisances.

Every lady of good family is schooled in the etiquette of the ancient Tea Ceremony as part of her classical education. At least three years of instruction and practice are considered necessary to acquire proficiency.

Tea Manners & Customs

The prominence given to tea drinking by the Japanese was further enhanced by the inauguration in 1623 of the picturesque and spectacular "Tea Journey," an imposing annual pageant for bringing the first of the season's new tea from Uji to the Shogun at Yeddo, now Tokyo, a three-hundred-mile journey.[9]

The Japanese have a worshipful regard for tea and always refer to it as *O Cha*—"Honourable Tea." Upon arising, it is the custom in the home to offer tea to one's ancestors by placing it before the altar, and to one's parents before partaking oneself.

Of course, ceremonial tea has nothing to do with ordinary tea drinking. The great mass of the people in Japan use Bancha, or ordinary tea, made from coarse leaves, and generally of such a cheap character that it would be denied admittance to the United States. They prepare it much as we do, only more often than not they use water that is merely hot, instead of freshly boiling.

British family portraits were often composed around a tea table, as modelled by this Glasgow family, c. 1888.

The entire population—men, women, and children—all drink tea constantly; in fact, the business of the Empire is said to be transacted over the teacup. Green tea is used mostly, but certain brands of Ceylon and India black teas are on the menus of the leading hotels, restaurants, steamship and railway lines. Tea is served in small handle-less cups, without sugar or milk. The manner of making it is to cool freshly boiled water to a temperature of about 176° F. before pouring it on the tea leaves in a heated teapot, where it is infused for from one to five minutes.

Tea houses abound throughout the country. They are democratic and comfortable and afford more amusement than the conventional hotel. To the Japanese, the home is too personal a place for receiving a guest; therefore, guests are entertained in tea houses, clubs, and restaurants. The tea houses are so much a part of the national life that one would be quite lost without them.

At the railway stations hawkers sell little green bottles of tea to travelers for four cents a bottle.[10] These bottles, containing about a pint of hot tea, are provided with a glass-cup top from which the beverage can be drunk or sucked—the popular but noisy way of drinking tea in Japan. Little brown teapots of ready-brewed Ceylon and India tea are offered in the same way for seven and a half cents, including the pot.

As in the beginning, boiled and churned butter tea continues the great standby of the Tibetans. No Tibetan drinks less than fifteen or twenty cups a day, and some even seventy or eighty.

Nowhere can a better or a more satisfying cup of tea be found than in England. Here the making and serving of the drink is an art. Every man, woman, and child in the United Kingdom seems to know how to brew a cup of good tea. This statement will provoke snorts of derision from the chronic grousers who are always complaining in the newspapers, but in the main it cannot be disputed.

The London tea gardens of the eighteenth century first brought tea out of doors in England. One of the reasons why gardens in the suburbs began to be more frequented than the centrally located but wholly masculine coffee houses was that they offered their attractions to the fair sex as well as to the men. All sorts of beverages were served, including tea, coffee, and chocolate; but tea soon acquired an outstanding vogue.

The public gardens of the seventeenth century, known only as *pleasure gardens,* were tea-less; many of them were pretty rough. But the tea gardens of the eighteenth century were places where the best people went for relaxation and amusement. Many of them incorporated the word *tea* in their names, like the Belvidere, Kensington, and Marlborough tea gardens—to mention only three—but all of them offered tea as one of several fashionable and popular beverages.

The tea gardens provided flowered walks, shaded arbors, a "great room" with music for dancing, skittle grounds, bowling greens, variety entertainments, concerts; and not a few of them were given over to gambling and racing. Their season extended from April or May to August or September. At first there was no charge for admission, but visitors usually purchased cheese, cakes, syllabubs, tea, coffee, and ale. Later the Vauxhall, Marylebone, and Cuper's gardens had a fixed admission charge of a shilling, in addition to the price of any refreshments that might be purchased. At Ranelagh, an admission charge of half a crown included "the Elegant Regale of Tea, Coffee, and Bread and Butter."

Vauxhall and Ranelagh gardens were the best-known. It was at Ranelagh that Emma Hart, "the teamaker of Edgware Road," who later became Lady Hamilton, scandalized her lover, the Honourable Charles Greville, younger son of the Earl of Warwick, by singing to the assemblage from the front of the box where he thought he had hidden her safely from prying eyes while he went to call upon some of his society friends in other boxes.

Today the eighteenth century tea gardens with their thousands of twinkling candle lanterns, exquisite belles, and perfumed beaux are but ghostly memories in the romance of tea. Not one remains. The names of some are retained by public houses, but fashionable London for the most part takes its tea indoors, except on those rare occasions when, "weather permitting," it

Tea Manners & Customs

A bucolic tea setting in one of London's many pleasure gardens. Painting by G. Morland, 1790.

may be *de rigeur* to sip it in some favored spot in the open, such as the lawn before the Fellows' Pavilion of the Zoological Gardens or at Lord's Cricket Ground.

The custom of serving afternoon tea dates back probably to the seventeenth century, but as a distinct and definite function the world is indebted for it to Anna, wife of the seventh Duke of Bedford. In her day—early in the nineteenth century—people ate prodigious breakfasts; luncheon was a light meal, and dinner was not served till eight. The Duchess had tea and cakes served at five o'clock because, to quote herself, she then had "a sinking feeling."

The 1830s saw tea recruited as the ally of temperance reformers for the overthrow of alcoholic beverages in England. *Tea meetings,* as they were called, were held in many cities. A contemporary account of one of them relates that "wealth, beauty and intelligence were present; and great numbers of reformed characters respectably clad, with their smiling partners, added no little interest to the scene."

The British prefer the Empire-grown teas of India and Ceylon, but some of the diehard connoisseurs still insist upon China teas. The tea—a teaspoonful for each cup and one for the pot—is placed in a previously warmed teapot and is infused for about five minutes with freshly boiling water. Unless an infuser basket is used, the liquor is sometimes poured off the leaf into another warmed teapot, to avoid too much astringency. Teabags are not used, as our English cousins think tea draws better when not confined in a bag; instead, the leaves are kept out of the cups by cup or spout strainers.[11]

Milk or cream is generally added to the beverage in the cup. Cold milk is used by most people, but some prefer hot. It is placed in the cup before the tea is poured. In Scotland, where the cream is thin, it is used as superior to milk. In western England, where the milk is rich, cream is not much used in tea. To a small extent, tea is also served Russian fashion—that is, in a glass, with a slice of lemon. Sugar is entirely a matter of taste.

In restaurants, it is customary to serve a jug of hot water—the jug matching the pot—which is added to the teapot as occasion demands. This makes the tea go much further, and people frequently have three cups of tea each from one individual pot—a very cheap drink.[12]

The extent to which tea is drunk in the United Kingdom is surprising, not only to the American or Continental visitor, but to the Britisher himself who pauses to take stock of his fellow countrymen.[13] Each stratum of British society has its own particular tea drinking habits. The afternoon tea of the upper classes is the most characteristic of British institutions, as well as the most charming reunion of the whole day; and the afternoon tea of old Betty, the charwoman and laundress, is the most refreshing meal she takes. With the well-to-do, teatime is the prelude to a late dinner, but with the poor it is the sequel of an early one, and so the extremes meet.

Morning Repast, *1750 English print by Richard Houston.*

Among the classes that keep servants it is the custom to have an early-morning cup of tea brought to the bedside.[14] This first cup is regarded as an awakener and stimulator, with which to start the day. It is a habit which is recognized and catered to by many hotels, and their tariffs usually state a price for the bedroom cup of tea.

When the ten hour working day was the rule, the working classes indulged in a cup of tea at about half past five in the morning. In most cases, the husband would rise at this early hour, light the fire or the gas ring, make himself a cup of tea and take one to his wife before he went out into the streets. His breakfast—again with tea—would be taken at his place of work about two and a half hours later. Nowadays the eight-hour-day worker eats his entire breakfast before leaving home, and nine times out of ten he drinks tea with it.

Among the higher classes coffee is more frequently taken with breakfast, but, nevertheless, a large number take tea, as is evidenced by the choice always offered at hotels, of tea or coffee for breakfast.

One would think that after the hour of seven or eight in the evening the tea pot would he laid to rest for the day, but there are those who cannot retire without a final cup of tea with a little bread and cheese at about ten o'clock. Night workers in the newspaper world and other trades can call for a cup of tea or

The tea room pioneers in London were the Aerated Bread Company, familiarly known as the A. B. C. Tea at the A. B. C. in 1884 cost two pence per cup or three pence per pot per person.

coffee at the all-night coffee stalls; and the lonely night watchman guarding in the street the tools of the road menders, surrounded by his red danger lanterns and seated in his little wooden hut before his glowing open-air fire, takes his tea with his meal in the stillness of the night.

Recent social changes in England have caused a spread of the habit of an early morning and a midday cup of tea among domestic servants, shoppers and business women. Tea drinking at midday is not frequent among the well-to-do, but is common among the working and lower middle classes. The midday meal is the chief meal of the day with these people, consisting of meat, vegetables, and a sweet course, followed by a cup of tea. The famous English "five o'clock tea" of the middle classes is more frequently taken at about four o'clock nowadays, or between four and five; and it is an extremely light meal, if meal it can be called at all, consisting of a cup of tea with cake, biscuits, or other pastry. For those whose main meal is consumed at midday, the third meal of the day takes its name from the beverage, but is a much more substantial meal than the four o'clock tea of the well-to-do because there is no evening dinner to follow it. This "tea" is usually served at about six o'clock, on the worker's return from business, and is called "high tea," "meat tea," or "ham tea."

On Saturday afternoons and Sundays, when the Londoner is free to roam afield, he will hire a boat on the Thames and, together with his picnic basket and spirit kettle, he will be found at the right hour partaking of his afternoon tea, with his boat moored under the riverside trees in delightful sylvan surroundings. Again, others who can afford a motorcycle and sidecar will be found with the vehicle drawn up on the quiet roadside in some beautiful woodland spot or on some hilltop twenty or thirty miles out of London, with picnic tea spread out on a tablecloth on the grass.

Recently the caravan teashop appeared in southern England. It is drawn by a small motor-car and makes stops and serves tea at places where motorists congregate. London abounds with all classes of restaurants that serve tea throughout the day and evening. Although wines and liquors are obtainable at most of the first-class restaurants and public houses, practically all of them make a specialty of afternoon tea.

The tea room pioneers in London were the Aerated Bread Company, familiarly known as the A. B. C. Tea at the A. B. C. costs two pence per cup or three pence per pot per person. This company, with its sixty-five shops, has many competitors. Lyons, operating the largest chain of tea shops in the world, has hundreds of ordinary tea shops in addition to many huge and handsome restaurants, in and out of London. Pioneer Cafes number more than fifty, and the Express Dairy Company has a score of refreshment shops. Other well-known London tea rooms are: Buszard's, Ridgway's, Cabin's, Callard's, Fleming's, Ruller's, "J. P.'s," Lipton's, the Mecca Cafes, Slater's, Stewart's, and Williamson's. Also, the big London department stores, such as Selfridge's, Whiteley's, Harrod's, Barker's and Ponting's, all operate enticing tea rooms in an endeavor to tempt women shoppers to remain on the premises rather than go out for tea and not return. Numerous smaller choice tea rooms are scattered throughout the London metropolis, where orchestras play and *thé dansants* are not infrequent. In the average London teashop, the price of a cup of tea ranges from two pence to three pence; a pot of tea can be secured at three pence to four pence per person.

The Lyons teashop may be considered as truly representative of the best English tea traditions. Built on a forty-year-old idea of "a good pot of tea for two pence," it still is possible to get in a Lyons shop a pot of tea for three pence (six cents), a cup for two pence. No account of the Lyons tea shop would be complete without a reference to the engaging waitress, nicknamed "nippy." The aim of the management was to dignify and, if possible, to "glorify" service. Yet nippies as an institution are quite different from Mr. Cochran's "young ladies," or Mr. Ziegfeld's "glorified" American girls. The Lyons management set out to remove from the dress of the waitresses every semblance of servitude, and to that end they caused to be designed an up-to-date frock, minus the high collar and cuffs and the flying apron-strings of the early Victorian era. They made their waitresses stylish, human, and comfortable. The choice of the name "nippy" occupied the attention of the firm for several months. The word in colloquial English means active, vigorous, alert. As applied to the Lyons type of waitress it quickly became popular and now is in common usage in London.

Tea Manners & Customs

No account of the Lyons tea shop would be complete without a reference to the engaging waitress nicknamed nippy. *The aim of the management was to dignify and, if possible, to "glorify" its London tea service. The Lyons management set out to remove from the dress of the waitresses every semblance of servitude.*

Almost anywhere in England during the summer season it is possible to enjoy one's afternoon tea in the open, amid surroundings which are at once restful and inspiring. Tea gardens are operated in the public parks of London, mainly in Hyde Park, Kensington Gardens, the Zoological Gardens, and Kew Gardens. A visitor can obtain a pot of tea in any of them for fourpence. At these public places one is likely to find people from all walks of English society enjoying their afternoon tea at tables under the trees or sheltered from the sun by spreading white umbrellas.

In the suburban districts one is always sure to find any number of private houses that turn their parlors and backyards into tea rooms or tea gardens during the afternoon tea hour. The signal to the passer-by is usually the one word "Teas" neatly displayed in window or on doorpost, and it is not uncommon to see the announcement cheerily waving from the top of a flagpole.

Tea Manners & Customs

In the lounges of many London hotels afternoon tea is served to residents and casual callers. The average price is one shilling sixpence per head or two shillings sixpence including sandwiches and pastry. At theatre and cinema matinees patrons will be found holding small tea trays during intermission. All clubs serve tea. Tea at important social affairs, such as the Ascot races, the Henley Regatta, Lord's Cricket Ground on Harrow vs. Eton day, the Cowes Regatta, and the King's annual garden party, is a colorful picture. Without afternoon tea, these events would seem very un-English.

At the great London railway terminals, the platform tea wagons and the tea rooms are always busy, but more so at night, when the passengers for the night trains want warm tea for a "send-off." The platform tea wagons, or trolleys, are surmounted by an urn containing water which is kept hot by means of a primus lamp fitted into the trolley. The trains generally stop in the dead of night at a station one or two hundred miles from London just long enough to enable the passengers to buy a cup of hot tea or coffee at the station buffet.

Teatime was one of the expected services offered in First Class compartments on British trains in 1890.

If he is to be happy, the Briton must have his tea—good tea—whenever he wants it, and it was with this in mind that the more important railroads of England inaugurated a plan to provide him with tea service *en route,* graded to suit his pocketbook, from a simple tray to a tea room or restaurant-car service deluxe—but all good.

It was not until many years after the English railways had been developed to a high degree of comfort and efficiency that someone first thought to attach a restaurant car to a through train or to serve trays of tea from the station platforms to passengers in the compartments.

On the London Midland & Scottish Railway the number of teas served in the restaurant cars is about 1,160,000 per year. In the dining cars a cup of tea is obtainable at fourpence, and tea with bread and butter, toast, or cake may be had for nine pence. On the Great Western Railway over 2,500,000 cups of tea and 17,000 tea baskets have been served in one year.

Owing to its convenience, the tea basket service to passengers in the compartments, without their having to leave their places on the train, is immensely popular, and a great number of baskets are served upon the arrival of the trains at stations at all the regular daytime tea hours, as well as throughout the night. The tea baskets are set aside or pushed under the seats after use, and are cleared from the train by a special staff at the large stations, to be returned to the station from which they were issued. On the Great Western Railway the tea basket, with an enameled iron lining, contains tea, with additional hot water, milk, sugar, three slices of bread and butter, cake, and a banana or other fruit, the charge for which is one shilling three pence (about thirty cents).

Teatime customs also prevail on all British-owned and operated ocean-going steamships. Afternoon tea is served in the dining saloon or on deck, where the deck steward performs the honors; and along about midnight the cabin steward will supply the passengers, if they desire, with tea. and cakes.

The first "tea in the air" service was inaugurated in England by the Imperial Airways, Ltd., operating between London and Paris, in 1927. For the Londoner who would experience the service of "tea in the air," planes of the Imperial Airways make regular afternoon trips over the city of London during the months from May to October. The inclusive charge is thirty shillings (about seven dollars and a half).

During the World War a new custom arose in many English factories—probably on account of the large number of women workers who then entered the industries—of sending round tea wagons, like those used on railway platforms, to the workers at their benches and machines at about eleven o'clock in the morning. Although this custom has practically died out, eleven o'clock tea drinking still survives in some form or other among the women workers in many factories, large shops, and offices. Men and women in offices which do not serve tea are usually given time off to go out and get it in some near-by teashop where freshly made tea may be had at a nominal price.

The London business man in his office at about four in the afternoon is almost certain to be interrupted by the entrance of a "lady typist" with two cups of tea—one for the visitor. Even board meetings of directors have been known to be invaded by the tea tray. If this sounds extreme, what shall be said of the thinning out of the House of Commons itself and the discovery of legislators in the tea room, or, when the weather is favorable, at *alfresco* tea on the famous terrace overlooking the Thames?

The people of New Zealand drink tea as many as seven times a day. In the preparation of the beverage, the New Zealand housewife follows much the same method observed in England, though in recent years the teabag has been used to an increasing extent. Those living in the rural districts known as the "back blocks," however, are prone to boil the leaves. Many people think the palm for tea drinking should be awarded to the workers on the great

Australian sheep farms in the back blocks. These men of the wide-open spaces, "four-meal, meat-fed men," who rank as the tallest of the civilized races, drink the strongest kind of tea on every possible occasion.

In few countries is tea more popular than in Australia, where blends of India, Ceylon, and Java are favored. In many homes and in most hotels tea is served seven times a day—before breakfast, at breakfast, at eleven o'clock in the forenoon, at lunch, at four o'clock, at dinner, and just before retiring. Practically all large offices and business houses serve tea to their employees at eleven o'clock in the morning and again at four in the afternoon.

In the average Australian home, tea is prepared in the same manner and with the same care as in New Zealand, but in the back blocks the bushman makes tea quite differently. He has a smoke-blackened tin "billy-can" in which he boils water as soon as he crawls from his bunk in the morning. He throws in a handful of tea and lets it go on boiling until his bacon is cooked. By this time the tea is well stewed and ready for breakfast. The meal over, the billy is left simmering; and when he returns to his cabin at dusk, he rekindles the fire, warms up the black concoction which has been stewing all day, and drinks it with the utmost enjoyment.

The billy-can, used by the bushman, "sundowner," or "swaggie," has been given the name of "Matilda," for reasons unknown. Under this sobriquet, it has been celebrated in an almost national song entitled "Waltzing Matilda," which has for its refrain: "You'll come a-waltzing Matilda with me."

Canada is the foremost tea drinking country of the Western Hemisphere. The beverage is served there at breakfast, with the other meals throughout the day, and before retiring. Teabags are being used in increasing quantities.

In New Brunswick, Nova Scotia and Newfoundland tea is prepared in the English manner, but there, too, teabags are growing in favor. Five o'clock tea is becoming more of a function in the new modern hotels of St. John, Digby, Halifax, and St. John's, N. F.

In Holland, where tea was introduced into Europe, its use as a beverage was well established by the middle of the seventeenth century. Late in that century it brought fabulous prices among the aristocracy—eighty to a hundred dollars a pound—and the craze for tea parties resulted in the ruin of many homes.

Today the people of the Netherlands lead the nations of Continental Europe as tea drinkers. Fermented teas of Java, India, Ceylon, and China are favored. In preparing the beverage the Dutch housewife, using only freshly boiling water, permits the tea to infuse not longer than five or six minutes and then places the pot under a cozy to keep warm. Tea may be had in all cafes and restaurants and in many bars throughout the country. In the homes, tea is the drink commonly taken at breakfast, and not a few households serve it at luncheon, although coffee is largely used. In the late afternoon and in the evening, about an hour after dinner, tea is served in most Dutch homes. The conventional afternoon tea is a family affair—women, men, children, and callers if they drop in.

From Holland the custom of afternoon tea crossed the Atlantic to New Amsterdam. With tea came also the tea boards, teapots, "bite and stir" boxes, silver spoons and strainers, and other tea table paraphernalia which were the pride of Dutch housewives.

The socially correct grand dame of New Amsterdam not only served tea, but she brewed several kinds in different pots so as to accommodate the tastes of her guests. She never offered milk or cream with tea—for this was a later innovation that came to America from France - but she did offer sugar, and sometimes saffron or peach leaves for flavoring. The guests would either nibble a lump of loaf sugar or stir powdered sugar into their tea; hence tea tables were provided with "bite and stir" boxes. These were partitioned in the center—one side for lump sugar, the other for powdered. The ooma, or sifter, also adorned the table. This was filled with cinnamon and sugar, with which they sprinkled hot puffets, pikelets, hot waffles, or wafers.

New Amsterdam having passed into English hands in 1674, it was rechristened New York and proceeded to acquire English manners. Copying the idea of the London pleasure gardens of the first half of the eighteenth century, tea gardens were added to the coffee houses and taverns. Then on the outskirts of the city were opened the Ranelagh and Vauxhall gardens, named after their famous London prototypes.

From advertisements of the period 1765-9 we learn that there were fireworks and band concerts twice a week at Ranelagh and Vauxhall. The gardens were "for breakfasting as well as the evening entertainment of ladies and gentlemen." Tea, coffee, and hot rolls could be had in the pleasure gardens at any hour of the day. William Niblo, previously proprietor of the Bank Coffee House in Pine Street, opened in 1828 a pleasure garden which he named Sans Souci.

Among other well-known pleasure gardens of old New York where tea was served were Contoit's, later the New York Garden, Cherry Gardens and the Tea Water Pump Garden. The latter was a famous "out-of-town" garden located at a spring near the junction of Chatham (now Park Row) and Roosevelt streets. This spring and its surroundings were made into an extremely fashionable resort for drinking tea and other beverages.

In order to make it possible to obtain good water for preparing tea, the corporation of New York erected a tea water pump over the spring at Chatham and Roosevelt streets. This water was considered much more desirable than that from the other town pumps and was peddled

Tea Manners & Customs

Knapp's Water Pump in lower Manhattan was one of several deep spring-fed wells that provided pure water for tea making during the 1700s. Tea wagons also delivered water directly to wealthy clients for a fee.

about the streets by carters whose cries of "Tea water! Tea water! Come out and get your tea water!" were characteristic of the day. By 1757 this business had grown to such an extent that the Common Council was constrained to enact "Law for the Regulating of the Tea Water Men in the City of New York."

Tea water was also pumped from several other springs. There was Knapp's famous spring, located near the present Tenth Avenue and Fourteenth Street; another spring that was well patronized was near Christopher Street and Sixth Avenue.

British governors and their wealthy Tory friends helped to give a note of formal dignity to the early tea manners of New England, but the price of the leaf was too high during the third quarter of the seventeenth century to permit its frequent use. By the turn of the century, however, tea drinking had an extraordinary vogue, which not only influenced the furniture of the period but required for its service silver, porcelain, or earthenware teapots and china teacups and saucers of great beauty and cost. With these went all the equipage of the tea tray, wrought by craftsmen whose artistry made them famous.

Many of the living rooms had several tea tables of various kinds. Around these much of the social life of the colonists was centered. The realization of this fact gives point to the irritation which led to the Boston Tea Party. Large tiptop tables, small kettle-stands, and tray-topped four-legged tables were made for this purpose. Made of rich woods and covered with dainty and artistic teapots and cups, they gave a beautiful variation of color to the rooms. Their disappearance caused many a sigh of regret when colonial women pledged themselves to give up tea as a patriotic duty.

In the early days of the Republic tea returned to the American table. From a coeval account, we learn that George Washington at Mount Vernon "ordinarily, for breakfast, had tea, English fashion, Indian cakes, with butter, and, perhaps, honey, of which he was very fond. His evening meal, or supper, was especially light, consisting of, perhaps, tea and toast, with wine." Tea remained for many years the principal table beverage at the evening meal in America, which was designated as either "supper" or "tea."

Today the people of the United States drink black, green and oolong teas, and, unlike the British, pay more attention to the appearance of the leaf than to quality in the cup. There is abysmal ignorance concerning differences in teas, popular education having progressed little beyond a notion that the term "Orange Pekoe" is synonymous with quality. Our English cousins tell us we buy poor teas in our blends and usually spoil the beverage in the making. Certainly, we seem to prefer the fancy Pekoes to the more substantial brokens, and we may as well admit that even our best hotels, restaurants, and homes as often as not use flat, stale water for brewing.

Indias and Ceylons, which together supply 42 percent of the American demand, are pretty generally consumed in all the states. Javas and Sumatras represent an additional 20 percent. Japans, supplying about 17 percent of the demand, are used principally along the northern border and in far Western States. Oolong teas are consumed chiefly in New York, Pennsylvania, New Jersey, and the Eastern states. Formosas, representing 12.5 percent of the tea imports, being especially favored in New York and Boston, while Philadelphia always has adhered to Foochows. China teas account for about 9 percent of the imports, the blacks still being sought after by connoisseurs throughout the Union, while the greens are consumed chiefly in the Middle States, such as Ohio, Indiana, Missouri and Kentucky.

During the transition period of the late nineties supper, or "tea," was displaced by dinner as the evening meal. The older generation will remember the light repast at the evening hour, when the teapot reigned supreme. Coffee held undisputed sway at the breakfast and noon dinner tables, but "tea" and "supper" were synonymous, inseparable, and ingrained parts of the American's daily habit throughout the nineteenth century.

There is great lack of uniformity in the use of tea throughout the country, some sections being heavy consumers, and others using very little, depending on racial descent. Also, some sections are seasonal consumers, like the Southern states, which drink only a little hot tea in winter, but off set this by liberal consumption of iced tea in summer.

Recently the ubiquitous American soda fountain has begun adding tea, hot or iced, to its menu, and this has opened up a new and important field for the public serving of tea.

The introduction of the teabag,[15] or teaball, has done much to popularize tea, not alone in the American home, but to an even greater extent among chefs and stewards. The latter believe that teabags simplify brewing and ensure a better and more uniform brew.

The American housewife prepares tea in practically the same manner in which it is prepared in England, but in the homes of immigrants of the first and second generations from the European continent tea is prepared after the manner of their mother countries. Infusion varies from three to ten minutes.

To the average American, tea for breakfast is "flat, stale and unprofitable." He must have his coffee. Many, however, prefer tea even for breakfast and invariably at luncheon.

Tea Manners & Customs

Afternoon tea in the American home varies greatly in its details. In many cases, all the traditions of the British "bun worry" are observed, but the younger generation has introduced some startling innovations. It is not unusual to find the same hostess serving hot tea in winter and iced tea in summer. In winter, most hostesses bring the pot of tea from the kitchen with the tea all brewed and serve it with nothing but crisp pieces of toast and home-made jam. In the summer, iced tea is served on the porch. Iced tea being a purely American development, almost any variation and accompaniment that one desires are proper. The tea wagon is popular, as it saves steps. Instead of the omnipresent muffin stand of the English tea, there is a nest of tables, which the hostess distributes among her guests, keeping the largest for the tea tray.

Tea drinking in the United States received considerable impetus when the idea of afternoon tea was revived with the dancing craze of the last decade, and when, for a while, afternoon tea drinking promised to become an American institution. Every city, town, and village has since inaugurated some form of the tea room, or, as it is often termed, tea garden. They really are light-lunch places. The average price of a cup of tea is ten cents, or twenty-five cents for a pot of tea for two, including sugar, cream or lemon, and hot water. There are two hundred tea rooms in New York City alone, and between twenty-four and twenty-five hundred tea rooms and tea gardens in the United States.

The Hotel Pennsylvania was one of many New York City hotels offering tea rooms in the first quarter of the 20th century.

In the cities, society folk frequent the restaurants of the leading hotels for afternoon tea. Nearly all these places serve black, green, and Oolong teas. New York society takes its afternoon tea in the refined, quiet, sumptuous surroundings of the best hotels. The price of tea at the Waldorf-Astoria, the Ritz-Carlton, and the Savoy-Plaza is fifty cents; at the St. Regis, forty-five cents; and at the Astor, twenty-five cents. At Ropemaker's the price is forty cents. Teabags are common, but not at Rumpelmayer's. A Gramercy Park hotel advertises to "serve tea from 3 to 6 afternoons and 8 to 12 evenings, in the solarium on the 17th floor overlooking the city"—which should appeal to any Australasian visitors.

The best hotels throughout the country provide an individual tea service, for which they charge on the average twenty cents per cup, or thirty cents per pot for two, including sugar and cream or lemon. Teabags are universal.

Tea Manners & Customs

In chain restaurants like Schrafft's, tea for one person costs fifteen cents per pot; at Childs' the charge is ten cents. Sugar and lemon or cream is included in both places. In the Fountain and Tea Room on the eighty-sixth floor of the Empire State Building tea is twenty cents per pot. In New York, "Gypsy" tea rooms serve tea with cinnamon toast or cake for fifty cents and read "a real fortune gratis from your teacup."

Well-dressed diners enjoy a stylish afternoon tea at a French chateau in 1905.

Germany has yet to acquire the tea drinking habit. Five o'clock tea is confined to very limited circles. Speaking generally, coffee has the preference as an afternoon drink, tea being taken with the evening meal.

Tea drinking in France is confined to the *bourgeois,* the poor classes preferring to use wines that can be had cheaply and in abundance. The large English, American, and Russian colonies in France, particularly on the fashionable Riviera, help to increase the Frenchman's per-capita consumption. The teas come from China, Indo-China, and the British Indies.

Tea is prepared much as it is in England. The use of teabags is not common. The tea hour is between five and six o'clock in the afternoon—somewhat later than in England. This is due to the fact that the dinner hour in France is later.

Afternoon tea in the hotels, restaurants, and cafes is usually served with milk, sugar, or lemon. The always delightful French pastry which accompanies it may be responsible for the tendency to demand a second cup.

The Parisian "five o'clock" started modestly and has been evolving gradually ever since the day in 1900 when the Brothers Neal, in their stationer's shop, now W. H. Smith & Sons, in the rue de Rivoli, began to serve tea and biscuits on two tables at the end of a counter. Since then afternoon tea has grown steadily in importance among the smart set in Paris. Tea rooms now are as numerous in the French capital as cafes and restaurants. The department stores have democratized the "five o'clock." Tea also may be had *alfresco* at the restaurants in the Bois.

Afternoon tea at from three to ten francs, with cakes from one franc each, may be had between four-thirty and six-thirty o'clock at any of the following favourite resorts: the Ritz, Rumpelmayer's, Colombin, Ciro's, Hotel de Crillon, Mirabeau, Carlton, Claridge's, The Volney-Chatham, Restaurant du Pre-Catelan, The Recamier, A la Marquise de Sevigne, Pihan, Compagnie Anglaise, W. H. Smith & Sons, Kardomah, Ixe, Dovet, Montaber, Rivoli, and the British Dairy.

The people of Soviet Russia now consume China, Japan, Ceylon, India, and Georgia teas. The term "Russian tea" for many years meant China tea imported into Russia. The beverage is made with boiling water drawn from a samovar, a large, graceful, copper, brass, or silver boiler, heated by charcoal in a metal pipe extending vertically through its center, and usually resolving itself into four legs and a tiny grate. The top is crowned by a saucer-shaped receptacle upon which the teapot rests and where it usually is to be seen keeping hot above the steaming urn, ready to fill the tall glasses in which tea is served *a la Russe*.

Before the samovar is brought to the table, the boiler is filled with water, lighted chips and charcoal are placed in the vertical pipe, and an extra length of pipe is placed on top to draw the flame. When the charcoal is glowing steadily and the water is boiling, this source of forty-odd cups of good cheer is borne into the room and placed upon a silver tray at the right hand of the hostess.

When Russians gather for tea, the host sits at one end of the table, while the hostess presides over the samovar at the other. Tea is made in a small teapot and this is placed on top of the samovar. As soon as the tea has drawn its full strength, the hostess fills each glass about one-quarter full of tea from the pot, and the other three-quarters with boiling water from the samovar. The glasses have silver holders with handles, similar to those used at American soda fountains. A slice of lemon is served with each glass of tea whenever lemons are obtainable, but no milk or cream. Each guest has a tiny glass dish of jam and another for sugar. Basins placed about the table contain large lumps of sugar. The guests supply themselves from the central sugar basins, using sugar tongs, and then break the lumps into small pieces with silver nippers. The peasants rarely place the sugar in the tea, but put a piece directly in their mouths before each sip of tea. Not infrequently a spoonful of jam is put in the tea in place of lemon; and in winter time a spoonful of rum is sometimes added as protection against influenza.

Connoisseurs of tea for three centuries, the Russians differ in their tea drinking from all other peoples. Mostly they eat but one substantial meal a day. Their breakfast is light, consisting of bread and tea; but dinner and lunch are combined into one enormous meal, which is eaten between three and six o'clock. Throughout all the rest of their waking hours they drink tea constantly, if they can get it.

Tea Manners & Customs

The tea room, or *chainaya* as it is called in Russian, abounds in the cities, towns, and villages and is liberally patronized during all hours of the day and night. Russian tea is not always drunk from glasses; in some districts cups and large mugs are used.

Tourists visiting present-day Russia have been impressed with the free early morning tea and rusks (dry biscuits) served them on railway trains by the Soviet authorities, and likewise by the rush of the natives for hot water for tea, supplied free, from a large boiler in the stations, every time the trains stop.

The other countries of Europe are not large tea-drinkers. Five o'clock tea may be had, however, in polite society and at the best hotels in Austria, Hungary, Belgium, Czechoslovakia, Denmark, Finland, Greece, Italy, Norway, Poland, Sweden, and Switzerland.

Siberia drinks both loose and brick teas from China after the Russian manner. The Mongols and the other Tatar tribes make a kind of soup from powdered brick tea, which they boil with alkaline steppe water, salt, and fat. Then they strain it and mix it with milk, butter, and roasted meal. Korea consumes mostly Japan teas, prepared by dropping the leaves into a kettle of boiling water. Raw eggs and rice cakes are served with the tea. The eggs are sucked between sips of tea, and the cakes are eaten when the eggs have been consumed.

The natives of Indo-China follow the Chinese method of preparing the beverage, and prefer strong acrid teas to those of delicate flavor.

In Burma the tea manufactured and consumed by the natives is the letpet, or pickled tea. It is prepared as a salad by being soaked in oil, with garlic and sometimes dried fish added. Newly married couples drink from the same cup a mixture of tea leaves steeped in oil, to ensure a happy union.

The population of Siam consumes enormous quantities of the native miang, or Siamese tea, which they chew with salt and other condiments.

Tea drinking is becoming a habit among the natives of British India through the persistent efforts of the Tea Cess Committee. The natives buy only the cheapest teas and dusts, but every bazaar and railway station now has its tea stall, and there are street venders who sell tea to passing pedestrians. The British residents use the best India teas and import small quantities of the leaf from Ceylon and Java.

In the native Indian state of Cashmere, churned tea and bitter tea, or *cha tulch*, are favored. The latter is boiled in a tinned copper pot, and red potash, aniseed, and a little salt are added. For churned tea, bitter tea is churned with milk.

Cream tea, or *vumah cha*, a product of Turkistan, is sometimes found in Cashmere. For this, only black tea is used. The tea is boiled in a tinned copper pot and a much stronger decoction made than ordinary tea. Cream is added to the tea while it is boiling or after it has been poured into the teapot. Bits of bread are soaked in the beverage.

The average native Ceylon villager relishes a cup or bowl of tea, which he drinks without milk, but with a little sugar or, more often, jaggery—, a strong extract of tea is made at the beginning of the day, and the kiosk-keeper puts a spoonful of this into each cup and fills it with boiling water. The foreign residents use the fine teas raised in Ceylon, and import some Indias and Javas.

Tea is the national drink of Iran. A native can live without meat or vegetables, but he must have seven or eight cups of tea each day. The home-grown variety is insufficient for local needs, so seventy-five percent is imported from India, China, and Java—mostly green teas.

In Arabia, the tea drinking habit is spreading and, as in Iran, green teas are mostly in demand. Every coffee house reserves a table for tea, in the drawers of which one finds the precious commodity, together with sugar and a hammer to break it up. The large cities have sumptuous tea rooms built in Moorish style. In these the tea and cakes are as good as those served in the larger tea rooms of London, Paris, or New York.

In Turkey, street venders brew tea by the Russian method and serve it in glasses. The outfit includes a brass samovar and a portable table with tea caddies, slices of lemon, glasses, spoons, and saucers. A European teapot also is carried for the occasional Occidental with different ideas of tea brewing.

In Bokhara, a Soviet state, the native carries his tea with him in a small bag, and when he is thirsty he looks for the nearest tea booth and has the proprietor brew it for him.

Tea seldom is purchased at these booths of which there are thousands—the proprietor being paid only for the water and his skill at brewing the beverage. The breakfast drink is tea flavored with milk, cream or mutton fat, in which bread is dipped. After drinking, it is customary for Bokharans to eat the tea leaves.

Green tea is the favorite beverage of Morocco and is an essential article of diet for all Moors of whatever degree or occupation. The Moors drink the beverage hot out of glasses, the liquor being almost saturated with sugar and strongly flavored with mint.

Most of the tea consumed in Algeria comes from China. It is prepared by the Europeans in much the same manner as in England, but the native population brew theirs with mint and much sugar.

Tea Manners & Customs

In Egypt, tea is prepared and served as in England, except among the natives, who prepare it in glasses and drink it with the addition of sugar only. Five o'clock tea is customary among the resident foreigners and Europeanized Egyptians.

In the Union of South Africa, the favorite teas are Ceylons and Indias, home-grown Natal, and a small proportion from Netherlands Indies. Tea is drunk not only in the afternoon and after meals, but also in the early morning on arising and at eleven o'clock. It is prepared and served in the English manner.

In the countries of Central America tea drinking is an exotic custom followed only by foreign residents.

The tea consumed in Mexico is imported from the United States, China, Great Britain, and British India, in amounts according to the order named. Most of the natives drink coffee. Tea is drunk by foreign residents and upper-class Mexicans. In Mexico City, a number of restaurants, tea rooms, and clubs serve afternoon tea.

In South American countries, tea is drunk mainly by foreign residents or the upper classes; the lower-class native populations almost invariably prefer coffee or yerba maté.

NOTES

1. What Ukers is describing here is called in China a *Gaiwan*; literally "covered cup." Both steeping vessel and drinking cup, the gaiwan is older than the teapot, having been used in China since before 1350 at least. It consists of a saucer, bowl and lid which function together when in use. Tea may be drunk from the bowl or decanted into smaller cups. Generally used for green and white teas, gaiwans are also suitable for any other type of tea.

2. Ukers is referring to Pu-Er (*puer*), one of the very few teas that improves with age. Pu-Er belongs to the dark tea (*heicha*) family, as opposed to the white, green, oolong or black families or types of tea. Chinese connoisseurs have always aged Pu-Er and prized extremely old cakes for which they willingly pay exorbitant prices. It has been produced since ancient times in Yunnan province and is finally gaining popularity in the West thanks to its healthfulness.

3. Shogun Ashikaga Yoshimasa (1436-1490) abdicated rule of Japan in order to cultivate the arts and their appreciation. As an important patron, he became a pivotal figure in Japan's history, responsible for the Japanese aesthetic which produced *ikebana* (flower arranging), *Noh* drama, *sumi-e* ink painting, and *chanoyu* "hot water for tea" or the Japanese tea ceremony. This practice of tea embodied the aesthetics and attitudes of Zen Buddhism which the retired shogun learned from a renegade Zen monk named Murata Shuko (1425-1502). The student of his student was the great Master Rikyu. Shuko's simple thatched tea hut still stands on the grounds of Yoshimasa's palace, the oldest teahouse in Japan.

4. *Teaism* was first explained in English by Okakura Kakuzo in his 1906 *The Book of Tea*. No Westerner can fully understand the spirit of Japan until they appreciate tea's significant influence upon Japanese architecture, art and etiquette. Okakura suggests that "Teaism is the art of concealing beauty that you may discover it, of suggesting what you dare not reveal."

5. Kakemono is a scroll painting or calligraphy usually mounted on silk fabric. It is hung in the tokonoma, an alcove in the tea room or in the reception room of a home or palace.

6. Sen no Rikyu (1521-1591) learned the way of tea from a student of Shuko. Rikyu's patron was also a ruler, Toytomi Hideyoshi (1536-1598). Hideyoshi was not only a brilliant politician and warrior but also a patron of tea and art. Rikyu became one of several tea masters at court, but he soon gained Hideyoshi's trust to become an influential confidant of the inner circle, on par with top generals and state advisors. Rikyu made an indelible impression on his time and left many students at the time of his death by suicide on orders from Hideyoshi. Through Rikyu, the tea experience in Japan had evolved from a game to a rite of acceptance and enlightenment, embracing our haunting longings, listening for the echo between Ego and one's right-sized self, where every moment is beautiful, because it is fleeting.

7. The Jesuit father João Rodrigues, a contemporary of Rikyu, whom he probably met in Kyoto, speaks of the tea ceremony as he knew it as a somewhat informal gathering of friends rather than the stylized and rather rigid rite into which it developed. He credits Yoshimasa with originating the practice and establishing a canon of taste to be observed. "The purpose," he writes, "of this art of cha is courtesy, good breeding, modesty and moderation, peace and quiet of body and soul.…"

8. It would take more diligence and time to unravel the mysteries of the Japanese tea ceremony than to write the rest of this book. Musashi, the greatest samurai Japan ever knew, recognized chado—the way of tea—as a vocation just as demanding as his warrior's way. The author of *The Book of Tea*, Okakura Kakuzo, tells us: "Chado is a religion of the art of life.… A subtle philosophy lay behind it. Teaism was Taoism in disguise." Contemporary students of tea can find branches of the Urasenke Foundation located in major cities around the world, organized and run by direct descendants of Rikyu's family and currently under the direction of the sixteenth-generation Grand Master.

9. Ichibancha, "Number One" or First Flush tea, was used ceremonially in Japan as *Tribute Tea* as it had long been in China. There are colorful woodblock prints depicting this procession. Another annual procession involved Dutch traders bearing "tribute" to the Emperor from their trading concession in Nagasaki. They were made to look fearsome with bushy red beards and blue eyes.

Tea Manners & Customs

10. These "hawkers" have long since been replaced by vending machines dispensing hot or cold ready-to-drink teas from companies such as Ito-En, Japan's leading tea brand.

11. "…bags were not introduced into the U.K. until Lipton patented a 'flo-thru' teabag in 1952. The British were slow to show interest, and by 1968, only three percent of all tea brewed in the U.K. was prepared using a teabag. By 1971, that had risen to a still negligible 12.5 percent. But by the end of the twentieth century, the total use of teabags accounted for approximately 96 percent of all tea brewed in the United Kingdom." Pettigrew/Richardson: *A Social History of Tea* (2014) Benjamin Press, p.183.

12. Even with briskly boiling water it is not easy to coax three steepings out of black tea leaf, regardless of the savings incurred. On the other hand, most green or oolong teas will yield three or more steepings with less than boiling water. Any oolong of distinction, for which a Chinese or Taiwanese would pay US$500 or more per pound, yields cup after cup at less cost than the price of common soda.

13. As a bathtub lined with white porcelain, when the hot water gives out or goes tepid, such is the slow cooling of the British passion for tea in recent generations. Though the per capita quantity is lower, the US has for some years imported and consumed more tea than the U.K.. The Irish have always drunk more tea than the British, but nobody drinks as much as the Turks, although Russians and Pakistanis try.

14. Thank Heavens for the "One Percent" without whom we should no longer have any classes that keep servants. Whether personal trainers, laundresses and chauffeurs can be trained as tea sommeliers remains to be seen. "Bed tea" is not uncommon thoughtfulness in middle-class homes in India and elsewhere.

15. World War II began when Japan invaded China in 1936, the same year *Romance of Tea* was published. The war changed the worldwide tea trade in every respect. In East and West alike, traditions centuries in the making were ruined and never revived but replaced by new beginnings. Beginning in the U.S. and the U.K. came the bag only to be ubiquitously accepted throughout the post-war West in the name of "modern convenience." The U.K. resisted for a time but after 1970 it was a walkover. It quickly became difficult to find tea that was not in teabags anywhere outside a few elderly and aristocratic firms that continued to cater to the carriage trade in cities. Very few tea businesses of any other sort survived. Tea was not purveyed but "marketed" like any other commodity, an anonymous brown beverage. Any differences between the mass-merchandised brands disappeared in a general race to the bottom. People simply forgot the taste of good tea. Teas that poets once praised—Ezra Pound's "hyson, congou, bohea and a few lesser divinities"—disappeared altogether from the market. Tea was drained of its romance.

The oft-touted myth about the invention of the teabag is attributed to a New York City tea importer Ukers knew named Thomas Sullivan. In 1908 he thought to economize on operating expenses by sending his samples to retailers and private customers in little silk bags sewn closed by hand. He was perplexed but delighted so many of them placed orders, but they then complained his tea was not packaged in those little bags that steeped so conveniently. Sullivan got the message, substituted gauze for silk, and realized handsome profits from a previous invention. It was not a new idea: The first teabag patent was issued to a certain Mr. Smith of London in 1896.

Tea Leaves, *Oil on canvas by William McGregor Paxton, 1909. Courtesy of the Metroplitan Museum of Art.*

TEA AND THE FINE ARTS

Tea as a drink has been a source of inspiration to artists and sculptors in many lands. Likewise, the fashionable demands of the tea table in the West and of ceremonial tea in the East have inspired the potter and the silversmith to supreme achievements, following strictly utilitarian beginnings.

When the Dutch introduced tea to Europe, they brought with it dainty Chinese teapots, delicately fragile teacups, and ornamental jars for holding the leaf. European potters and silversmiths, attracted by the high prices of the imported Chinese wares, began to copy them in order to satisfy a rapidly-growing demand for tableware of the highest artistic excellence.

Early Chinese paintings on tea subjects are rare, but there is one in the British Museum entitled *Preparing Tea for His Majesty,* by the artist Chiu Ying of the Ming dynasty (1368-1644). The best-preserved Chinese paintings of the subject belong to the eighteenth century and represent scenes of cultivation and manufacturing. They depict each step in the preparation of the leaf from the sowing of the seed to the final packing into chests and sale to a tea merchant.

Japanese pictorial art is largely Chinese in its origin, but has developed great originality in treatment of themes. The point at which it exhibits the closest resemblance to Chinese art is in a nobly austere type of religious painting, the product of a special phase of Buddhism which developed along somewhat new lines after it came to Japan.[1] An example is the painting of Saint Myōe, which was one of the treasures of Kozan Temple. It has been preserved in the Municipal Museum at Kyoto. Saint Myōe, who planted the first tea in Uji, is shown seated meditating in a grove of pines—emblems of immortality.

A rare and valuable *makimono,* painted on silk and presented to me on one of my visits to Japan, depicts twelve scenes connected with the historic "Tea Journey."

The artists of Japan have preserved for future generations many scenes showing tea manufacture. A series of unmounted colored drawings by the nineteenth century artist Uwa-hayashi Seisen, in the British Museum, show *The Processes of Tea Preparation*. The pictures are drawn in ink on silk and painted in colors. But motives chosen from nature hold the preponderant interest, as in *Chrysanthemums and Tea,* painted by the eighteenth century artist Nishikawa Sukenobu. The first European pictures of tea subjects were steel engravings—now rare—that were published to illustrate early accounts of the China plant.[2]

In the eighteenth century, when tea became a fashionable beverage in northern Europe and America, *genre* artists frequently painted tea drinking scenes in the new environment. William Hogarth (1697-1764), London's preeminent eighteenth century satirical artist, lived close to the famous Vauxhall tea gardens and painted a number of pictures for the rooms. None of these were on the subject of tea, but three of his other pictures, which he first painted and then engraved, illustrate tea drinking and the tiny teacups then in use.

The accomplished French artist Jean Baptiste Chardin (1699-1779) painted his *Lady Making Tea* at about the same time that Hogarth was rising to celebrity. This canvas is in the art collection of the Hunterian Museum at Glasgow.[3]

Two fine examples of line engraving depicting eighteenth century tea drinkers are *Cafee und Thee,* an oval bookplate in a square frame from Martin Engelbrecht's *Sammlung von Folgen figürlichen Inhalts,* published at Augsburg, Germany (1720-50), and *Le Phlegmatique,* engraved by R. Brichel, also of Augsburg, in 1784, after a painting by Joseph Franz Goz (1754-1815). *Le Phlegmatique* is a Johnsonian tea drinker, clay pipe in hand, and with teapot and cup beside him, whose rapt expression bespeaks an imagination unleashed and far afield.

The painting *Tea a l'anglaise* in the Grand Salon of the Temple, with the *Court of the Prince de Conti Listening to the Young Mozart,* by Olivier, in the Louvre, represents a stately formal tea in the time of Louis XV. The assembled guests are grouped about tables having tea as they listen to a harpsichord recital by the seven-year-old German musical prodigy.

Nathaniel Hone (1730-84), the Irish portrait painter, has left us a charming picture of a tea drinker of 1771 in the portrait of his daughter, which he painted in that year. This young tea devotee, in shimmering satin, with a snowy lace fichu about her shoulders, and another bound modishly about her head, is holding by its saucer a steaming handle-less dish of tea, which she stirs gracefully with the tiniest of silver spoons.

A Tea Party at Bagnigge Wells (p. 123), painted by George Morland (1764-1804), offers a delightful glimpse of a family group enjoying *alfresco* tea at the famous pleasure garden.

Edward Edwards (1738-1806), a London artist, painted a picture of a couple about to take tea in a box at the Pantheon, Oxford Street. This canvas, painted in 1792, shows a richly bedizened coquette about to accept a tiny cup and saucer from the hand of a no less resplendent gallant.

Tea & The Fine Arts

A tray on a bare table in the foreground brings into prominence the tea service of the period, while another female figure in the rear seems to be whispering discretionary advice in the lady's ear. Other tea drinkers are to be seen in the boxes on the opposite side of the house.

The canvas *A Cottage Interior,* by W. R. Bigg, R. A. (1755-1828), signed and dated 1793, in the Victoria and Albert Museum, London, shows a rural housewife, in middle life, seated before a huge open fireplace with a small tea table at her elbow, and an iron tea kettle singing on the crane.

The painting *Delights of the Tea Table,* by Sir Daniel Wilkie (1805-41), the celebrated Scotch artist, portrays the solid comfort of an English family at their tea in the beginning of the nineteenth century.

The famous races of the swift China clippers, bringing the first of the new season's teas from Foochow and other Chinese ports to London and New York, furnished inspiration for innumerable canvases by both contemporary and modern painters of sea pictures.

Visitors to the Metropolitan Museum of Art, New York, are familiar with two tea pictures that hang there. They are *The Cup of Tea*, by Mary Cassatt, and *Tea Leaves,* by William M. Paxton (p. 42).

There are a number of paintings in the Musee Royal des Beaux Arts at Antwerp showing groups of tea drinkers. They include Oleffe's *Springtime,* Ensor's *Afternoon in Ostend,* Miller's *Figure and Tea Service* and Portielje's *Teasing.*

The substitution of "people's palaces," with their *chainaya,* or tea rooms, for the vodka dram-shops of pre-war days in Russia, supplied the artist A. Kokel with the inspiration for *Chai-naya,* which hangs in the Academy of Art, Leningrad.

When the cartoonist looks at tea, he is nearly always amusing, but never more so than the late Phil May, of *Punch* and the London *Graphic,* with his famous Lipton drawing, which showed a country couple standing aghast before a derelict sandwich-man

The Cup of Tea *by Mary Cassatt, oil on canvas. Courtesy of the Metropolitan Museum of Art.*

Tea & The Fine Arts

whose sign bore the one word: "Lipton," the old lady exclaiming: "Oh, is that 'im? No wonder 'e ain't married."

The Buddhist patriarch Daruma is frequently to be met with in Chinese and Japanese paintings and in the shape of images that range all the way from good-sized effigies to children's toys. Some show serious purpose and have a lofty expression, while others—and their name is legion—are given humorous treatment. He became the original of the Japanese toy that is so weighted that nothing can destroy its poise. In humorous treatments of his sensational vigil, the *netsuke-carvers* show him indulging in prodigious yawns, stretching his arms above his head, one hand clutching a fly-swatter, or as a not unpleasant mass of flesh, sitting Buddha-like in benign contemplation. Some less reverent representations show him as a spider in a web, or gazing at a pretty geisha with an expression that has in it nothing of the patriarchal. Following legendary accounts, he often is represented as crossing the Yangtze on a reed, or standing on the waves supported by a millet stalk, bamboo, or reed.

London cartoonist Phil May pokes fun at a sandwich board advertising Thomas Lipton's tea.

It is a curious fact that tea has not supplied the same inspiration to musicians as coffee. Tea never caused any great composer to write a cantata celebrating its allure as did Bach for coffee;[4] no comic opera such as Meilhat and Deffes produced in Paris, nor lilting *chansons* like those praising coffee in Brittany and other French provinces. The best that music has done for tea is represented by the pluckers' songs of the East, and in the West by a few temperance hymns and various ballads—comic and otherwise—dealing with social festivities rather than praise of the beverage.

The tea pluckers' songs of China and Japan serve to keep the pluckers—usually women and girls—in the best of spirits and to stimulate their activities. At a public reception to me on a recent visit to Japan, the schoolchildren at Tsu, in Miye Ken, sang one called *Cha-Tsumi* that is typical. Its burden was: "Pick all you can, you young maidens! If you don't pick, we Japanese will have no tea."

The English have occasionally, though rarely, sung of tea. The Temperance movement during the nineteenth century yielded a few such songs, and they were sung with great enthusiasm at what were known as "tea meetings."

Tea & The Fine Arts

"Tea in the Arbour" is the title of a comic song, set to rollicking measure by J. Beuler, and "sung with great applause by Mr. Fitzwilliam," about the year 1840. George Cruikshank, the celebrated caricaturist who illustrated some of Dickens's hooks, drew the humorous cover design for it.

"Poezie en Proza in de Thee," or "Poetry and Prose on Tea," a declamation in the Dutch language with piano accompaniment, closing with a song, was composed and presented by the well-known Dutch *chansonniers* J. Louis Pisuisse and Max Blokzul when they toured Netherlands Indies in 1918.

A modern American composer, Louise Ayers Garnett, has written the words and music for a charming little solo for soprano entitled "A Tea Song." In it a "little brown maid" from far-away Nippon tells how she delights to serve Japan tea to appreciative American men.[5] Japan has also dramatized tea in a graceful dance performed by geisha.

The art of the potter was first applied to articles of the tea service in China with the concurrent discovery of tea and of the materials and process for making artistic porcelains in which to serve it.

The world owes a lasting debt to the Chinese for discovering the materials and methods for producing this hard, translucent, glazed ware known to us as "china" or "porcelain" and in China as *tz'u*. Their successes in this direction date from the Tang dynasty (A.D. 620-907). There are few specimens of porcelain known, however, that are older than the Ming dynasty (A.D. 1368-1644), though there is a stoneware tea bowl of the Sung dynasty (A.D. 960-1280), from Kian, in Kiangsi, displayed in the British Museum.

The principal Chinese porcelain-manufacturing center of Kingtehchen, located near Nanking, dates from 1369, when a factory was built there for the express purpose of producing superior articles of the tea service for the Imperial court.

From China, the art of the potter spread to Japan,[6] where glazed stoneware—often of fabulous worth—became the accepted pottery of the Tea Ceremony, but where beautiful and artistic porcelain tea sets also are made and appreciated. Like every other country, Japan had its primitive pottery, but artistically it lagged far behind China, whence its culture and arts were derived, until two events in the thirteenth century combined to provide the necessary stimulus. The first of these was the spread of tea drinking in Japan, and the second was the return from China of Kato Shirozaemon, or Toshiro, as he is commonly called, after a thorough study of Chinese ceramics. Kato settled at Seto and was succeeded by many generations of potters, who maintained the family tradition in the production of Seto ware.

No further progress was made by Japanese ceramics, however, until the end of the sixteenth century, when a number of Korean potters followed Hideyoshi's army upon its return to Japan and, about this same time, Sen-no Rikyu established the ritual for *Chanoyu,* the Tea Ceremony, which had a far-reaching influence on Japanese ceramics. The pottery used for *Chanoyu* included: the small jar for holding the powdered tea, the drinking bowl, the wash bowl, the cake dish, and frequently a water container, an incense box, an incense burner, a fire holder, and a vase to hold a single spray of flowers. The utmost in the line of anxious care was lavished on the production of pottery for this use. Several of the great tea masters were potters and had kilns of their own, where they produced vessels that now are almost priceless.

The most highly prized tea jars are the old Seto stoneware ones, nearly or quite black in appearance, and some of them attributed to Tashiro. These are not considered complete unless they are in their original silk wrappings and wooden boxes.

The tea bowls for *Chanoyu* have a body of coarse, porous clay, with a soft, cream-like glaze. This material acts as a non-conductor of heat and serves to preserve the temperature of the tea as the bowl is passed about for each guest to sip. It does not become too hot for the hands, and the glaze offers an agreeable surface to the lips. The bowls vary in color from salmon pink to a deep, rich black, with a treacle-like glaze of wonderful color and depth.

A celebrated type is the Raku ware that was first made by Chojiro, a Kyoto potter, after a design by Rikyu, the great tea master.[7] While the most extreme taste requires that the tea bowl be without decoration, there are some notable examples, by Ninsei and other great masters who have achieved decoration with the utmost simplicity. Among the undecorated *Chanoyu* wares that were especially valued was one known as Hagi, from the chief town in the province of Nagato.

Other highly prized and much-sought-after Japanese art wares associated with tea are the pearl-grey crackled glaze made at Matsumoto; pottery from Kaga; Takatori and Zeze products; specimens named after famous tea masters, such as Furuta Oribe and Shino Lenobu; and Arita and lmari wares, much copied by the Dutch, Frence and English.

The Dutch brought the first delicate Chinese teapots and teacups to Europe with the first teas, and shortly afterwards Continental potters began to imitate them in a tin-glazed decorated earthenware known as *faience*. The Delft ware of the seventeenth century was a beautifully decorated faience in which Dutch artists successfully captured the color and charm of Chinese blue-and-white porcelain.

With the advent of the tea set, about the middle of the seventeenth century, numerous French and German faience-makers turned their attention to the production of pseudo-Chinese teapots and other articles of the tea service. Scandinavian potters in Denmark, Sweden, and Norway followed. Examples of these early European teapots are preserved in existing collections.

About the year 1710, the famous Bottger, at Meissen, Germany, made the first true porcelain teapots and teacups produced outside of China and Japan. His factory continued in existence until 1863 and the ware produced there, although the factory was located at Meissen, is commonly known as Dresden ware. Holland, Denmark, and Sweden followed in the production of tea sets in the German style. The French at Vincennes and Sevres developed a peculiar, glassy porcelain of great translucence, in which they imitated the Japanese Imari tea sets extensively.

Meissen porcelain tea bowl and saucer made in 1716.

The notorious Madame Pompadour is said to have influenced some of the beautiful designs to be seen on articles for the tea table that have been preserved in art collections, and the beautiful shade of rose appearing as the ground color on some of the pieces was named in her honor.

The first teapots made in England were produced by the pioneer potter John Dwight at Fulham about the year 1672. They were of red stoneware in imitation of the Chinese *boccaro* teapots. He also made other articles for shelf and table in "tortoise-shell" and "agate" variegated wares.

There followed imitations in English *faience* of Dutch specimens; English cream-colored ware, ware with the Staffordshire salt glaze by Elers and Whieldon, and the lovely English porcelains, including the works of Spode, Minton, and Wedgwood at Stoke-upon-Trent and of Davenport at Longport, as well as the famous Worcester, Staffordshire, Lowestoft, Chelsea, Leeds, Caughley, Coalport and Swansea productions.

The willow pattern, in the traditional Chinese blue and white, is supposed to have originated at the Caughley, Shropshire, porcelain works about 1780. It was quickly copied by migratory engravers in the factories of Staffordshire and other parts of England. A story differing in detail at the hands of various raconteurs but retaining its main essentials is told about the willow pattern, which is said to illustrate the legend of Koongse and her lover Chang.

Koongse was the beautiful daughter of a wealthy mandarin, who lived in the two-storied house in the center of the pattern. There is an orange tree behind the house. A willow tree overhangs a footbridge. Koongse lost her heart to her father's secretary, Chang. This greatly angered the proud mandarin, who ordered Chang to keep away from the place. As a further precaution, he betrothed Koongse to a wealthy but dissolute old *Tajin* (Duke). The father then built the palisade, or fence, that appears across the foreground of the picture, in order to keep Chang and Koongse apart. He allowed her only the freedom of the garden and tea house encircled by the stream.

The lover, Chang, floated messages of love and devotion down the little stream in a coconut-shell to his fair one. On the evening of Koongse's first meeting with her hated fiancé, he presented her with a box of jewels. After the guests had feasted and the *Tajin* was drunk with wine, Chang slipped into the banquet-hall disguised as a beggar and signaled Koongse to flee with him. Three figures are shown running across the footbridge. These are: Koongse, holding a distaff, the symbol of virginity; Chang, carrying the box of jewels; and the old mandarin brandishing a whip.

Chang hid Koongse in the house across the stream while he went for a boat. Just as her father's guards were closing in, the lovers pushed off. The boat is shown in the design. It drifted far downstream to an island shown in the upper left of the pattern. Here they built a house, Koongse helping, and Chang brought the land to a high state of cultivation. This can be seen in the design, for the whole of the ground is furrowed and every scrap of it is utilized—even narrow strips of land being reclaimed from the river.

They were very happy, and Chang become a celebrated writer, but his name at length reached the *Tajin,* who had his soldiers slay Chang. Koongse, in despair, set fire to the house and was burned to death. The gods cursed the Duke, but in pity transformed the souls of Chang and Koongse into two immortal doves, emblems of constancy, shown in the upper part of the pattern.

America developed a pottery manufacture of its own, based on English methods and carried on at first by English potters. In this way factories were established at Trenton and Flemington, New Jersey; East Liverpool, Zanesville and Cincinnati, Ohio; and Syracuse, New York. At all these centers, earthenware tea and dinner sets have been manufactured after the best English traditions, and there have been some individual efforts at artistic production.

While the first European teapots were of porcelain, silversmiths soon began to design teapots, teaspoons, and other articles for the tea service in silver. The first silver teapots were sterling, or "solid" silver. Plated-ware pots—some of them highly decorative—did not make their appearance until 1755-60.

Of the English silver, that made during the eighteenth century is the most interesting. It has a higher quality of workmanship than the English silverware of any other period, and it was during this time that the largest amount of English ware was exported to the American colonies.

Most of the early examples of silver teapots were small, on account of the scarcity and dearness of tea. Those that have been preserved are plain in design, being either lantern- or pear-shaped. The earliest is lantern-shaped, dating back to 1670, but has no claims to artistic design, being perfectly plain, and is practically identical in shape with the earliest coffee pots.

Tea & The Fine Arts

The pear-shaped teapot first appeared during the reign of Queen Anne (1702-14) and never has gone entirely out of style. The earliest American teapot of which we know is of this type. It is in the Clearwater collection at the Metropolitan Museum of Art, New York, and was made by John Coney (1655-1722) of Boston. Plain teapots with this same pear-shaped outline were common down through the reign of George I (1714-27), but in the closing years of that reign they were ornamented with chasing in the rococo style then prevalent in France.

Silver teapot by John Coney. Courtesty of the Metropolitan Museum of Art.

From early in the eighteenth century until the end of its third quarter, a globular body on a molded foot was favored. In the first examples the spout was straight and tapered. The later pots of this form have a cast spout, gracefully tapered and curved. The handles, like those of most of the early silver teapots, usually were of wood, but a few were of silver with ivory non-conductors inserted.

About 1770-80, Glasgow silversmiths created a new form by reversing the Queen Anne pear-shape, placing the larger part uppermost. Their pots were decorated with an embossed design, faintly suggesting the rococo. In this same period, there was a pronounced movement in favor of silver teapots that were beautiful in their simplicity. They were either octagonal or oval, with straight, vertical sides, flat bases, straight tapering spouts, scroll-shaped handles and slightly dome-shaped lids.

The necessity for the tea caddy passed with extreme high prices for tea, but when the leaf cost six to ten shillings per pound, it was kept under lock and key—often in little silver caddies, one for each kind of tea. Sometimes these were contained in a box ornamented with silver handles, lock-plates, and delicately chased corner pieces.

Beautiful caddies may be found in every style and shape, following in general the prevailing fashions of the times. Many are so dainty and of such exquisite workmanship that mere words fall short of doing them justice. They date mostly from the eighteenth century, when silver-smithing was at its best.

The teaspoon is only a miniature in spoon history, but the fashionable auspices under which it first appeared made it the favored child of the family. It was carefully wrought by silversmiths of the seventeenth and eighteenth centuries, and there are thousands of beautiful examples in all of the larger collections. Tea caddy spoons were common in the eighteenth century. They varied from broad, squat shapes to cockle-shells and leaves, all in dainty silver, delicately engraved. Sometimes the handles were of wood, sometimes of ivory; more often they were silver.

A silver creamer and one of four surviving teapots made by Paul Revere in Boston. Courtesy of the Metropolitan Museum of Art.

Fashions in the design of silverware have moved in cycles. The ornateness of the closing years of the nineteenth century has given way to a preference for simplicity of design. Among the various styles now offered in period tea sets are the Elizabethan, Italian Renaissance, Spanish Renaissance, Louis XIV, Louis XV, Louis XVI, Jacobean, Queen Anne, George I, George III, Sheraton, Colonial (Paul Revere) and Victorian. One finds in modern silver the graceful curved line and the broad, plain surface of silverware that might have been made in the days of Queen Anne, or the straight lines and oval shapes of our own versatile Paul Revere.

Literature gained in tea a new and fruitful theme. Beginning with early Chinese and Japanese commentaries and continuing down to the present, through a period of twelve hundred years, a galaxy of writers—occasional opponents along with more numerous advocates—have treated its many angles.

To Chinese literature we owe our all too meager knowledge of the genesis of tea; to the literature of Japan, the history of its expansion into a cult; and to the literature of the West, a thousand sidelights on the progress of its adoption as one of the world's greatest temperance beverages. We owe the preservation of many early writings on tea to the lucky chance that printing was invented contemporaneously with the spread of the new drink. Books began to be bound during the Tang dynasty (A.D. 620-907); previous to that time only scrolls were used. The *Cha Ching* (p. 14), or *Tea Classic,* by Lu Yu, was published in the Tang period.

There are so many charming myths attaching to Lu Yu that some Chinese scholars question whether such a person ever really existed. They say that one or more of the tea merchants of the eighth century may have written the book attributed to him, or have hired some scholar to write it, and then credited it to Lu Yu, who has come to be known in China as the patron saint of tea.

According to the *Cha Ching,* "the effect of tea is cooling. As a drink, it is well suited to persons of self-restraint and good conduct." Dr. Johnson should have had that line to hurl at Jonas Hanway in the great tea controversy of 1756. Further along, Lu Yu cautions his readers that "the first and second cups are best, and the third is the next best. One should not drink the fourth and the fifth cups unless one is very thirsty."

Tea & The Fine Arts

Ancient Chinese literature abounds in stories about tea. Typical is the one about Li Chiching, the Chinese general, and Lu. The general was passing through Yangchow on his way to Huchow Prefecture when he met the famous tea master near the confluence of the Nanling and the Yangtze. "I have heard that the water of the Nanling is exquisite for making tea," said Li, "and Mr. Lu is the nationally renowned tea expert. We should not miss an opportunity that may happen but once in a thousand years." He then dispatched a few of his faithful soldiers to sail away to the Nanling to get water, while Lu prepared the tea making implements.

After the water was brought, Lu spilled some with a ladle and said at once: "This is not Nanling water." The water was ordered to be poured into a basin. When about half of it was poured, he suddenly ordered the pouring stopped. He again spilled the water with the ladle and said that the remainder was true Nanling water. The soldiers who had brought it showed amazement, and confessed having first filled the receptacle with Nanling water, but having subsequently lost half by the rolling of the boat and fearing the wrath of their master if they appeared with so small a quantity, they had filled the jar with other water near the shore.

Since tea occupies a supreme position in the social and religious life of the Japanese, their literature, as might be expected, is rich in references to tea. One of the earliest now extant is to be found in the *Ogisho*, written by the poet Kiyosuke Sugawara (1178). There are important references to tea in the ancient Japanese history *Ruishu Kokushi*, compiled in 1552 by Michzane Sugawara, one of the foremost men of letters of his time.

The first Japanese work devoted exclusively to tea was the *Kitcha Yojoki*, or *Book of Tea Sanitation*, in two volumes, by the abbot Yeisai. The learned abbot wrote: "Tea is a sacred remedy and an infallible means of longevity. The soil of the mountains and valleys where the tea plant grows is sacred."

The tea goddess has inspired the muse from the earliest days of the "cup with vapours crowned." The Chinese poet Chang Meng-yang of the Chin dynasty wrote in the sixth century: "Fragrant tea superimposes the six passions." It was during the brilliant Tang dynasty, when outside influences and the break with iron-bound tradition found expression in China's Age of Poetry, that the Honan poet Lu Tung sang:

> The first cup moistens my lips and throat;
> The second cup breaks my loneliness;
> The third cup searches my barren entrail but to find therein some five thousand
>   volumes of odd ideographs;
> The fourth cup raises a slight perspiration—all the wrongs of life pass out through my pores;
> At the fifth cup I am purified;
> The sixth cup calls me to the realms of the immortals.
> The seventh cup—ah, but I could take no more! I only feel the breath of the cool

wind that rises in my sleeves.
Where is Elysium? Let me ride on this sweet breeze and waft away thither.

Among the best of the Chinese tea ballads, in so far as sentiment and metaphor are concerned, is one entitled the *Ballad of the Tea Pickers* that is sung by the girls and women as they pluck the leaves. The Chinese original, by Le Yih, a native of Haeyang, was written sometime during the early part of the Tsing dynasty (1644-1912). The entire ballad has been rendered into English verse by S. Wells Williams, LL. D. (1812-84), Professor of Chinese Language and Literature at Yale, who lived for many years in China. Here are typical stanzas:

Ballad of the Tea Pickers

Where thousand hills the vale enclose, our little hut is there,
And on the sloping sides around the tea grows everywhere;
So I must rise at early dawn, as busy as can be,
To get my daily labor done, and pluck the leafy tea....
Ye twittering swallows, rise and fall in your flight around the hill,
But when next I go to high Sunglo, I'll change my gown, I will;
And I'll roll up the cuff and show arm enough, for my arm is fair to see;
Oh, if ever there were a fair round arm, that arm belongs to me.

The scholar-Emperor Chien Lung (1710-99) was an inveterate and tireless versifier who wrote on a wide range of subjects, including tea. Many of his shorter poems adorned Chinese teapots in the eighteenth century. He sang: "You can taste and feel, but not describe, the exquisite state of repose produced by tea, that precious drink, which drives away the five causes of sorrow."

In Japan, Prince Junna, brother of the Emperor Saga (A.D. 810-24), found inspiration in tea for many of his verses. Koreuji, in the year 827, wrote an ode on tea. Sanyo, the poet-historian, wrote of tea brewing, and the poet Onitsura composed several tea *haiku*.

English letters had barely entered upon a fresh phase, under the influence of the secondary French poets in the last quarter of the seventeenth century, when Edmund Waller (1606-87) wrote the first English poem on tea, as a birthday ode to Catherine of Braganza:

Venus her Myrtle, Phrebus has his bays;
Tea both excels, which she vouchsafes to praise.
The best of Queens, and best of herbs, we owe
To that bold nation, which the way did show
To the fair region where the sun doth rise,
Whose rich productions we so justly prize.

Tea & The Fine Arts

> The Muse's friend, tea does our fancy aid,
> Repress those vapours which the head invade,
> And keep the palace of the soul serene,
> Fit on her birthday to salute the Queen.

As a satire on Dryden's "The Hind and the Panther," Matthew Prior and Charles Montague wrote the poem "The City Mouse and the Country Mouse," in 1687, in which the rhyme gives the word "tea" its modern sound, "tee," although this may have been mere poetic license.

> "And I remember," said the sober Mouse,
> "I've heard much talk of the Wits' Coffee House";
> "Thither," said Bundle, "you shall go and see
> Priests sipping coffee and Poets tea."

A rollicking Dutch ballad of the year 1697, entitled *The Merry Wedding Guest,* acclaimed tea for the medicinal virtues that were always foremost in the minds of early tea drinkers.

Dr. Nicholas Brady (1659-1726), the learned chaplain to the court of William III and Mary, was the author of a poem "The Tea Table," in which he called tea "the sovereign drink of pleasure and of health," one of the most graceful tributes ever paid to the beverage.

In 1709 Pierre Daniel Huet, the learned Bishop of Avranches, published at Paris a *Poemata* in Latin, including a lengthy ode to tea in elegiac verse.

Tea was still "tay" in 1711, when Alexander Pope (1688-1744) wrote *The Rape of the Lock*. The poem contains the oft-quoted reference to Queen Anne:

> ... There stands a structure of majestic frame,
> Which from the neighbouring Hampton takes its name....
> Here thou, great Anna, whom three realms obey,
> Dost sometimes counsel take—and sometimes tea.

In Pope's verses *Bohea* was another term for the tea in use by fashionable people. Like "tay" the word was pronounced "Bohay," and was so rhymed in *The Rape of the Lock*:

> Where the gilt chariot never marks the way,
> Where none learn ombre, none e'er taste Bohea.

Again, in 1718 Pope draws a pleasing picture of an aristocratic lady of the time who drank tea at nine o'clock in the morning: "She pretends to open her eyes for the sake of seeing the sun, and to sleep because it is night; drinks tea at nine in the morning, and is thought to have said her prayers before."

Peter Antoine Motteux, a French litterateur residing in London, wrote "A Poem upon Tea," published in 1712. It portrays a discussion among the gods on high Olympus as to the virtues of wine and tea. Fair Hebe proposes to substitute tea for the more heady wine. The author introduces the argument with this salutation to tea:

> Hail, Drink of Life! How justly shou'd our Lyres
> Resound the Praises which thy Pow'r inspires!
> Thy Charms alone can equal Thoughts infuse:
> Be thou my Theme, my Nectar, and my Muse.

Further along in the poem tea is again acclaimed as follows:

> Tea, Heav'ns Delight, and Nature's truest Wealth,
> That pleasing Physic, and sure Pledge of Health:
> The Statesman's Councellor, the Virgin's Love,
> The Muse's Nectar, and the Drink of Jove.

After a lengthy presentation of the claims of tea on the one hand and wine on the other, Jove decides the debate in favor of tea in these words:

> Immortals, hear, said Jove, and cease to jar!
> Tea must succeed to Wine as Peace to War:
> Nor by the Grape let Men be set at odds,
> But share in Tea, the Nectar of the Gods.

The pronunciation of the word "tea" must have changed pretty generally to "tee" after Pope wrote *The Rape of the Lock,* for not only did Motteux so rhyme the word in 1712, but Prior wrote in 1720 of "A Young Gentleman in Love:"

> He thanked her on his bended knee;
> Then drank a quart of milk and tea.

Dean Jonathan Swift (1667-1745) described a lady serving tea:

> Surrounded with the noisy clans
> Of prudes, coquettes, and harridans.

Tea & The Fine Arts

An allegorical poem of more than nine thousand words entitled *Tea, a Poem in Three Cantos,* was published anonymously at London in 1743.

At this time the serving of tea had become an important social function of the boudoir. The ladies of English high society had adopted the French custom of not rising until well toward noon and of receiving their friends and admirers in their boudoirs, while their costuming progressed. The poet John Gay (1688-1732), who began his career as secretary to the Duchess of Monmouth, refers to this custom in the lines:

> At noon (the lady's matin hour)
> I sip the tea's delicious flower.

Dr. Samuel Johnson was responsible for the following verses extemporized in ridicule of the ballad form of poetry, about the year 1770:

> So hear it then, my Rennie dear,
>   Nor hear it with a frown;
> You cannot make the tea so fast
>   As I can gulp it down.
> I therefore pray thee, Rennie dear,
>   That thou wilt give to me
> With cream and sugar softened well,
>   Another dish of tea.

Beautiful in its homely simplicity, after the stilted elegance of the earlier eighteenth century English poets, is William Cowper's tribute to "the cups that cheer." This famous phrase, borrowed from Bishop Berkeley, appears in "The Task," published in 1785. In its context, it reads:

> Now stir the fire, and close the shutters fast,
>   Let fall the curtains, wheel the sofa round,
> And while the bubbling and loud-hissing urn
>   Throws up a steamy column, and the cups
> That cheer but not inebriate, wait on each,
>   So let us welcome peaceful evening in.

Byron in the next century sighed that he grew pathetic, "moved by the Chinese nymph of tears, green tea."

In America after some of the prejudice against tea had cleared away, an early but unknown protagonist of the temperance cause wrote and printed a broadside entitled: "The Jug of

Rum" and "Dish of Tea." The original is preserved in the Ticknor Room of the Boston Public Library. "Let some in grog place their delight," wrote the unknown bard, but—

> A dish of tea more pleases me,
> Yields softer joys, provokes less noise,
> And breeds no base design.

John Keats (1795-1821) refers to lovers who "nibble their toast, and cool their tea with sighs."

William Hone (1779-1842) published an *Extract from Ancient Mysteries, Christmas Carols, Etc.* in 1823, in which there is included a curious Christmas carol on "Peko Tea," said to have been dedicated by one Francis Hoffman to Queen Caroline.

Hartley Coleridge (1796-1849) asked that someone "inspire my genius and my tea infuse," and later wrote:

> And I who always keep the golden mean,
> Have just declined my seventh cup of green.

Shelley (1792-1822) exulted:

> The liquid doctors rail at, and that I
> Will quaff in spite of them, and when I die
> We'll toss up which died first of drinking tea.

Tennyson (1809-92) sang of Queen Anne's reign as:

> The teacup times of hoop
> And when the patch was worn.

The charming custom of afternoon tea was mentioned by Browning (1812-89) as:

> That circle, that assorted sense and wit,
> With five o'clock tea in a house we know.

Mrs. Browning spoke in less kindly vein of the woman who:

> Then helps to sugar her Bohea at night
> With your reputation.

Tea & The Fine Arts

A patriotic poem entitled "Boston," read upon the occasion of the one hundredth anniversary of the Boston Tea Party, December 16, 1873, by Ralph Waldo Emerson, begins:

> Bad news from George on the English throne;
>   "You are thriving well," said he;
> "Now by these presents be it known
>   You shall pay a tax on tea;
> 'Tis very small,—no load at all,—
>   Honor enough that we send the call."
>
> The cargo came! and who could blame
>   If 'Indians' seized the tea,
> And, chest by chest, let down the same
>   Into the laughing sea?
> For what avail the plow or sail,
>   If land, or life, or freedom fail.

Oliver Wendell Holmes (1809-94) in his *Ballad of the Boston Tea Party,* has this comment on the event:

> The waters in the rebel bay
>   Have kept the tea leaf savor;
> Our old North-Enders in their spray
>   Still taste a Hyson flavor;
> And freedom's teacup still o'erflows
>   With ever-fresh libations,
> To cheat of slumber all her foes
>   And cheer the wakening nations!

Harking back to tea's mystic origin is one of the finest poems about tea in English, a sonnet by Francis Saltus Saltus (d.1889) in *Flasks and Flagons:*

> From what enchanted Eden came thy leaves
>   That hide such subtle spirits of perfume?
>   Did eyes preadamite first see the bloom,
> Luscious Nepenthe of the soul that grieves?
>
> By thee the tired and torpid mind conceives
>   Fairer than roses brightening life's gloom,
>   Thy protean charm can every form assume
> And turn December nights to April eyes.

Thy amber-tinted drops bring back to me
   Fantastic shapes of great Mongolian towers,
Emblazoned banners, and the booming gong;
I hear the sound of feast and revelry,
    And smell, far sweeter than the sweetest flowers,
   The kiosks of Pekin, fragrant of Oolong!

The Tea and Coffee Trade Journal published in 1909 this tribute in verse to the charms of India tea, by E. M. Ford:

"A Tea Idyl"

In Assam dwelt her ancient family,
And there heart-free grew graceful India Tea;
Till one who long for love of her had pined,
Drawn by the sun and driven by the wind,
From Ocean's realm, Prince Crystal-Water came,
But Falling Dew stepped forth the bride to claim.
"This blooming flower was pledged from birth to me,
And Nature gave assent"—but India Tea
Turned to the one she loved and sobbing said,
"Prince Crystal-Water only will I wed."
Then on the scene, as ever in each place,
Stepped meddling Man, "I will decide this case,"
He told the rivals, and, at his command,
A prison's outlines rose by fire spanned.
A scorching blast enwrapped the shrinking maid,
And soon, thereto by many hands conveyed,
Teapot received her form. Cried Man, "Behold,
The altar where ye wed, oh suitors bold!"
Cold Falling Dew gave up his hopes and fled,
But Crystal-Water scorned the ordeal dread,
And, fearless, plunged into the threatening gloom,
"Make way," called Steam—and lo, a happy groom
Passed through the prison's door and in his arms
Lay India Tea, with tenfold added charms!
The world applauds their union and they live
Steeped in the bliss which cream and sugar give.

In her poem, "The Old Tea Master of Kyoto" Antoinette Rotan Peterson gives us the best English interpretation of the Japanese Tea Ceremony in terms of poetic imagery. The

Tea & The Fine Arts

The Tea Plantation of Katakura *from the series* The Thirty-six Views of Mount Fuji, *1830 woodcut by Katsushika Hokusai. This iconic scene is situated in Shizuoka Prefecture, the largest tea-producing area of Japan.*

following excerpt is presented by permission of the author and of the publishers of *Asia* magazine, in which it first appeared in 1920:

> We sat on the soft matting;
> Another bow;
> Bearing a vase for water now,
> A rich brown triumph of the glazier,
> The master came
> And set it near the brazier
> With deft, slow care; the same
> Measuring steps, a sort of delicate shuffle,
> When next he brought a slender tea jug
> Of much prized white with streaks of sea slug
> And sparks of red as in a pheasant's ruffle,
> And then a bowl
> Whose colours "warm as jade" were young
> When the dynasty was Sung.

He seemed so very simple, even humble,
As he made the minute motions
Of those complicated notions;
Not to falter once or fumble
Showed his thoughts were not of self at all.
More grace than we possessed was needed
As the ceremony quaint proceeded,
But—at length—we sipped the bowl
Where east and west with disparate soul
Do meet, for all the world drinks tea.

When I visited Shizuoka, on the occasion of my second world-tour of the tea countries, in 1924, Mr. Seiichi Ishii composed a Japanese acrostic, which was set to the music of an old folk-song and prettily sung and danced by geisha. Translated, it recites:

"TEA, when analyzed, means the delectable go-between that binds the friendship of Japan and America."

Balzac was the possessor of a limited quantity of a tea that was both unique and fabulously valuable. He never served it to mere acquaintances; rarely even to his friends. This tea had a romantic history. It had been plucked at dewy dawn by young and beautiful virgins who, singing as they went, carried the leaves to the Chinese Emperor. An Imperial gift of the tea had been sent from the Chinese court to the Russian Tsar, and it was through a well-known Russian minister that Balzac received his precious leaves. This golden tea had, moreover, been further baptized, as it were, in human blood during its transfer to Russia; a murderous assault having been made on the caravan that bore it, by a native tribe seeking to seize it. There was also a superstition that more than one cup of this almost sacred beverage was a desecration and would cost the drinker his eyesight. One of Balzac's greatest friends, Laurent-Jan, never drank it without first observing dryly: "Once again I risk an eye, but it's worth it."

Congreve (1670-1729) was the first English writer to associate the terms "tea" and "scandal," in his play, *The Double Dealer,* written in 1694. One of the characters says: "They are at the end of the gallery; retired to their tea and scandal."

The prevailing vogue for tea gave rise to all manner of satires. Sir Richard Steele (1671-1729) wrote a comedy, *The Funeral, or Grief a la Mode,* in which he ridicules the "juice of the tea." One of the characters exclaims: "Don't you see how they swallow gallons of the juice of the tea, while their own dock leaves are trodden under foot?"

Tea as a loosener of female tongues was celebrated by Colley Cibber (1671-1757), the gay

Tea & The Fine Arts

English dramatist and comedian, in these lines from *The Lady's Last Stake:* "Tea! thou soft, thou sober, sage, and venerable liquid, thou female tongue running, smile smoothing, heart opening, wink tipping cordial, to whose glorious insipidity I owe the happiest moments of my life, let me fall prostrate."

There is still extant a copy of a comedy performed at Amsterdam in 1701, and printed the same year, which is entitled *De Thee-Zieke-Juffers,* or *The Tea Smitten Ladies.*

Henry Fielding (1707-54) declared in his first comedy, *Love in Seven Masques*, published about 1720, that "love and scandal are the best sweeteners of tea." About this same time, Dean Swift averred that "the fear of being thought pedants hath taken many young divines off from their severer studies, which they have exchanged for plays, in order to qualify them for the tea table."

Isaac D'Israeli (1766-1848), the English litterateur, in his *Curiosities of Literature* quoted from the *Edinburgh Review* on the subject of tea: "The progress of this famous plant has been something like the progress of truth; suspected at first, though very palatable to those who had courage to taste it; resisted as it encroached; abused as its popularity seemed to spread; and establishing its triumph at last, in cheering the whole land from the palace to the cottage, only by the slow and resistless efforts of time and its own virtues."

Looking back over his past life, Sydney Smith (1771- 1845), divine, essayist, and wit, was moved to exclaim: "Thank God for tea! What would the world do without tea? How did it exist? I am glad I was not born before tea."

Washington Irving (1783-1859) painted a vivid picture of a sumptuous tea table of the early days of New York—then New Amsterdam—in his *Legend of Sleepy Hollow.*

"Tea," wrote De Quincey (1785-1859), "though it is ridiculed by those who are naturally coarse in their nervous sensibilities, or are become so from wine-drinking and are not susceptible of influence from so refined a stimulant, yet it will always be the favorite beverage of the intellectual." Again, he wrote: "Surely everyone is aware of the divine pleasures which attend a wintry fireside: candles at four o'clock, warm hearthrugs, tea, a fair tea maker, shutters closed, curtains flowing in ample draperies to the floor, whilst the wind and the rain are raging audibly without."

Dickens was a tea devotee, though by no means in Dr. Johnson's class. In *Pickwick Papers* (1836-7) he describes a meeting of the Ebenezer Temperance Association at which some of the leading members caused Mr. Weller great alarm by the inordinate amounts of tea they consumed.

Thackeray paid glowing tribute to "the kindly plant" in *Pendennis* (1849-50). He wrote: "What a part of confidante has that poor teapot played ever since the kindly plant was introduced among us! What myriads of women have cried over it, to be sure! What sickbeds it has smoked by! What fevered lips have received refreshment from it! Nature meant very kindly by women when she made the tea plant; and with a little thought, what a series of pictures and groups the fancy may conjure up and assemble round the teapot and cup."

Henrik Ibsen (1828-1906), the Norwegian dramatist and poet, thus lyricizes on tea in *Love's Comedy*:

> HAWK: Far in the dreamy East there grows a plant Whose native home is the Sun's Cousin's garden.
> THE LADIES: Oh, it is tea!
> HAWK: It is.
> THE LADIES: To think of tea!
> HAWK: Its home lies in the Valley of Romance, A thousand miles beyond the wilderness. Fill up my cup. I thank you. Let us hold on tea and love a good tea table talk.

Sir Edwin Arnold (1832-1904), author of *The Light of Asia,* paid a fine tribute to the spiritual aspect of the teacup of the Japanese in one of the longest sentences from his tireless pen: "Insensibly, the little porcelain cup becomes pleasantly linked in the mind with the snow-pure mats, the pretty prostrate *musumes* (serving girls) the spotless joinery of the walls, the exquisite proprieties of the latticed *shojis,* adding to all these a charm, a refinement and distinguished simplicity found alike amid high and low, emanating, as it were from the inner spirit of the glossy leaf and silvery blossom of the tea plant—in one word, belonging essentially to and half constituting beautiful, wonderful, quiet and sweet Japan."

Lafcadio Hearn (1850-1904), the Irish-Greek writer who became a naturalized subject of Japan, was, as he expressed it, only a "humble traveller into the vast and mysterious pleasure ground of Chinese fancy," but the Daruma legend of the origin of the tea plant appealed to him. He made it the theme of his weirdly beautiful "Tradition of the Tea Plant" in *Some Chinese Ghosts*, published in 1887. After describing the penitential severance of his eyelids, which has been popularly ascribed to Daruma, Hearn tells of the wondrous shrub which sprang up from the ground where the eyelids had been cast and tells how, after naming it "Te," the sage spoke to it, saying: "Blessed be thou, sweet plant, beneficent, life giving, formed by the spirit of virtuous resolve! Lo! the fame of thee shall yet spread unto the ends of the earth; and the perfume of thy life be borne unto the uttermost parts by all the winds of heaven! Verily, for all time to come, men who drink of thy sap shall find such refreshment that weariness may not overcome them nor languor seize upon them—neither shall they know the confusion of drowsiness, nor any desire for slumber in the hour of duty or of prayer. Blessed be thou!"

Tea & The Fine Arts

"Nowhere is the English genius of domesticity more notably evidenced than in the festival of afternoon tea," declared George Gissing (1857-1903) in *The Private Papers of Henry Ryecroft*. "One of the shining moments of my day is that when, having returned a little weary from an afternoon walk, I exchange boots for slippers, out-of-doors coat for easy, familiar, shabby jacket, and, in my deep, soft-elbowed chair, await the tea tray.... Now, how delicious is the soft yet penetrating odour which floats into my study, with the appearance of the teapot! What solace in the first cup, what deliberate sipping of that which follows! What a glow does it bring after a walk in chilly rain! The while I look around at my books and pictures, tasting the happiness of their tranquil possession. I cast an eye towards my pipe; perhaps I prepare it, with seeming thoughtfulness, for the reception of tobacco. And never, surely, is tobacco more soothing, more suggestive of humane thoughts, than when it comes just after tea—itself a bland inspirer. ... I care nothing for your five o'clock tea of modish drawing rooms, idle and wearisome like all else in which the world has part; I speak of tea where one is at home in quite another than the worldly sense. To admit mere strangers to your tea table is profanation; on the other hand, English hospitality has here its kindliest aspect; never is friend more welcome than, when he drops in for a cup of tea."

In 1883, Dr. W. Gordon Stables, a Scottish author and M.D., published: *Tea: The Drink of Pleasure and of Health*. The book contains numerous quotations in praise of tea. Among them is one that has appeared in different forms and been credited to different authors. Dr. Stables credits it to Lu Yu, as follows: "Tea tempers the spirits, calms and harmonizes the mind; it arouses thought and prevents drowsiness, lightens and refreshes the body, and clears the perceptive faculties." Arthur Gray, in his *Little Tea Book*, credits it, with slight amplification, quite erroneously, to Confucius. Simpler is the version given by Alfred Franklin in *La Vie Privée* (Paris, 1893), who credits it to Shen Nung's *Pen Tsao*: "It quenches thirst; it lessens the desire for sleep; it gladdens and cheers the heart."

In 1884, Arthur Reade, the author of *Study and Stimulants*, published at London *Tea and Tea Drinking*, a scholarly compilation of references to tea by poets and writers of the old school. In the same year, Samuel Francis Drake of Boston published *Tea Leaves, a history of the stirring events culminating in the Boston Tea Party*.

It has been said that tea drinking fills all the gaps in English novels. An American essayist points out that the technique of such novelists as Mrs. Humphry Ward, Mrs. Oliphant, Mrs. Riddell, Miss Yonge, and even the undomestic Ouida is simply to open the door, and have a neat-handed Phyllis or two men in livery, as the case may be, bring in the tea urn, and everything stops while this immovable feast takes place. Tea is drunk twenty-three times in *Robert Elsmere*, twenty times in *Marcella*, and forty-eight times in *David Grieve*.

The Russian novelists Gogol, Tolstoy and Turgenev were not behind the English writers in filling gaps in their stories with tea drinking; the only difference was that they added

Tea & The Fine Arts

Born in Yokohama in 1862, Okakura Kakuzo interepreted the art spirit of Japan to generations of Westerners via his 1906 book The Book of Tea.

the picturesque background of the steaming brass samovar.

In 1901 there was published anonymously in Calcutta a collection of essays supposedly written by an assistant on a tea estate in Assam. They had appeared previously in the Englishman, and were entitled *Rings from a Chota Sahib's Pipe*, a *chota sahib* being a junior assistant. They are written in humorous vein and possess marked literary flavor.

In 1906, Okakura Kakuzo, founder and first president of the Imperial Academy of Fine Arts at Tokyo and subsequently connected with the Oriental department of the Boston Museum of Fine Arts, published in English *The Book of Tea*, an exquisite volume that has held the interest of Western readers. The author traces the inception and development of teaism, a religion of aestheticism; the evolution of the successive schools of tea; the connection of Taoism and Zennism with tea; and discusses *Chanoyu*, the Japanese Tea Ceremony, as only a gifted writer and artist could treat of a truly aesthetic rite.[8]

May Sinclair, the English poetess and novelist, in *A Cure of Souls* (1924) gives a charming pen-picture of the afternoon tea service. The locale is an English country town where the social life centers in the parish church, the rectory, and the bachelor rector, Canon Chamberlain. Canon Chamberlain is calling on Mrs. Beauchamp, a wealthy and attractive widow, who has only recently taken a house in the parish:

> At that moment the parlor-maid came in, bringing the tea things.[9] There was a flutter of snow-white linen and the pleasant tinkle of china and of silver, and a smell of hot butter.
> He rose.
> "Oh! Don't go just as tea's coming in.... Please stay and have some." ...
> It was, delicious, sitting there in the deep, soft-cushioned chair, eating hot-buttered scones, drinking China tea with the smoky flavour that he loved, and watching the plump, but dainty hands hovering about the teacups and the dishes. Mrs. Beauchamp enjoyed teatime and was determined that he should enjoy it too.
> The teacups—he noticed such things—were wide and shallow and had a pattern of light green and gold on white, with a broad green and gold band inside, under the brim. His nostrils drank in the fragrance.

"I wonder why it is," he said, "that a green lining to a cup makes tea so much more delicious. But it does."

"I know it does," she said with feeling.

"There's a house where they give you strong Indian tea in dark-blue china. You can't imagine anything more horrible."

"It would be."

"And all teacups should be wide and shallow."

"Yes, it's like champagne in wide glasses, isn't it?"

"A larger surface for the scent, I suppose."

"Funny that there should be light green tastes and dark blue tastes, but there are. Only, I didn't think anybody noticed it but me."

Delightful community of sense. And, like himself, she felt that these things were serious.

In a new account of the famous tea controversy between King George III and the American colonists, Hendrik van Loon commented in his *America* (1927): "True enough the tax was very light, only three pennies on the pound, but it was a nuisance, for every time a peaceful citizen made himself a cup of the delectable brew he knew that he was aiding and abetting a law which he felt to be unjust. In the end, the humble teacups (the proverbial scenes of so many storms) provoked a hurricane that was to rock more than one ocean, and all that for an expected annual revenue of only $200,000."

The Dream of the Red Chamber, a curious novel of Chinese life written in English by Tsao Hsiieh-chin and Kao Ngoh, and published in 1929, gives us an idea of what it means to be a real connoisseur of tea. A nun is offering tea to a couple of guests named Black Jade and Precious Virtue: "The matriarch asked her what water it was, and the nun answered that it was rainwater saved from the year before. . .. The nun then took Black Jade and Precious Virtue into another room to make some special tea for them. She poured the tea into two cups of different patterns, of the rare Sung period. Her own cup was of white jade. 'Is this also last year's rainwater?' Black Jade asked. 'I did not think you were so ignorant,' the nun said, as if insulted. 'Can't you tell the difference? This water is from the snow that I collected from the plum trees five years ago, in the Yuan Mu Hsiang Temple. It filled that blue jar there... . All this time it was buried under the earth and was opened only this last summer. How could you expect rainwater to possess such lightness and clarity?'"

Included in William Lyon Phelps's *Essays on Things* (1930) is an "Essay on Tea" containing this pleasant commentary on the English custom of afternoon tea:

"At precisely 4:13 p.m. every day, the average Englishman has a thirst for the astringent taste of tea. He does not care for hot water or hot lemonade colored with tea. He likes his tea so strong that to me it has a hairy flavor.... . There are several good reasons (besides bad coffee) for tea in England. Breakfast is often at nine (the middle of the morning to me), so that early tea is desirable. Dinner is often at eight-thirty, so that afternoon tea is by no means superfluous. Furthermore, of the three hundred and sixty-five days in the year in England, very, very few are warm; and afternoon tea is not only cheerful and sociable, but in most British interiors really necessary to start the blood circulating.

"There are few more agreeable moments in life than tea in an English country house in winter. It is dark at four o'clock. The family and guests come in from the cold air. The curtains are drawn, the open wood fire is blazing, the people sit down around the table and with a delightful meal—for the most attractive food in England is served at afternoon tea—drink of the cheering beverage."

Agnes Repplier published in 1932 a charming book of tea table talk entitled *To Think of Tea,* which records the development of tea drinking in England since the beginning of the practice in the seventeenth century.

Among latter-day British writers Beverley Nichols, author of the *American Sketch,* writes glowingly of tea. J. B. Priestley, in his *English Journey,* bemoans the fact that it should ever be made in slovenly fashion. There is but one dissenter. Bernard Shaw views it with distaste, as might be expected from a confirmed vegetarian and a water-drinker.

There are of course many fugitive and anecdotal references to tea in literature and in the lives of famous writers, actors, and statesmen. A few of the more notable ones follow:

Dr. Johnson always lived up to his reputation as a "shameless tea-drinker." Richard Cumberland, the dramatist, relates an amusing incident which took place in his own home, when Sir Joshua Reynolds ventured to remind Johnson that he had drunk eleven cups of tea. "Sir," replied the doctor, "I did not count your glasses of wine; why, then, should you number my cups of tea?" And then, laughing, he added: "Sir, I should have released the lady from further trouble if it had not been for your remark, but you have reminded me that I want but one of the dozen; I must request Mrs. Cumberland to complete the number."

Both Victor Hugo and Balzac drank tea when working at night, but they found their later slumbers more peaceful if they mixed brandy in it. Longfellow said: "Tea urges tranquillity of the soul." William Ewart Gladstone was a noted tea drinker. He once said that he drank more tea between the hours of midnight and four in the morning than any two members of the House of Commons put together.[10]

John Ruskin not only was a tea drinker, but at one time opened a tea shop in Paddington Street, London, for the purpose of supplying the poor with packets of pure tea as small as

Tea & The Fine Arts

The Tea *by American artist Mary Cassatt. Courtesy of the Museum of Fine Arts, Boston.*

they chose to buy. The well-meant enterprise was not appreciated, however. Ruskin records that it had to be terminated because "the poor only like to buy their tea where it is brilliantly lighted and eloquently ticketed."

Henry Thomas Buckle, the historian, was a most fastidious tea drinker; he insisted that his cup, saucer and spoon be well warmed before the infusion was poured.

NOTES

1. Ukers here means Zen, the Japanese offshoot of Chan Buddhism which had been introduced to China by Bodhidharma (Daruma in Japanese) around 550 CE. Chan or Zen is a transmission of enlightenment outside the scriptures or prescribed observances. The Japanese monk Yeisai brought both Chan Buddhism and tea back to Japan from his sojourn in Chinese monasteries. It was Yeisai who sent Myōe the tea seeds he planted in Uji.

2. As early as 1583, the Dutch trader Jan Huyghen van Linschoten (1563-1611) was busily recording detailed accounts and drawing maps of his Portuguese employer's secret trade routes, navigation, ports of call, cultural observations and possible trade goods of the many countries he visited. When he published *Reys-gheschrift vande navigatien der Portugaloysers in Orienten* (Travel Accounts of Portuguese Navigation in the Orient) in his native Dutch in 1596, his work of espionage broke the nearly century-long maritime trade dominance of the Portuguese.

Nearly sixty years after van Linschoten's 1596 *Orienten*, Olao Worm (Ole Worm), a Danish physician, scientist, and historian with impressive talents in 'natural philosophy' (precursor to modern science), authored a catalog of his walk-in 'Cabinet of Curiosities' published in Latin in 1655 *(Museum Wormianum),* with descriptions and images of wonder to behold: penguin, narwhal, Egyptian sarcophagus, cashews, strawberries, Inca art, tarantulas, pineapples, Chinese luopan (the Feng Shui compass), and perhaps the first tea leaf illustration to be identified as such. He also writes of tea ('Thea') from China as well as Japan, includes instructions for brewing, visual observations of the 'made' leaf, and offers tasting notes. Among other observations noteworthy in Worm's passage on tea, he ascribes the source of the different teas that he writes of as coming from two different plants.

3. A charming canvas, now in The Frick Collection, New York, by Chardin's contemporary in France, the frivolous Francois Boucher (1703-1770) depicts his wife relaxing at home beneath a shelf that displays her dainty tea wares, connoting the status and *a la mode* sophistication befitting the wife of the portraitist of Mme. de Pompadour.

4. Bach spent a lot of time with amateur musicians (often his students) and kept up on the latest trends, which in Saxony in the 1730s meant Baroque instrumental music and coffee, then first filtering down from the ruling class. Every Friday evening, Bach and his students would assemble outside of Gottfried Zimmerman's Café in Leipzig. It was for Zimmerman that Bach composed a special vocal work—the "Coffee Cantata" (Opus BWV 211) which is clearly a lighthearted musical plug for Zimmerman's Cafe and for coffee. The young heroine sings to her old-fashioned father, suspicious of her new-fangled craze, "I've got to have it."

5. Why no tea for two? Ukers strangely omits mention of Vincent Youman's and Irving Caesar's "Tea for Two" from the 1925 Broadway musical, *No, No, Nanette.* This hit song capitalized on the then-current craze for the tango and also for the Tea Dance, an invention of fashionable hotels in London which, like the tango, became popular throughout the UK and US shortly after World War I.

Tea & The Fine Arts

6. In fairness, the Japanese admittedly made pottery before learning from China how to make porcelain. Rikyu and subsequent masters of *chanoyu* inculcated appreciation of the early, unsophisticated wares made by unknown craftsmen in Korea and Japan.

7. Rikyu's shogun sponsor, Hideyoshi, presented the tile maker's family with a seal bearing the Chinese character for "enjoyment," "comfort" or "ease." Now in their fifteenth generation, Kichizaemon XV and the family still proudly handmake the tea wares stamped with the family name awarded them: *Raku*.

8. Okakura Kakuzo was born in the emerging seaport of Yokohama in 1862, eight years after Commodore Matthew Perry's "Black Ships" pried Japan's gates open to international trade. Christian missionaries taught him to speak English and sing Methodist hymns, while Buddhist monks schooled him in Confucianism and the drinking of green tea. Working alongside his teachers at Tokyo University, all of them imported from Harvard and other New England schools, Okakura helped save countless Japanese artistic treasures (now housed in Boston's Museum of Fine Arts) from being tossed aside in favor of modern Western-style objects.

By 1904, Okakura had made his way to Boston, where he became the Director of Asian Arts at the Museum of Fine Arts and the favorite companion of Back Bay society's *grande dame*, Isabella Stewart Gardner. A man with one foot in the East and one foot in the West, he found in tea the perfect metaphor for the spirit which Japanese art expresses. He summarily infused his "cup of humanity" to a Boston culture thirsty for a counterpoint to America's headlong rush into materialism and wealth. Since Okakura published *The Book of Tea* in 1906, it has never been out of print. The work had tremendous influence on Frank Lloyd Wright and Georgia O'Keeffe, to name only two of the countless artists and teaists who have been inspired to infuse *teaism* into their lives.

9. Jane Austen used the term "tea things" in her novels as well. The Regency period writer often used tea as a literary tool to bring the sexes together, and "tea things" were frequently employed to set the stage for conversation. In *Sense and Sensibility*, Elinor attends a social gathering at Lady Middleton's, eager to have a chat with Lucy, but "the insipidity of the meeting was exactly such as Elinor had expected; it produced not one novelty of thought or expression; and nothing could be less interesting than the whole of their discourse both in the dining-parlour and drawing room … they quitted it only with the removal of the tea things."

The ceremonial brewing of the tea took place in the drawing room. A servant would carry in all the tea equipage and any food to be offered but would leave the lady or daughter of the house to brew and serve the tea. In *Mansfield Park*, Austen wrote: "The next opening of the door brought something more welcome; it was the tea things … Susan and an attendant girl … brought in everything necessary for the meal.…"

10. William Gladstone (1809–1898) served as British Prime Minister on four separate occasions and was Britain's oldest Prime Minister when he resigned for the final time at age 84. His contribution to tea literature is this perfect description of tea's most immediate benefits:

> *If you are cold, tea will warm you;*
> *If you are too heated, it will cool you;*
> *If you are depressed, it will cheer you;*
> *If you are excited, it will calm you.*

A Lipton tea taster at work evaluating teas in the company's San Francisco cupping room, c.1930.

THE SHINING HOUR OF THE DAY

The shining hour is the teatime hour. In England and America, it may be celebrated as an afternoon tea festival; or it may have a more intimate connotation. It may be, as it is for many tea lovers, the hour when, in the company of a friend or alone, we loaf and invite our souls.

Before proceeding with a discussion on the preparation of the beverage it may be illuminating to look into the chemistry and pharmacology of tea and so learn something of its healthfulness. It wasn't until about the turn of the present century that scientific studies of the chemistry of tea began to assume some definite form. Since then considerable progress has been made, but our knowledge of the subject is still incomplete and vague.

In recent years, much earnest work has been done by British, Dutch, Japanese, and Chinese chemists at experimental stations in the tea growing districts, but little of consequence has been accomplished with the beverage itself in the countries where it is most favored. Perhaps after all, at least in so far as tea drinkers themselves are concerned, it isn't required. The normal person drinks tea because he finds it a pleasant drink. He needs no pseudo-scientific argument to make him want to continue its use. Tea, like good wine, needs no bush. But that doesn't appeal to the hard-pressed copywriter looking for new angles for advertising tea. Recently Americans were astonished to learn that there was a sex urge in tea. How our grandmothers would have been scandalized! But it was just another copy man's aphrodisiac treatment of the subject.

In an age where debunking is the order of the day, an American debunker has said: "People are no longer misled by impressive scientific-looking statements about animal experiments or by pictures of gentlemen in white coats peering through microscopes." And that goes for tea. An English writer summed it up when he said: "I do not drink tea to cure the Willies, nor do I imbibe it as a mildly stimulating drug. No, I drink tea because I find it a pleasant drink—just that; and were I not a perfect gentleman I would join with James Joyce's old mother Grogan and say that 'when I makes tea I makes tea and when I makes water I makes water.' As admirable a piece of straight reasoning as one could ever wish to encounter."

Dr. C. R. Harler, former chemist of the Indian Tea Association, has published some findings on the chemical changes taking place in the manufacture of black and green teas and on the pharmacology of tea. His scientific conclusions in regard to the manufacturing processes are chiefly interesting to those engaged in the industry, but anyone who drinks tea cannot fail to be interested in his conclusions regarding the use of tea as a beverage.

"Arguments used against the healthfulness of tea," says Dr. Harler, "are frequently founded on the experience of individuals or on the assumption that tea is taken in excess. Tea is the beverage of people in many parts of the world, living in every kind of climate. Although the general use of tea cannot, in itself, be used as an argument in favor of its healthfulness, nevertheless, it indicates that tea has a very general appeal."

In China, where tea drinking started, the four hundred odd million inhabitants drink about two pounds per capita, while the people of the United Kingdom, which adopted the custom centuries after, drink about five times as much. Why the difference? It cannot be charged altogether against the moist English climate, for Australia and New Zealand, which are hot and dry, consume about the same amount. In India the Englishman prefers hot tea and the native Indian has lately been taking to it in increasing quantities. Of course, patriotism may have had something to do with the popularity of tea among the English and the Dutch, tea being colonial sources of great wealth in both instances, and that also applies to China and Japan. But these reasons do not explain the use of tea in Germany, France, Russia, the United States, and South America. We must seek deeper for the essential causes. We shall find them in the pleasure the beverage gives and the health it promises. Tea is consumed for its warmth, easy digestibility, piquant flavor and aroma, its gentle stimulation of the nervous and muscular system, and the easy repose which it promotes.

Other scientific conclusions reached by Dr. Harler in reviewing experiments in British India and in Holland are as follows:

A cup of tea contains, on the average, a little under a grain of caffeine and about two grains of tannin. The medical dose of caffeine suggested in the British Pharmaceutical Codex is 1 to 5 grains and of tannin 5 to 10 grains. It will be realized, therefore, that in the average cup of tea these two most important constituents of tea are present in very small amounts, especially when it is remembered that the caffeine is injected gradually and the tannin is fixed by proteins during its journey through the alimentary tract. The tea infusion is faintly acid, almost neutral. The gastric juice is at least a thousand times as acid as tea.

The Shining Hour of The Day

A tea taster samples imported teas for quality and adulterations in this 1924 photo. The U.S. Board of Tea Examiners office was in operation from 1893 until 1993.

When milk is added to tea, the tannin is fixed by the casein in the milk. Sugar added to the tea merely sweetens it and adds to the value of the drink as a food. The addition of milk to tea robs it of practically all its astringency.

When the infusion is drunk, it passes first into the stomach, where the sugars are absorbed as ordinary foods, and the ingestion of caffeine begins. The comforting effect of the warmth of the drink is at once felt, but the stimulus due to the caffeine comes about a quarter of an hour later.

The compound of tannin and casein may be digested like any other coagulated protein, and the free tannin thus liberated passes into the smaller intestine, where it exhibits a mildly astringent action.

Although many people are opposed to tea drinking on account of the tannin content, small though it be, this constituent with its fermented products is such an essential to the beverage

The Shining Hour of the Day

Scientific studies touting tea's healthy attributes became a marketing strategy for tea in the 1930s.

that a tannin-free tea is difficult to imagine. In the same way, the stimulus from the caffeine is such an essential, that caffeine-free tea would make no appeal to tea drinkers.

Tea is something more than a beverage. It is an adjuvant food. It promotes appetite, and good digestion waits on appetite. Men and women drink tea because it adds to their sense of well-being. It not only smells good and tastes good, but it at once stimulates and refreshes.

Like all good things in life tea drinking may be abused. Indeed, those having an idiosyncratic susceptibility to alkaloids should be temperate in the use of tea, coffee, or cocoa. Generally speaking, children do not require them.

In every high-tensioned country there is likely to be a small number of people who, because of certain individual characteristics, cannot drink tea at all; they are caffeine sensitives. These belong to the abnormal minority of the human family. Some people cannot eat strawberries; but that would not be a valid reason for a general condemnation of strawberries. One may be poisoned from too much food. Overfeeding causes most of our ills. Over-indulgence in meat is likely to spell trouble for the strongest of us. Tea is, perhaps, less often abused than wrongly accused. It all depends. A little more tolerance!

So many things that are not so have been published about tea, as about coffee, that it would be illuminating to assemble the best answers to such intolerances as have persisted since the early days of the beverage. As it is, we must content ourselves here with a few notable observations by authorities who ought to know whereof they speak when tea is the subject. From the march of tea:

Early Chinese and Japanese writers celebrated many of tea's virtues, not the least among which were that it promoted wakefulness; that it made for sobriety; that it "superimposed the six passions"; and that it was in itself a complete medicine chest, because it was a specific for practically all the ills that flesh is heir to. Travelers, historians, the literati, priests, and medical men rang the changes on these ideas for over a thousand years.

The Shining Hour of The Day

In the seventeenth century tea was highly acclaimed in England as a remedy for colds. It still is. In 1702 Dr. Louis Lemery, Regent Doctor of the Faculty of Physic, Paris, pronounced tea a wholesome drink, and added: "It agrees at all times with any age and constitution."

In 1842 Baron Justus von Liebig, the distinguished German chemist, hailed tea as a "liver food."

The London Lancet was the first to stress the psychological value of tea, in 1863. The battle of life produces in us moods of frustration—feelings under the influence of which the bodily tissues wear out rapidly. Tea, the *Lancet* said, "has a strange influence over mood, a strange power of changing the look of things, and changing it for the better, so that we can believe and hope and do under the influence of tea what we should otherwise give up in discouragement and despair." Thus, it becomes the servant of civilization, after having already figured in the history of Europe as the savior of civilization.

It was Dr. W. Gordon Stables, of London, who, in 1883, announced that he found tea more cooling, calming, and invigorating than wine.

In 1884 Professor Edward A. Parkes, of London, hailed tea as the drink par excellence of the soldier on service.

The caffeine in tea was found to lessen the waste of tissue by William B. Marshall, of the United States Museum, in 1903.

In 1904, Sir Jonathan Hutchinson, M.D., F.R.C.S., of London, declared tea a "nerve nutrient."

In 1905 Dr. George F. Shrady, of New York, pictured tea as the machine-age tranquillizer.

Dr. Woods Hutchinson was one of the first to announce the value of tea as an adjuvant food, in 1907.

Referring to the stamina displayed by the armies of opposing nations of tea drinkers during the war in Manchuria, Captain Carl Reichmann, of the United States Army, observed, in 1908, that tea was the ideal "stuff to feed the troops."

Dr. C. W. Saleeby, M.D., F.R.S., of Edinburgh, is one of the strongest advocates of tea among the medical profession. In 1908 he acclaimed it as "a pure stimulant with no second stage of depression," and later hailed it as a "good Samaritan."

"It's good for the aged," said Dr. George M. Niles, Professor of Physiology in the Southern College of Pharmacy, at Atlanta, Georgia, in 1912, and the announcement added greatly to the comfort and cheer of millions of elderly persons who had long since proved it so.

Scores of medical men in many civilized countries have from time to time confirmed the findings of their fellows as to the healthfulness of tea. In 1927 Sir James Crichton-Browne, M.D., of London, called it "the great consoler," and "the best of cocktails;" in 1928 Dr. Arthur L. Holland, of New York, famous stomach specialist, said that it wasn't true, as had so long been alleged, that tea produced an acid condition in the stomach; and in 1930 Dr. Hugh A. McGuigan, pharmacologist of Chicago, announced that, of all things, tea actually promoted slenderness, because it lessened the sense of hunger and so prevented overeating.

When approaching the subject of the proper preparation of tea as a beverage it is necessary to take into consideration the local background. For example, the most popular method of making tea in England is not necessarily to be recommended for Americans, any more than it should be thought that the manner of making coffee most favored in Brazil is best for Americans—because it is not.

We have seen how the tea drink was made and served in the beginning, and how it is prepared in the principal tea consuming countries today. Now let us examine briefly what science and epicureanism have indicated is the best procedure to obtain the cup that cheers in the two great English-speaking countries, Great Britain and the United States; for here, in the last analysis, tea manners and customs are to be found at their best among the Caucasian peoples. Let us not be surprised to find that considerations of climate and national characteristics indicate one thing for England and something quite different for America.

My friend Dr. Harler says it's hard to define "tea goodness." The connoisseur drinks tea for its delicate flavor and aroma and for him the stimulating and comforting qualities are secondary factors. On the other hand, the settler in the back blocks of Australia who is, perhaps, the world's heaviest tea drinker, cares little for the finer qualities of the beverage, to judge by the way in which he makes his tea. It is common in these places to put the tea in a billy-can and let it stew. This process produces a stimulating, strong, thick liquor, but one lacking all the subtleties of a carefully prepared infusion. Quite different from the tea made by the lonely colonial is that drunk, at all hours of the day, in China and Japan. In these countries, the brew is usually so weak that the beverage becomes little more than a thirst-quencher.

In the British Isles, Australasia, North America and Holland, where most of the black tea of India, Ceylon and Java is consumed, the beverage is drunk primarily for its stimulating effect and then for the peculiar sour-harsh taste or pungency given by the astringent tannin and tannin compounds which are present in a black tea infusion. This taste becomes palatable by use. The alkaloid caffeine, responsible for the stimulus in tea, has a slightly bitter taste when taken in medicinal quantities, but the small amount present in the usual cup of tea is practically tasteless.

The Shining Hour of The Day

Caffeine taken in small doses increases mental and muscular power and has no after, depressant effect on the system. Tannin in large doses has a deleterious effect on the mucous membrane of the mouth and on the alimentary canal, but in the amount present in a cup of carefully made tea its harmful effect is negligible.

The ideal preparation of tea, then, is one which extracts a maximum of caffeine and a not excessive amount of tannin. Such a preparation also conserves the aroma and flavor—evanescent qualities easily lost by careless preparation.[1]

Tea may be served for breakfast, luncheon, dinner, or supper, but its particular place in the American dietary would seem to be in the afternoon, say about four o'clock, when it will be found a most refreshing drink to relieve fatigue at home or in the office or factory, to promote efficiency and carry one's workday through to a happy and successful conclusion. Its magical properties also recommend it to the hostess as a social custom tried and proved in England and certain to become the socially correct thing in America.

In conclusion: Be modest, be kind, eat less and think more, live to serve, work and play and laugh and love—it is enough! Do this and you may drink tea without danger to your immortal soul.

NOTES

1. The list of beneficial compounds discovered in a cup of tea has expanded tremendously since Ukers' day. Studies indicate that drinking tea promotes an 'attentive serenity' energy boost which can be conducive to meditation or conversation; that it combats the growth of cancer cells, improves blood sugar and digestion, fights diabetes and weight gain, improves cholesterol balance and blood pressure, circulation, heart and brain health. Tea is an important part of a healthy diet, but some conditions may be improved by certain teas more than others. Today's best medical advice suggests drink plenty of tea of several types. Camellia sinensis is undoubtedly humankind's most benign plant ally.

A Chinese tea vendor dispenses hot water from an oversized teapot on the street in Shanghai, c.1890.

TIMELINE OF TEA HISTORY
James Norwood Pratt

Before Common Era (BCE)

4100 — Bronze made in Armenia is first metal hard enough to hold an edge. Earliest known wine-making also occurs in Armenia.

4000 — Chinese cultivation of both long and short grain rice is already well established.

2737 — According to a book of ancient lore compiled during the Three Kingdom Era (220-65 CE) the legendary emperor Shen Nung discovered tea this year, about the time of the Biblical Moses. Other Chinese legends attribute the origin of tea to individuals like Gan Lu or Bodhidharma well after the time of Christ. Ethnic peoples in Yunnan and south China have legends of their own about tea originating in dim antiquity as a culture hero's discovery or as a gift from a deity.

c.1500 — Aryan people from the Eurasian steppes lead herds of cattle and flocks of sheep into India and begin to take over, eventually codifying wisdom traditions in the Vedas (800-600 BCE) and inaugurating veneration of the cow and milk products in most of India. Egyptian civilization slowly approaches its crescendo with Ramses II (1279-1213).

1046 — A history written later in 350 CE describes the victory in 1046 BCE by which King Wu established the Zhou dynasty. Mair and others think at this time Sichuanese offered the first tea tribute to the Emperor, depending on how an archaic character is interpreted. Native to the Yunnan/Sichuan region, tea was first cultivated as a crop in Sichuan.

551 — Birth of Confucius (K'ung-fu-tzu 551-479), traditionally considered a contemporary of Lao-tzu (Laozi, dates unknown).

528 — Buddhism has its beginnings in north India, where Prince Siddhartha Gautama at age 35 finds enlightenment at Bodhgaya near Benares. The Enlightened One ("Buddha") promulgates his teachings throughout the Ganges Valley for the next 45 years. The Buddha's marvelous century was a time when enlightenment sprouted around the world with Confucius in China, Zoroaster in Persia, Pythagoras in Greece, and notable Hebrew prophets.

490	First mention of tea in cooking appears in Yan's *Stories of the Chun Qiu Period*.
330	Alexander the Great of Macedon conquers Persia, sacks Persepolis, and in the next year takes Samarkand in Central Asia, the furthest extent of his Greek-governed empire. First statues of the Buddha are made by Greek-influenced artists in Afghanistan.
221-207	Ch'in (Qin) gives his name to China by becoming the first Emperor (Huang-di) after 25 years of fighting to unify the country. While Hannibal crosses the Alps and invades Italy in Europe, the 14 year-long dynasty of Qin and son sees the Great Wall partially completed along with lesser projects like the just-excavated tomb at Xian. Under the Qin, Sichuan tea, probably drunk as a tonic, enters mainstream Chinese life; tea cultivation begins to spread down the Yangzi from Sichuan.
165-160	Tea is found in the ancient Ma Wang Dui tomb of this date.
100	Silk Road brings China new crops—alfalfa, grapes, cucumbers, peas, pomegranates and walnuts—from the Mediterranean and Central Asia. Soon Rome begins receiving Chinese silks, ceramics and lacquer wares. By the time of Augustus (27 BCE-14 CE), Rome's poet laureate Horace calls Chinese by the name latin name "Seres."

Common Era (CE)

c.50	Tea buying is first documented in *Directions to a Sevant,* a satire by Wang Pao stipulating his tea has to come from near Chengdu in Sichuan. He writes around the time the Emperor Nero is persecuting early Christians in Rome and the Emperor of China is receiving the first emissaries from Japan.
168	Tea Ridge (Chaling, still pronounced *tu-ling*) County is established in Hunan, evidence of major tea growing halfway down the Yangzi from its most ancient areas of cultivation in Sichuan. Tea growing soon extends to the coast.
220	During reign of the Western Han dynasty emperor Xuan, the Buddhist monk Wu Lizhen is later said to have planted "seven fairy tea trees" on Mengdingshan in Sichuan. This legendary monk is commemorated more than 1200 years later when the Song dynasty emperor Xiaozong awards him the title Gan Lu, Master Sweet Dew.
c.265	Poem by Da Yu, China's first poet to praise tea, hails "a marvelous plant from magnificent mountains." Zhang Yi's book *Guang Ya* describes how to make tea cakes and use them with ginger and green onion in a drink.

Timeline of Tea

c.270	As recorded in the *History of Three Kingdoms* (San Guo Zhi), Emperor Sun Hao (232-283) serves guests tea instead of alcohol. Although sometimes used as a beverage, tea's main use for three centuries to come is for medicinal and healing purposes.
350	The great scholar Guo Po compiles a Chinese encyclopedia, *Erh Ya,* which defines tea as a beverage and a tribute paid to emperors. Incorporating very ancient material, this work is the first to describe tea cultivation and preparation of the beverage. Ealier, a Chinese contemporary of Constantine, the first Christian Emperor of Rome, builds a Buddhist monastery on Lushan, where he presumably propagates Lushan Yunwu, the "cloud-mist" tea celebrated ever since by China's seekers and poets.
c.390	Tastes evolve in the later Wei dynasty as people of the southern border areas make tea into cakes to be ground into powder later for infusing. Just as Christian monasteries grow famous for their wines in Europe, the names of nearly all early teas are associated with Buddhist mountain retreats. The great up-surge of Buddhism in China, which begins in the mid-300's and lasts until the reign of the Empress Wu Tse-tien (690-705), converts China into a tea drinking society. Tea culture finally outgrows its ancient hermit and herbalist origins as tea becomes a prized commodity produced for the faithful by monastic communities. The proverb arose "Ch'an (Zen) and Cha (tea) have one same taste." Farmers begin growing tea to sell.
476	First record of China tea bartered to Turkish people across the Mongolian border. In centuries to come, even Arabs and Persians will sometimes obtain China tea through peoples of Central Asia.
581-618	Sui dynasty again unifies China and sees tea, spread by Buddhists, becoming widely used as a social beverage. Emperor Sui Wen cures his hangovers with tea.
593/622	Japan begins absorbing Chinese culture and Buddhism.
610	China's Grand Canal—1100 miles long, 100 feet wide, with roads along both banks—is completed, joining the Yangzi and Yellow Rivers and connecting north and south China.
618-907	Tang dynasty sees largest expansion of Chinese rule across Central Asia. It is considered the Golden Age of Chinese culture.
632	Mohammed's *Hegira* from Mecca becomes the founding date of monotheistic Islam, a faith which forbids alcohol but has blessed the drinking of tea.
640	Tibet's first tea arrives when Wen-cheng, daughter of the founder of China's Tang dynasty, marries the King of Tibet. This royal marriage of cultures is baptized in tea, which soon becomes Tibet's principal import and article of trade, thus inaugurating the "Southern Tea Route." Tibet still imports South Route Teas from Yunnan and Sichuan.

Timeline of Tea

676	Korea's first tea is brought to a newly-united Silla kingdom from Tiantai Temple in Zhejiang by Tang Buddhist monks. Earlier Korea-China cultural exchanges date to the 400s.
725	*Cha*, the character for tea, first appears in a Chinese dictionary. Obviously, the term had long been used by Buddhists and farmers in the countryside and now finally reaches the urban literati. This dictionary entry probably follows widespread adoption of this rustic term.
771	Emperor Tang Dai Zong decrees establishment of first imperial tea garden near Yixing. This emperor later befriends Lu Yu.
780	Lu Yu (733-804), an orphan prodigy raised by Zen monks, publishes the *Chajing* or *Classic of Tea,* the world's first book on tea, which he began in 758. Lu Yu gave the literate urban elite the word—cha—to signify one single sort of drink from one single source producing one certain effect. His Chajing is a hymn of praise beginning "Tea is the most wonderful tree growing in the south." Lu Yu is soon considered tea's patron saint as tea grows popular not merely as a medicinal or even spiritual drink but as a luxury and, ultimately, a daily necessity. In Lu Yu's time, tea leaf was processed by steaming leaf to be dried and compressed into cakes. To prepare tea, the cake was crumbled, ground fine and boiled briefly. Spoiling good tea through imperfect preparation is a sin, Lu Yu says, or at least a crime.
805	Tea seeds are brought to Japan from China by Denyo Daishi (in life called "Saicho" 767-822) upon his return from studying Buddhism at China's Tiantai Temple. Saicho's tea dies out but his teachings of Tendai Buddhism last to this day.
815	Japan's Emperor Saga, inspired by Saicho, orders tea cultivation in five provinces near the capital. This was a false start for, within a few generations, tea is forgotten in Japan.
c.830	*Hints on Water Used for Making Tea* (Jian Cha Shui Ji), a book by Zhang You-xin, discusses the different types of water suitable for making tea. He concludes the best water is generally that from the area where the specific tea grows. *Shui Liu Tong Pin* written by Su Yi at the close of the Tang dynasty also discusses waters and skills required to prepare tea.
c.850	*Drawings Illustrating Tea Picking* by Wen Ting-yun (812-870) records how the famous poet and high official Bai Yuyi (772-846) used to drink tea to sober up. Sulieman's *Account of Tea* in Arabic becomes the first report of tea to the non-Chinese world. According to legend, the goatherd Khaidi in southern Ethiopia was led by his goats to discover *kahve* or coffee about this time. Strange claim, as coffee drinking is neither mentioned nor recorded until after 1450.

Timeline of Tea

900	England receives spices from Asia for the first time since Roman days 500 years earlier. Spices in Europe are used mainly as medicines. Europe's imports from Asia mostly flowed through Constantinople to Venice.
1060	*Tea Record* (Cha Lu), China's second comprehensive tea book in line of succession after the *Chajing*, is written by Song dynasty official Cai Xiang (1012-1067). Cai describes the method of preparing tea by grinding the leaf into a fine powder and whipping it into a froth in hot water using a fine bamboo whisk. Cai describes wares for whisked tea and new imperial tribute teas from his home province of Fujian. The teahouse is a Song dynasty creation.
1071	Venice is the first European city to use forks at meals, a skill learned from a Byzantine princess who marries the Doge and brings the practice with her from Constantinople, where forks have long been customary. It will take another 400 years before forks are used beyond the Alps.
1100-26	The reign of Song Huizong, "poet-Emperor" and last of the Northern Song dynasty, who wrote his *Treatise on Tea* (Da Guan Cha Lun) detailing enjoyment of tea. A gifted artist, husband to 3912 wives and concubines, and the leading tea lover of his day, Huizong died in exile as a prisoner of nomadic Jurchen invaders, far from his beautiful capital of Hangzhou.
1191	Zen Buddhist Yeisai (posthumously named "Senko-Sochi" 1141-1215) brings Ch'an and Cha—Zen and tea—home with him from China to Japan, establishing Rinzai Zen and re-introducing tea in Japan. In 1211 Yeisai writes the first Japanese tea book, *Treatise on Tea Drinking to Preserve Health,* and wins the shogun's patronage.
1200	Buddhist monk Myōe plants tea seeds (given to him by Yeisai) near Kyoto at Togano. Chinese culture and traditions begin to permeate Japan and tea is closely associated with Buddhist spirituality. Tea is finally planted in Uji around 1400.
1215	Genghis Khan (1162-1227) captures Beijing, eastern-most capital city of an empire that eventually stretches to Budapest and Warsaw. From end to end, the Silk Road is now under a single ruler.
1225	Japanese Buddhist Dogen achieves enlightenment at a Zen monastery on Mt. Tientai in China. He brings Soto Zen and the *Luohan Gong Cha* tradition home with him to Japan's Eihei-ji temple.
1241	Hanseatic League of trading cities surrounding the Baltic Sea founded in North Europe.
1270	Kublai Khan overthrows the Southern Song dynasty in 1270, proclaims the Mongol Yuan dynasty and proceeds to conquer all China. It was a Southern Song writer who listed tea, along with rice and vinegar, among the seven daily necessities of Chinese life.

Timeline of Tea

1294   Marco Polo returns to Italy after his epic 24-year journey to China where he lived for two decades. Taken prisoner by Genoa, then at war with his native Venice, he dictates his travel memoirs to a cellmate without mentioning at all the tea in China—a puzzling omission.

1313   A book on agriculture by Chinese scholar Wang Zhen mentions loose leaf tea for the first time in listing three types of tea: loose leaf, powdered and "wax tea" (*lacha*), which was the most expensive but only made as imperial tribute tea.

1348   Having devastated Europe, the Black Death finally ends, leaving two-thirds of the population dead.

1368   Ming Hongwu founds Ming dynasty after anti-Mongol revolts, starting around 1350, liberate much of China.

1391   Emperor Ming Hongwu decrees that loose leaf tea, not cake tea, is to be paid as an imperial tribute, greatly accelerating improvements in processing loose tea.

1473   In Japan, Shogun Yoshimasa retires and becomes the patron of the early Tea Ceremony and of Murata Shuko (1423-1502), its first promulgator, who cultivates a taste for "cold and withered" style of simplicity.

1492   Columbus discovers the New World. Old World's first teapots are produced in Yixing, Jiangsu, of unglazed stoneware. Artists, tea lovers and potters begin collaborating on *gongfu* teapot design.

1502   Portuguese seafarers become the first Europeans to reach Asia by sea. They land in Cochin, India, in 1502, the islands of Indonesia by 1512, and Guangzhou, China, in 1517. In China, the Portuguese introduce maize, peanuts and sweet potatoes, which are adopted more quickly than in Europe. China acquires her first cannons from Portuguese; in 1521 the Ming forbid foreign trade.

1541   *Cha Pu,* Ming dynasty tea book by Gu Yuan-qing, becomes the major description of loose leaf tea from manufacture to preparation. Over 100 works on tea were written between Lu Yu's day and the sequel to the *Chajing* by Lu Ting-can written about 1700. Taken together, these untranslated books represent a trove of historical and cultural wealth probably unparalleled outside China.

1557   Macao is ceded to the Portuguese as an enclave on China's mainland, to remain a Portuguese possession until 1999. Macao was considered principally valuable as a way-station en route to Japan, which the Portuguese first reached in 1543.

1559   In Europe, tea is first mentioned by Giovanni Ramusio of Venice, who collects reports from abroad. He records a hear-say account of the cultivation,

Timeline of Tea

preparation and pleasures of tea in *Voyages and Journeys* (Navigazione e Viagi)i. Portuguese Jesuit Gaspar de la Cruz writes about his years as a missionary in Japan and publishes the first mention of tea in Portuguese in 1560, confessing himself a tea lover also. Later, Portuguese Jesuits in Japan continued to practice *chanoyu*.

1578   In Tibet, the title of Dalai Lama is bestowed on abbots of Lhasa's principal monasteries by the Mongol Alta Khan at Lake Kokonor. The then abbot became the third Dalai Lama since the title was posthumously bestowed on his two previous incarnations. Mongols receive Ming permission to purchase tea direct from China again after 200 years of relying on Tibetan traders for tea.

1584   In America, Sir Walter Raleigh plants England's first colony on Roanoke Island, North Carolina, later dubbed "The Lost Colony."

1585   In Japan, warlord Hideyoshi serves tea to the Emperor, a great honor for Hideoshi's tea master Rikyu, now established as the foremost tea practitioner in Japan.

1587   Hideoshi commands a Japan-wide tea gathering at Kitano presided over by Rikyu. All tea people, whether samurai, townspeople, peasant farmers or even Chinese, are invited without regard to social distinctions. More than 800 guests have tea together in one day.

1591   Japan's culture hero who perfected and popularized *Chado* or the "Way of Tea," Sen no Rikyu (1521-1591) commits *seppuku* or ritual suicide by order of his patron Hideyoshi.

1595   In England, tea (*cha*) is first heard of in an English language translation of Dutch navigator Jan Huyghen van Linschoten's *Travel Accounts of Portuguese Navigation in the Orient*. Linschoten's descriptions inspire Dutch and English to covet the rich Portuguese trade and possessions in Asia. Holland sends 14 ships to India in 1598.

The Seventeenth Century

1600   England's Queen Elizabeth the Great charters the Honorable East India Company (EIC) on New Year's Eve granting it a complete monopoly on all English trade with Asia. This same year smugglers circumvent the Arabian monopoly on coffee growing by taking seeds, seven unroasted coffee berries, from the Arabian port of Mocha to south India where they thrive and quickly multiply.

1601	In China, Matteo Ricci, Italian Jesuit, moves to Beijing and publishes, in Chinese, an *Atlas of the World*, astonishing the emperor and court. Ricci becomes influential among Chinese intelligentsia.
1602	Holland's Vereenigde Oostindische Compagnie (VOC), modeled on the British EIC (EIC), is founded and takes over Dutch interests recognized in Java since 1596. The Dutch gradually establish themselves in India, Sri Lanka, Japan, Africa and elsewhere.
1610	Holland imports Europe's first tea. This green tea from Japan arrives in Amsterdam on a VOC ship from Java. Having no direct access to China, VOC acquires China goods in Java. In 1611 Japan grants VOC privilege of a trading post on Hirado island, up the coast from Nagasaki.
1618	In Russia, emissaries return from China with a gift for the Czar, the first tea ever tasted in Russia.
1623	In Japan, the first annual ceremonial "Tea Journey" is inaugurated by Shogun Iyemitsu to bring tribute tea from Uji to Tokyo.
1624	In Taiwan, Dutch ship *Zeelandia* lands and establishes a fortified port sheltered from typhoons. The port is ruled by 12 Dutch governors in succession until Qing China conquers Taiwan in 1683. In 1626, the Dutch acquire another island, Manhattan, and plant a colony that is later lost to the British in 1664.
1637	Europe's first regular imports begin as tea "begins to come into use" by the Dutch and the VOC's "Lords Seventeen" order "Some jars of Chinese as well as Japanese teas with every ship." Only wealthy Europeans ever drink tea, doing so mainly for therapeutic reasons as it is primarily sold in pharmacies.
1638	German diplomat Albrecht von Mandelslo, returning from Persia and Gujarat, reports that drinking tea in those lands is commonplace. They obtained China tea both by Silk Route and by sea.
1647	Peter Stuyvesant, a director of the Dutch East India Company, arrives in New Amsterdam on Manhattan Island to serve as governor. His household goods include teapots, teacups and other tea wares—the first to appear in the New World.
1652	Chinese Ming loyalist and Zen monk Ingen flees to Japan. At the Obaku temple at Uji he produces loose leaf tea and introduces Japan to the use of the teapot and the steeped tea enjoyed in Ming China. Baisao (1675-1763), an Obaku monk, will much later become famous as the old tea seller of Kyoto who popularizes sencha.
1657-58	In England, tea is first sold at Garraway's Coffee House the same year London's first chocolate house opens with "an excellent West India drink… where you may have it ready at any time, and also unmade." England's first advertisement of tea

Timeline of Tea

	(available from Garraway's) appears in September in a paper announcing Cromwell's death.
1660-62	England's Restoration of the monarchy overthrows the Puritan Commonwealth and installs the Merrie Monarch Charles II. A tea drinker himself, he marries the tea drinking Portuguese Princess Catherine of Braganza in 1662. England finds tea smart, royal and expensive. The diarist Pepys first drinks "a Cupp of Tee" (a China drink) …" in 1662. The first poem on tea in English is written by one of Catherine's favorites, court poet Edmund Waller. Tea is a luxury confined to aristocrats and privileged Londoners.
1669	English EIC imports its first tea, 140 pounds in all, procured through Java and intended chiefly as a gift to King Charles II and Queen Catherine.
1670	England's first known silver tea pot is given to EIC directors by Lord Berkeley. France's first café opens on Paris' Left Bank. Café Procope, serving coffee as well as wines, sherbets, and sweetmeats, becomes the haunt of generations of writers, from Racine to Voltaire and the revolutionaries. By 1700, Paris will have over 300 cafés but none that serve tea.
1679	EIC gluts the London market with 5000 pounds of tea and holds its first tea auction on March 11.
1680 I	In Scotland, The Duchess of York, wife of the future James II and London court sophisticate, introduces the custom of serving tea to the Scots.
1684	In China, English EIC is allowed a trading post alongside other foreigners at Canton. In Java Dr. Andrew Cleyer (VOC) grows tea plants and sends a German colleague the first drawing of the plant ever seen in Europe. It is published in 1685 in Brandenburg as *True Depiction of the Fruit Tea*.
1685	Qing Emperor Kangxi (1661-1722) restricts all European trading activities to Canton and closes all of China's other ports to foreign trade. His decree remains in effect until 1841, making Canton with its onerous co-hong system Europe's only legal access to China, except for Portuguese Macao. The Dutch are not allowed trading privileges in Canton until 1729.
1689	England imports tea direct from China for the first time and her thirst grows. Tea is no longer drunk primarily for health but is now sold, as in Holland, in grocery stores in larger cities, where the upper crust increasingly enjoys it simply as a stimulating drink.
	By treaty Russia and China establish an entrepôt for caravan trade at a border crossing a 16-month trek from Moscow. Every fourth year a Russian caravan is allowed to enter Beijing.
1698	In France, sparkling Champagne is invented at the Abbey d'Hautvilliers by the 60-year-old blind Benedictine Dom Pierre Perignon who remains the Abbey's cellar master until 1715.

The Eighteenth Century

1700 — France welcomes her first ship home from China, the *Amphitrite,* loaded with tea and other commodities. Vienna has four coffeehouses and soon will have ten. This year England consumes 20,000 pounds of tea. Almost all European countries have competing East India Companies. Even Denmark acquires a port in India (which it holds until 1845).

c.1700 — National preferences for tea in Holland and England and coffee in France become entrenched due to recent history. France under Louis XIV was at war with Holland and England in 1672-1679 and again from 1689-1697. France cut off trade at the very time Holland was Europe's leading importer of tea. At the same time Holland and England were cut off from coffee imports via the Mediterranean, which France controlled.

1702 — England receives first EIC ship fully-laden with tea. England consumed 66,738 pounds of tea in 1701; by 1730 EIC imports will pass one million pounds. England's surging demand for tea (plus cocoa and coffee) creates increased demand for slave-produced sugar from Caribbean colonies.

1708 — In Europe, porcelain or "china" ware is first produced for Saxony's Grand Duke Augustus III at Meissen near Dresden.

1705-15 — Green tea predominates in general use in England. In 1705 an Edinburgh goldsmith advertises green tea at 16 and black at 30 shillings the pound. In 1711 Addison writes in his *Spectator* that all "better" London households enjoy tea in the mornings. In 1712, even colonist Z. Boylston, Boston apothecary, advertises "Green & Bohea" and "green and ordinary" teas for sale. Due to import duties, Dutch tea costs far less than English, resulting in widespread smuggling throughout the American colonies.

1717 — Thomas Twining opens England's first shop devoted exclusively to tea on the Strand in London next door to his original Tom's Coffee House (established 1706). Ladies are welcome to shop for tea and enjoy it on the premises. The costliest of Twining's original fourteen teas was "Finest Hyson." Thomas Gainsborough painted his portrait before he died, a rich man, on May 19, 1741.

1720 — Caffe Florian, Italy's oldest coffee house, opens on Piazza San Marco, Venice. Second oldest is Rome's Caffe Greco, 1760.

1725-27 — England passes law against "smooch," recycled adulterated tea. Treaty of Kiakhta

Timeline of Tea

establishes the trading post between China and Russia in southern Siberia. Tea is now the principal article of trade.

1735 — Russia's Czarina Elizabeth greatly expands overland caravan tea trade with China, where Emperor Ch'ien-lung (*Qianlong* 1736-1795) comes to the throne. China is the largest, wealthiest and most civilized country on earth. Qialong indulges a lifelong passion for tea and art, ruling 60 years.

1738 — Japanese farmer Soen Nagatani, in Uji, invents process for Sencha manufacture. His friend Baisao, the old tea seller of Kyoto, popularizes his loose-leaf tea. In the Netherlands, tea becomes the most valuable import-export commodity.

1750 — Frederick the Great establishes Prussia's East India Company and, in 1753, the company's ship *King of Prussia* arrives in Emden from Canton with a cargo of over 500,000 pounds of tea. Frederick is later forced to liquidate his company due to the Seven Years War (1756-1763). Meanwhile black tea is gradually surpassing green's popularity in Holland.

1753 — Swedish botanist Carl Linnaeus gives tea the botanical name *Thea sinensis* in his classic work *Species Plantarum*. But in his second (1762) edition, he classifies it as two separate genera, *Thea bohea* for black tea and *Thea viridis* for green tea plants. In the interim Linnaeus has become the first European to succeed at growing a tea plant.

1756 — In India, British EIC's army defeats French-led forces at battle of Plassey, clearing the way for India to become, by degrees, an EIC fiefdom. The wealth plundered from India by the "nabobs" finances Britain's nascent Industrial Revolution.

1760 — Frederick the Great opens the magnificent Chinese tea house he has created on the grounds of his Potsdam palace, Sanssouci. Porcelain collecting and manufacture become all the vogue with monarchs after Meissen ware began to appear. In imitation come Sèvres in la Pompadour's France, Lomonosov in Czarina Catherine's Russia, and other royal examples, soon to be followed by Spode, Limoges, and similarly non-royal porcelain factories.

1764 — Josiah Wedgwood founds a pottery and soon develops Black Basalt, Queensware, and other ceramics. American colonies now consume tons of tea annually, the third most valuable American import. Illegal trade in smuggled Dutch tea grows as British taxes increase and colonists protest. Finally, in 1770, all import duties are abolished except for the most important—the Tea Tax.

1773 — American Revolution begins to gather steam and results in the Boston Tea Rebellion, when colonists disguised as Native Americans board three ships and dump 342 chests of British EIC Chinese tea into the harbor to protest George III's tax on tea. News of Boston reaches London via John Hancock's ship *Hayley*. Similar protests break out in Charleston, Philadelphia, and New York. Fifty years later, a newspaper reporter will for the first time call the incident *The Boston Tea Party*. Britain has lost control of events and is drawn into war.

1778   In Russia, first factory dedicated to production of samovars is set up by gunsmith Ivan Lisitsyn 100 miles from Moscow in Tula.

1784   British tea smugglers are effectively put out of business when tea merchant and EIC Director Richard Twining persuades Prime Minister Pitt to reduce import duty from 120 to 12 percent, spurring an instant drop in prices and dramatic increase in consumption. As one consequence of increased tea drinking, British sugar consumption reaches 12 pounds per capita per year, up from four pounds in 1700. Sugar is made by slaves in British West Indies.

1785   Legal tea imports in Great Britain rise from 12 to 33 million pounds; the trade accounts for five to ten percent of Britain's total economy. Though still a luxury item "far-fetched and dear bought," tea begins to be affordable for all levels of society. EIC now has about 30,000 registered wholesale and retail "dealers of tea", which has become the English grocers' most profitable item. In America, direct trade with Canton opens with arrival of *Empress of China* in New York with a cargo mainly of tea. America's first three millionaires will make their fortunes in the China trade.

1789   France sees beginnings of Revolution. The U.S. levies its first tea tax 15 cents a pound on black tea, 22 cents on Imperial green, and 55 cents on Young Hyson green. First Bourbon whiskey distilled by Baptist minister Elijah Craig near Georgetown, Kentucky.

1793   England's first "willow ware," a blue and white *chinoiserie* pattern, is designed by Thomas Minton. At the same time, England's trade mission to China led by Ambassador Lord MacCartney fails. His expedition's diarist Aeneas Anderson brings home the deathless tale of monkey-picked tea. Anglo-Chinese trade rests increasingly on opium.

         Paris has 500 restaurants. British tea consumption approaches an annual rate of two pounds per capita, an amount that will increase five-fold over the next century.

         Working class Britons already spend an average of two Pounds Sterling on tea annually, out of just 40 in total income.

1795-96   In China, Qianlong, longest ruling emperor of Qing dynasty, dies. Czarina Catherine the Great dies in Russia. Russian caravans import some 3.5 million pounds of tea, about one-tenth the amount Britain takes in.

1798   In Europe, from the outset of the French Revolution, trading companies have faced growing challenges to their monopolies. In 1797, England for the first time allows ships from friendly nations to enter EIC controlled ports like Bombay, effectively

Timeline of Tea

launching free trade. The heavily indebted VOC or Dutch East India Company collapses and is dissolved by the Dutch Government, which assumes its properties and debts of more than 50 million dollars. In its 198-year history, VOC stockholders have received dividends averaging 18 percent per annum. London now becomes the world's spice and tea trading capital.

1800 China's new Qing Emperor, succeeding the long-ruling Qianlong, issues first edict forbidding import of "foreign mud," opium. China's social stability, standard of living and level of culture are unsurpassed anywhere. Opium imports will only grow in volume until about 1910. In New York, John Jacob Astor makes his first fortune, earning $50,000 profit from his first China trade venture.

The Nineteenth Century

1803 In France, the world's first guide to restaurants and food shops, *Almanach des Gourmands,* appears in Paris. Gastronome Alexandre-Balthazar-Laurent Grimod de la Reyniere lovingly reviews over 500 spots annually for the next eight years. Grimod considers it quite reasonable to spend five hours over a good meal.

1813 In Britain, Parliament ends EIC monopoly of the India trade but continues its monopoly of the China trade for another 20 years.

1815 Ceylon becomes a fully occupied Crown Colony after British depose the 186th and last native Sinhalese king whose dynasty reined since the time of Buddha.

1819 Singapore on Malaysia's Malacca Straits is claimed by Sir Stamford Raffles for the EIC. The port makes the perfect way-station for "Tea Wagons," as East Indiamen ships are called. EIC is by this time the world's most powerful corporation ever.

1823 "October 14: This evening I went for the first time to a large tea-party at Goethe's," writes Johann Eckermann at the opening of *Conversations with Goethe,* often considered "the best book in German." Similarly, James Boswell first met Samuel Johnson over tea (1763), resulting in the best biography in the English language. In the 1820's, romantic geniuses like E.T.A. Hoffmann and Thomas De Quincey do their best work on tea, which is universally appreciated by Europe's intelligentsia. In Assam bordering British India, EIC Major Robert Bruce meets Maniram Duta and 'discovers' tea, locally known as "Fanap," grows wild. EIC officials ignore his discovery.

1824	Britain's Royal Navy adds tea to the daily ration and reduces daily rum ration from a half-pint to a quarter-pint. Tea has become the petroleum fueling British life and work.
1826	English Quaker John Horniman markets the first packet tea, sealed to protect against adulteration and to guarantee net weight. Horniman acquires an enviable reputation which in time makes his firm the largest U.K. tea business.
1827-30	In Java, Dutch plant tea seeds brought from Japan. J.I.L.L. Jacobsen is commissioned to explore China in search of tea plants and information. Experimental tea is produced in 1828; Jacobsen returns from a second China trip with seeds and plants in 1829. First Java tea factory is built 1830.
1832	Tea is planted experimentally in Nilgiri Hills of South India by Dr. Christie of Madras. Up north, Charles A. Bruce, brother of the deceased Robert, again informs EIC officials in Calcutta of the indigenous tea plants growing wild in Assam.
1833	J.I.L.L. Jacobsen returns to Java from his sixth and last trip to China bringing millions of tea seeds along with tea production equipment and fifteen skilled tea workers. Appointed manager of all government tea enterprises, he ships to Amsterdam the world's first tea made commercially by a European in 1834-35. EIC loses its prized monopoly on trade with China. England now imports over 30 million pounds of tea annually, paying China from the proceeds of over 30,000 chests of EIC-grown opium shipped annually from India.
1834	England's first public tea auction is held in Mincing Lane in London following termination of the EIC monopoly on tea imports. EIC sends Indian Tea Committee secretary George James Gordon to China in search of tea seeds, artisans and information on tea cultivation and manufacture.
1835	In Japan, method for producing Gyokuro by shading plants is perfected by Yamamoto Tokuo-o. First consignment of Java tea reaches Amsterdam. It is Europe's first tea not from China or Japan.
1837	England's Queen Victoria, aged 18, ascends the throne which she will occupy for 64 years, until 1901. Brothers Joseph and Edward Tetley, who began by peddling salt and tea on horseback in Yorkshire, open their first tea shop in Huddersfield. Lea & Perrins is launched in Worcestershire.
1838	First eight chests of Assam tea are sent to London by Charles A. Bruce and, in January 1839, are sold at auction in Mincing Lane, bringing record prices and prompting the formation of the Assam Company, the world's oldest tea-growing company.

Timeline of Tea

1839   EIC "annexes" Assam, deposing the last Ahom king but hiring his Prime Minister Maniram Dutta. Assam tea seeds are sent to Ceylon from Calcutta.

1840   Assam Company is granted EIC experimental tea gardens in Assam. British scientists in India recommend planting China tea in Assam and 42,000 plants raised from China seed in Calcutta are distributed to Assam and elsewhere. Charles A. Bruce is appointed Superintendent of tea culture in Assam. Privately he starts a nursery of indigenous Assam tea plants at Sadiya.

1840-42   China loses the Opium War to Britain and *de facto* loses her sovereignty, being forced by Treaty of Nanjing to cede Hong Kong to Britain and open ports of Shanghai, Ningbo, Fuzhou, and Xiamen (Amoy) to opium imports. The co-hong trading system in Canton established in 1687 is abolished and opium imports are legalized, to remain legal until 1908.

In London, actress Fanny Kemble enjoys the novelty of afternoon tea in 1842. In the U.S. Sylvester Graham invents the Graham cracker and fathers anti-tea propaganda and food faddism in America

1842-44   British India's first tea is planted at Dehradun in Himalayan foothills. Maniram Dutta Dewan, Assamese nobleman, establishes first private Assam tea garden "Cinnamora." Tea cultivation is undertaken experimentally in the British-owned island of Mauritius. J.I.L.L. Jacobsen publishes handbook for tea-growing in Dutch.

1847   Robert Fortune, Scottish botanist spying for EIC, leaves China after "Three Years Wandering in the Northern Provinces" (mainly Anhui), where he fails to learn secret of black tea production but manages to ship 2000 live plants back to India.

On Black Sea coast first tea is planted in Russian Transcaucasia (Georgia).

1848   In Britain, Samuel Ball publishes *An Account of the Cultivation & Manufacture of Tea in China derived from Personal Observation during an Official Residence in the Country from 1804 to 1826*. EIC's ex-tea buyer divulges all he knows about tea.

1854   In India, George Williamson replaces Charles A. Bruce as head of the Assam Company operations and promptly begins propagating indigenous Assam, not China, tea plants.

U.S. Navy Commodore Matthew Perry's "seven black ships" establish direct commercial relations with Japan, opening the way for the future tea trade. Kay Oura is first Japanese to send tea samples abroad.

1858   Robert Fortune makes his third trip into China on a commission from the U.S. government, which planned to send his plants to test gardens in southern states. U.S. tea growing is revived in 1880 when John Jackson, brother of the inventor of the tea-roller machine, experiments with tea in South Carolina without commercial success.

Queen Victoria is named Empress of India as the British Crown takes over all possessions (and debts) of the EIC, which is dissolved following India's Sepoy Rebellion of 1857. Some EIC retirees remain in India to become early tea planters.

1859　The Great Atlantic & Pacific Tea Company (A & P) is founded in New York City by partners who buy whole clipper shiploads of tea at a swoop, sell it for a third less than other merchants, and expand their business into America's first chain of groceries. America begins importing Japanese tea into San Francisco from Yokohama.

1860　British and French colonial armies enter Beijing and pillage and burn the Summer Palace by way of enforcing legalization of opium imports. China's addict population soon grows ten-fold and annual imports approach 75,000 chests, a three-fold increase since 1840. Incessant punitive invasions, acts of war and encroachments by Western powers between 1840 and 1894 cripple China.

1861　Revolutionary discovery in France, Louis Pasteur discovers pasteurization, scientifically describes chemical fermentation, etc. In China, the first Russian-owned brick tea factory is built at Hankow. In India, the first Calcutta tea auction is held. In Britain Mrs. Beeton's *Book of Household Management* becomes an instant classic which sells over half a million copies by 1890.

1866　"The Great Tea Race" involves eleven tea clippers sailing from Fuzhou, China, to London. Three ships leave Fuzhou on the same tide and reach London's docks on the same tide 99 days later, a close race technically won by the *Ariel*. Hamburg, Germany's free port city, has the largest number of ships in the tea trade after Britain and the U.S.

1867　Scotsman James Taylor plants Ceylon's first 19 acres of tea on Loolecondera Estate near Kandy. As "Father of Ceylon Tea" he sets up the first factory in 1872, installs the first tea-rolling equipment in 1880, and recruits Tamil workers from South India.

1868　First Formosa oolong exported to New York by Scottish opium dealer James Dodds.

First tea cultivation in Japan's Shizuoka Prefecture, eventually to become Japan's leading tea producer.

1869　Suez Canal opens, transforming world shipping from sail to steam. By 1882 the voyage from Shanghai to London takes just 30 days. The last tea clipper race is in 1871 and the winner *Cutty Sark* is retired to Australia's wool trade.

Timeline of Tea

1870 — Coffee blight descends on coffee plantations in Sri Lanka at the same time the *phylloxera* blight is destroying the ancient vineyards of Europe. Mr. A. Holle in Java becomes the first to roll tea mechanically.

1871 — New York's Fifth Avenue Hotel serves iced tea in summer.

1872 — Assam tea planter William Jackson pioneers tea machinery and sets up his first mechanical tea roller at Jorhat, Assam. A Jackson roller could do the work of 60 men in a day, ending the previous era where all the world's tea was entirely made by hand.

1874 — Lt. Col. Edward Money invents first tea drier, followed by the "Sirocco" tea dryer Samuel C. Davidson invents in 1877. The mechanization and industrialization of black tea production make tea estates the most profitable investment in the British Empire after gold mines and make Dutch tea growers in Java rich.

1875 — U.S. tea imports reach 60 million pounds, up from 20 million in 1862 thanks to removal of import duties imposed during the War of Northern Aggression. Stuart Cranston creates the first tearoom in Scotland.

1877 — Java tea first sold at London Tea Auction in Mincing Lane

1878 — Dutch switch to growing Assam, not China, tea plants in Java, laying foundations for eventual triumph of tea in Indonesia.

Stuart Cranston's sister Kate opens the first of five tearooms in Glasgow. She eventually employs art nouveau artist Charles Rennie Mackintosh to design her popular establishments, including The Willow Tearoom on Sauchiehall Street, still in business today.

1879 — Haelssen & Lyon is founded in Hamburg, Germany, shortly before the death of Gustav Haelssen. Alfred Moritz Lyon realizes that over 20 percent of Europe's tea already comes from colonial plantations, not China, and plans accordingly.

1880 — Ceylon's first tea-rolling machine is manufactured by John Walker & Co. In Paris, Mary Cassatt paints *Five o' Clock Tea*.

1881 — Indian Tea Association (ITA) is formed in Calcutta.

1882 — In France, first shop to sell India and Ceylon teas opens in Paris.

1883 — Colombo's first tea auction is held on July 16 in the office of Somerville & Co. as Sri Lanka's coffee output falls to 150,000 bags, down from 700,000 in 1870. The last Ceylon coffee is sold in 1899.

1884 — London's Aerated Bread Company establishes the ABC tea rooms, opening a new era in tea service in England with Lyons and other tea room chains to follow.

1885	Japan patents two rolling machines for Sencha manufacture, the first step toward industrialization of Japan tea production. After seizing Taiwan in 1895, Japan gains some 40 percent of America's tea market by 1915.
1886	Chinese tea exports reach their maximum at 144,360 tons, up from an average 90,000 tons per year between 1850 and 1860. Approximately 54 percent went to Great Britain, 27 percent to Russia and 14 percent to the U.S. Colonial machine-made tea quickly undersells China's mostly handmade artisanal tea. China's farmers suffer untold hardship as China falls from supplying 85 percent of the world's tea in 1870 to just 10 percent in 1910.
	In Canada, Salada Tea Co. is founded by Peter Larkin to sell India and Ceylon teas. By 1920 Salada is Canada's leading brand and second largest in the U.S. In the U.S., Coca-Cola goes on sale in Atlanta, Georgia, and Dr. Pepper in Waco, Texas. "Soft drinks" will become tea's greatest worldwide competition.
1888	William Jackson invents his first tea sorting machine. America now consumes much more green and oolong (mainly Japanese) teas than black. British sugar consumption reaches 76 pounds per capita, up from 60 in 1875.
1890	England's leading grocer, Thomas Lipton, visits Ceylon and begins buying tea estates to assure low cost tea for his 300 shops, where he undersells all competition.
	Dr. Charles U. Shepard plants acres of tea and builds a tea factory at Summerville, S.C.
1891	Ceylon tea brings record price at London auction when a fine lot sells for 25 pounds 10 shillings per avoirdupois pound.
1893	Chicago World's Fair showcases teas from Japan, India, Ceylon and other new tea lands. Okakura Kakuzo, Director of the Tokyo School of Fine Arts and future author of *The Book of Tea,* helps design the Japanese pavilion.
	Liu Junzhou of Zhejiang, China, visits Russia to advise the Russian tea industry.
1894	London's first J. Lyons & Co. tearoom opens. By 1904 there will be 96 Lyons tearooms, all with the same menu, prices and "nippies".
1895-98	Japan seizes Taiwan. In China, first tea equipment factory is built in Fuzhou. First individual teabag patent is issued in U.K.. Britain's annual tea consumption averages 10 pounds per capita, up from under 2 pounds in 1800. Black teas from India and Ceylon now outsell China greens and black congous, which are still preferred by connoisseurs. In the U.S., first consumer protection law establishes the U.S. Tea Examiners Office. Annual U.S. tea consumption reaches 1.5 lbs. of tea per capita, an historic high not yet surpassed.

Timeline of Tea

The Twentieth Century

1900   In Iran, tea cultivation begins near coast of the Caspian Sea. Last Russian camel caravan departs from Beijing; Trans-Siberian Railway nears completion. In India, Tocklai is established as first tea research center.

1901   *Tea and Coffee Trade Journal* is founded in New York by William Harrison Ukers, who begins assembling materials for his monumental *All About Coffee* and *All About Tea*.

          East Africa's first tea is planted in Kenya and Malawi.

          Queen Victoria dies January 22 at age of 81 after a reign of nearly 64 years. J. Lyons & Co. assumes the task of catering for all the troops drafted into London for Her Majesty's funeral.

1903   Japanese establish tea research center in occupied Taiwan.

1904   Tea merchandizing at the St. Louis World's Fair popularizes iced tea in U.S. Dr. Shepard's South Carolina tea wins prize for Best Oolong.

1905   Japan establishes National Tea Experimental Station.

1906-07   *The Book of Tea* by Okakura Kakuzo is first published in U.S. and never goes out of print. The Plaza Hotel opens in New York City. The Laurel Court Tearoom opens at the Fairmont Hotel in San Francisco—after the earthquake.

1908   Sir Thomas Lipton begins operations in New York, a business he will incorporate separately in 1915. The Palm Court at London's Waldorf Hotel opens and becomes a popular setting for tea dances which became a new craze.

1910   Dutch begin tea planting on a large scale in Sumatra.

1912   Republic of China is proclaimed with Sun Yat-sen as President, ending Qing dynasty which has ruled since 1644. China is in ruins, her tea trade in collapse, her population in misery.

          In the U.S., Wenham Village Improvement Society of Wenham, Massachusetts opens a tearoom—now the country's oldest.

1914   As World War One begins, black tea represents about 30 percent of tea consumption in U.S. and 90 percent in U.K..

          Alva Vanderbilt Belmont hosts a suffragette tea at her fashionable Marble House in Newport, Rhode Island. British porcelain maker Maddock & Sons designs a complete tea set bearing the slogan "Votes for Women" especially for the event.

1915 First tea plucking shears are patented in Japan.

1920-21 Overproduction forces India and Ceylon planters to adopt fine plucking as industry policy to reduce production.

1923 J. Lyons & Co. opens the world's largest tea facility near London using barges to haul tea chests from the London docks on the Grand Union Canal and producing over 1 million packets of tea daily.

The Tea Room Institute of the Lewis Hotel Training Schools in Washington, DC, launch their *Pouring Tea for Profit* classes with the enticing promise that "skilled tea room managers often make … $35 to $50 per week!"

1924 Japanese chemist announces the discovery of Vitamin C in the green teas of Japan.

1925 Tea Research Institute of Ceylon is established.

Africa's total tea exports exceed one million pounds. Brooke Bond and James Finlay & Co. Ltd. undertake extensive tea plantations in Kenya.

1929 Britain's Chancellor of the Exchequer Winston Churchill abolishes the Crown's 325-year-old tea duty, knocking four pence off the price of a pound of tea.

1930 CTC machine invented by W. McKercher in Assam, "the most significant invention in the history of Indian tea" according to Sir Percival Griffiths' *History of Indian Tea*.

1932 China establishes Rural Revival Committee with tea as a primary focus. Sir Thomas Lipton dies at 81 and within 24 months his picture begins to appear on Lipton packages, where it remains.

1933 As a Depression measure, an International Tea Committee is created to administer export regulations adopted by British India, Ceylon and the Dutch East Indies.

Cloning (vegetative propagation by "layering") of tea developed by Mr. A. C. Tunstall of Tocklai.

1935 W.H. Ukers' monumental *All About Tea* is published in two-volume sets intended for the trade. Only 600 copies were printed.

International Botanical Congress meeting in Amsterdam acknowledges tea as camellia and unites the genera Thea and Camellia into a single genus Camellia, with over 80 species.

1936 *The Romance of Tea* by William H. Ukers is published by Alfred A. Knaupf in New York City.

1939 W.H. Ukers estimates that China consumes about 900 million pounds of tea annu-

Timeline of Tea

ally, the U.K. about 450 million, India 111, the U.S. 97, Japan 75, Russia 63, Australia 51, Canada 43, the Netherlands 29, Eire 23, and Dutch East Indies 21.

1941 China's first Tea Research Institute is established in Wuyishan, Fujian.

1946 R.C. Bigelow Company has its genesis when Ruth Campbell Bigelow begins blending and selling her "Constant Comment" tea packages from a lower Manhattan apartment.

1947 In India, Cochin Tea Auction center is established in Kerala.

1949 People's Republic of China is proclaimed at Beijing by Mao Zedong on October 1. China Native Products & Animal By-Products Import-Export. Corp. aka "China Inc." is put in control of all the tea in China.

In India, the first three tea clones released by Tocklai Experimental Station in Assam mark start of revolution in plant material improvement.

1954 Tea Board of India is established in Calcutta.

1955 In China, Mao Zedong decrees rapid collectivization of agriculture and orders peasants who resist to be liquidated. His commune experiment is a costly disaster for rural life.

1958 Tea Research Institute of the Chinese Academy of Agricultural Sciences is established in Hangzhou.

The first China tea since the 1930s is sold in the London Auction, marking 300th anniversary of the first sale of China tea in U.K.

1960 In Kenya, Mombasa tea auction center is established.

1963 "King Tea Tree," a 1700-year-old wild tea tree, 105 feet high and 10 feet in diameter, is found growing on Mt. Badadahei, Yunnan province, China.

In India Conoor Tea Auction center is established in Nilgiri mountains of Tamil Nadu.

1965 Muslim countries in the Middle East and North Africa are estimated to absorb approximately one-fourth of the world's tea.

1970 Hotelier John Harney purchases Sarum Tea from Stanley Mason and eventually changes the name to Harney & Sons Fine Teas.

1972 Chinese tea production exceeds pre-Revolution levels for the first time. U.S. resumes trade with China.

Timeline of Tea

1972   Stash Tea is launched in Portland, Oregon, by Steve Smith. This tea entrepreneur eventually sells Stash and founds Tazo, later sold to Starbucks. Smith launched the elite Smith Teamaker in 2009, four short years before his untimely death.

1974   World's first organic tea estate created in Sri Lanka's Uva district at Needwood Estate under direction of Manik Jayakumar. Before 1980, Korakundah and Oothu in Tamil Nadu and Makaibari in Darjeeling will become India's pioneer organic estates. Organic tea gradually becomes an established category

1982   *The Tea Lover's Treasury* by James Norwood Pratt, published in San Francisco, is the first comprehensive guide to the teas of the world in English since Uker' *Romance of Tea*; it proves to be an inspiration for America's Tea Renaissance. In Germany, a German Tea Renaissance has produced about 500 specialty tea shops nationwide by 1982, up from about 50 in 1967. Flavored teas from Haelsen & Lyon in Hamburg begin booming in the U.S. market.

1984   China's National Tea Cultivar Accreditation Committee under the Ministry of Agriculture registers the first 30 tea cultivars.

1986   Zhejiang Agricultural University and Tea Research Institute, Chinese Academy of Agricultural Sciences, combine to offer a Ph.D. in tea under Professor Chen Zongmao, Tea Research Institute director and Control Committee member.

         Jane Pettigrew opens her stylish teashop Tea-Time in the London borough of Clapham.

1987   The Taiwanese tea culture is reborn with the legalization of tea houses when martial law is lifted. In China, archeologists at Famen Temple near Xian discover a trove of treasures bestowed by the Tang Emperor in 867. Included is an imperial tea set in gilded silver—grinder, sifter, caddy, spoons, etc.—implements such as Lu Yu used and described.

1990   China National Tea Museum opens in Hangzhou and first modern edition of *China Tea Encyclopedia* (Zhongguo Chajing) edited by Chen Zhong-mao is published.

         Shelley and Bruce Richardson open the Elmwood Inn Tea Room in Perryville, Kentucky. In 2002, it would be the first North American venue named to the prestigious list of *Best Tea Rooms*, published by the U.K. Tea Council.

         Devan Shah, a recent immigrant from India and a tea professional, establishes International, originally India, Tea Importers (ITI) in Los Angeles. With his wife Reena, they help fuel America's Tea Renaissance.

1992-95   In China, Chairman Deng Xiaoping ends export monopoly of China, Inc. and revives free enterprise and open tea markets. In U.S., the Republic of Tea paves the

Timeline of Tea

way for specialty tea companies. Roy Fong opens America's first traditional Chinese tea house, the Imperial Tea Court, in San Francisco's Chinatown. LA's first Chado Tea Room opens. Harney & Sons Fine Teas host annual "Harney Tea Summits," which give added impetus to the country's nascent Tea Renaissance. American Premium Tea Institute (APTI) the precursor of STI is founded in San Francisco

1996   The largest ancient wild tea growing area, covering approximately 1,600 acres, is discovered in a high-altitude area of Zhengyuan county in Yunnan, China. Included is perhaps the oldest wild tea tree, approximately 2,700 year in age, standing 84 feet high and 9 feet in diameter. It is a thousand years older than the King Tea Tree discovered in 1963.

1998   In England, the last London Tea Auction is held June 28 at Sir John Lyons House, Mincing Lane, a sign of changing times like the 1996 dissolution of U.S. Board of Tea Examiners and the closing of Jardin Matheson & Co. in Hong Kong.

1999   U.S. Specialty Tea Institute (STI) is formed when American Premium Tea Institute (APTI) and Specialty Tea Registry (STAR) merge.

The Twenty-first Century

2003   World Tea Expo, originally Take Me 2 Tea, launches in Las Vegas.

2005   World tea production stands at 3.2 million tons, as against 7.2 million for coffee. Total world acreage for tea is about 2.34 million hectares compared to 7.89 million hectares planted in vineyards. There is obviously more acreage for wine production than for tea, but the critical factor in making comparisons is yield. Mankind drinks more tea than coffee and wine combined.

2010   James Norwood Pratt's *Tea Dictionary* is released at World Tea Expo. U.S. tea consumption has climbed over 10 percent per year for two decades; U.S. now leads U.K. in tea imports and consumption.

2013   Starbucks purchases Teavana and the company's 300 North American stores for $620,000,000. Total U.S. tea market estimated at $13 billion as specialty tea sales and tea culture grow together.

2017   In U.S., Northwest Tea Festival in Seattle celebrates its tenth consecutive year, having inspired similar regional tea festivals in cities such as San Francisco, Los Angeles, Kansas City, Portland, Philadelphia, and New York. The United States is becoming a tea consuming society again.

INDEX

Aerated Bread Co., 125-6, 197

Afternoon tea, 119, 123, 124-39, 158, 165-8, 173, 195

Anglo-Ceylon & General Estates Co., Ltd., 45

Arabia, 21, 79, 138, 187

Argentina, 47, 122

Arnold, Sir Edwin, 164

Assam Company, 28, 40-1, 49, 194-5

Assam tea, 33, 37, 39-46, 48-9, 86, 106, 109, 160

Astor, John Jacob, 89, 134

Australia, 38, 97-8, 101, 130, 178, 196, 201

Ball, Samuel, 15, 26-8, 48, 71, 195

Balzac, Honoré de, 162, 168

Bancha, 140, 212

Banks, Sir Joseph, 39, 48

Batavia, 30, 33, 35-6, 55-7, 66

Board of Tea Examiners, 175, 203

Boccarro, 149

Bodhidharma, 22, 24, 30, 170, 181

Bohea tea, 24, 64, 66-7, 70, 84, 141, 155 158, 190

Book of Tea, The, 11, 140, 153, 166, 198-9,

Book of Tea Sanitation, 27, 171

Boston: tea first sold in, 70, 190

Boston; tea party, 72-3, 84, 132, 159, 165, 191-2

Brazil, 39, 47, 78

Brick tea, 75, 117, 137, 196

Broken Orange Pekoe, 113

Browning, Elizabeth Barrett, 158

Browning, Robert, 158

Bruce, Charles, 39-41, 106, 194-5

Bruce, Robert, 39, 49, 106, 193

Burma, 23, 47, 111-2, 137

Caffeine, 174-9

Camellia, 22, 29, 48, 115, 179, 200

Cassatt, Mary, 145, 169, 197

Catherine of Braganza, 55-6, 76, 83, 154, 189, 191-2

Ceylon tea: 33, 38, 40-6, 49, 109-10, 121, 124, 130-3, 136-9, 178, 193, 195-200

Cha, 14-8, 28-9, 53-5, 61, 106, 137-8, 140, 146, 183-4, 186-7

Cha Ching, 16, 18-9, 21, 152

Cha Pu, 22-3, 185

Chanoyu, 119-20 147-8, 166, 171, 187

Charles II, 38, 56, 65-6, 76, 83

204

China tea: history of, 15-31

Cleyer, Andreas, 33

Coffee houses, 60-7, 76, 79, 83, 131, 138, 155, 188, 190

Confucius, 16, 21, 28, 165, 181

Cream in tea, 124, 131, 134-6, 138, 157, 160

Dance, tea in the, 170

Daruma, 24, 30, 146, 164, 170

Davidson, Sir Samuel C., 41-2, 49, 197

Delft ware, 148

Duchess of Bedford, 123

Dutch East India Co., 33-4, 55-8, 61, 75-6, 80,

East Indiamen (ships), 79-81, 89, 94, 193

Edenton, NC 72

Elizabeth I, 75, 80-1, 105-6, 187

Emerson, Ralph Waldo, 159

English East India Co.: 30, 37-40, 55, 61-2, 65, 71, 73, 75, 79-80, 83-85

Faience, 148-9

Fielding, Henry, 163

Fortnum & Mason, Ltd., 67

Fortune, Robert, 37, 40, 195

France, 54, 58-9, 61, 131, 135, 151, 174, 189

Garway, Thomas (Garraway), 61-3, 76, 188

Germany, 57, 61, 130, 148, 174, 197, 202

Gisignies, L.P.J., Viscount du Bus de, 34-6

Gladstone, William Ewart, 168, 171

Gray, Arthur, 165

Green tea: 17, 18, 27, 67, 72, 84, 108, 113, 121, 138, 156, 171, 188, 190-91

Gypsy tearooms, 135

Ham tea, 125

Hanway, Jonas, 69, 152

Hearn, Lafcadio, 164

High tea, 125

Hogarth, William, 144

Holland, 34, 56-8, 61, 65, 69-70, 130-1, 19, 174, 178, 187-91

Holmes, Oliver Wendell, 159

Hugo, Victor, 168

Ibsen, Henrik, 164

Iced tea, 11, 133-4, 171, 199

India tea history of, 16, 22-4

Iran, 47, 75, 112, 138, 199

Irving, Washington, 163

Jackson, William, 42

Jacobson, J.I.L.L., 30, 34-36, 48

James II, King of England, 67, 189

Japan, 22, 24-6, 30, 33-4, 52-5, 74, 80, 93, 108, 110-14, 119-21, 140-3, 147, 152, 164

Jardine, Matheson & Co., 91, 97, 103, 106

Jesuit missionaries, 52-53, 57, 61-2, 74, 140, 186-7

John Company, 79, 86-8, 106

Johnson, Samuel, 67, 157, 193

Kakuzo, Okakura, 11, 140, 166, 171, 198-9

Keats, John, 158

Kenya, 47, 112

Korea, 137, 183

Kyoto (Heian-kyō), 25-27, 119, 140, 143, 160, 188, 191

Kuo Po, 16-17, 29

Lamb, Charles, 88, 105

Levant Company, 56, 80, 105

Linnaeus, 191

Linschoten, Jan Huyghen van, 54, 61, 170, 187

Little Tea Book, 165

London Tea Auction, 46, 77, 197, 203

Longfellow, Henry W., 95, 168

Lu Tung, 153

Lu Yu, 17-21, 29-30, 155, 162, 184

Lyons tea-shops, 116, 126-7, 197-8

Marco Polo, 51, 174, 185, 190

McKay, Donald, 94-6, 101

Mercurius Politicus, 64

Milk in tea, 58, 60, 117, 121, 124, 129, 131, 135-8, 175

Mincing Lane, London, 45-6, 49, 99-100, 194, 197, 203

Monkeys gathering tea, 23-4

Morocco, 138

Myōe, Saint, 27, 143, 170, 185

Netherlands Trading Company, 34-5

New Amsterdam, 69-70, 131, 188

New York, 130-4, 138, 141, 145, 150-1, 163, 170, 173, 192, 196-7, 199

Nippies, 126-127

Oolong teas, 110, 113-4, 132-4, 139-41, 160, 196, 198

Orange Pekoe, 114, 133

Paris, 58-9, 114, 129, 135, 138, 146, 155, 165, 189, 192, 197

Paxton, William M., 142, 145

Peet, John, 48

Pen tsao, 16, 165

Pepys, Samuel, 23, 66-7, 76, 189

Pleasure gardens, 122-3, 131

Polo, Marco, 51, 174, 185

Porcelain, 132, 141-50, 171, 190

Raku ware, 148, 171

Ranelagh, 122, 131

Repplier, Agnes, 168

Reynolds, Sir Joshua, 168

Ricci, Matteo, 53, 74, 187

Ruskin, John, 30, 168-9

Sablière, Mme de le, 60

Saicho (Buddhist saint), 25, 184

Sans Souci (Sanssouci), 131, 161

Scotland, 45, 49, 67, 124, 189, 197

Sen-no Rikyu, 120, 140, 147-8, 171, 187

Sévigné, Mme de, 60

Sèvres, 191

Shaw, Bernard, 168

Shelley, Percy, 158

Shen Nung, 15-16, 29, 165, 181

Shepard, Dr. Charles U., 47, 198-9

Shuko (tea master), 119, 140, 186

Siam, 23, 47, 111, 137

Smuggling tea, 71, 81-2, 85, 105, 190

"Sons of Liberty," 72

Stamp Act of 1765, 70-1, 77

Stuyvesant, Peter, 188

Sugar in tea, 56-59, 67, 117, 121, 124, 129, 131, 134-9, 175

Sultaness Head coffee-house, 64

Taylor, James, 45, 49, 196

Tea, origin of word, 24

Teabags, 11, 121

Tea caddies, 138, 151

Tea Ceremony, 19, 74, 118, 11-20, 140, 147, 160, 166, 186

Tea gardens: 23, 25, 37, 40-1, 74

Tea houses: 149, 191, 203

Teaism, 119, 140, 166, 171

Tea wagons, 134

Tea water pumps, 131-2

Tennyson, Lord Alfred, 158

Tewk, Maria, 67, 76

Tom's Coffee-House, 67, 190

Tribute tea, 17, 28, 30, 49, 140, 186, 188

Twinings in the Strand, 67, 190

Washington, George, 132

Wedgwood, Josiah, 69, 149

White tea, 22

Wickham, R.L., 55, 75, 83

Willow pattern, 149, 191

Yeisai, abbot, 25, 27, 153

Front cover illustration: *Silent Advocates of Temperance,* 1891 (oil on panel) by Edward George Handel Lucas, London. Permission granted by Bridgeman Art.

BENJAMIN PRESS TEA BOOKS

The New Tea Companion
Jane Pettigrew & Bruce Richardson

A Social History of Tea
Jane Pettigrew & Bruce Richardson

The Book of Tea
Okakura Kakuzo, edited by Bruce Richardson

Tea & Etiquette
Dorothea Johnson & Bruce Richardson

Green Tea
Kevin Gascoyne

Children's Tea & Etiquette
Dorothea Johnson

www.BenjaminPress.com

THE JESSE TREE STORY

A FAMILY ADVENT DEVOTIONAL

By Grace Claus
Illustrations by Kristen Morrison

The Jesse Tree Story: A Family Advent Devotional

Copyright © 2022 by Reformed Church Press. All rights reserved.

Written by Grace Claus

Edited by Becky Getz and Grace Ruiter

Illustrations by Kristen Morrison

Design and cover art by Erica McCary

No part of this publication may be reproduced without the prior written permission of Reformed Church Press, except for the use of brief quotations in a book review.

To request permissions, contact info@faithward.org.

Scripture quotations are from the New Revised Standard Version Bible, copyright © 1989 National Council of the Churches of Christ in the United States of America. Used by permission. All rights reserved worldwide.

ISBN 978-0-916466-24-4

www.faithward.org